THE UNEASY CENTURY

International Relations 1900-1990

Margaret MacMillian
Arne Kislenko

Ryerson Polytechnic University

KENDALL/HUNT PUBLISHING COMPANY
4050 Westmark Drive Dubuque, Iowa 52002

Kendall/Hunt Publishing Company

ISBN 0-7872-2217-8

Printed in the United States of America
10 9 8 7 6 5 4 3 2 1

CONTENTS

INTRODUCTION

Penicillin, television, the compact disc, airplane travel, all these are products of the twentieth century. But so too are death camps, ethnic cleansing, and urban terrorism. Industrialization and modernity have spread around the globe and also intolerant ideologies which condemn whole groups because they come from the wrong class, the wrong race, or the wrong religion. How can we characterize a century which has seen great advances in human knowledge as well as great barbarity? A distinguished British historian, Eric Hobsbawm, who has lived through many of the events you will be studying, calls it The Age of Extremes.

It is easy to see what he means. On the one hand, for example, modern communications have helped to bind distant parts of the world closer together; on the other, we have seen the rise of passionate nationalisms which have turned neighbours against each other. Advances in medicine, in food production, and in organization have brought greater prosperity and healthier lives to people all over the world. There has also been progress in another area: war. Along with new ways of saving lives have come much more efficient ways of taking them.

Death, on a huge scale, has been part of the history of this uneasy century: the millions of men dead in the First World War; the more millions, this time civilians, who died in the great flu epidemic of 1918-19; the dead on the battlefields and in the bombed cities of the Second World War; and the hundreds of thousands killed in the more than fifty smaller wars since 1945. And we must not forget the citizens killed by their own governments; the Jews and other victims of the Nazi state; the Soviet citizens who died, perhaps 20,000,000 of them, because of Joseph Stalin; and the millions more who died in Mao's China or Pol Pot's Cambodia.

A century of extremes and also of great change. That is as true of international relations as it is of the rest of this age. The nineteenth century pattern with states vying for power and influence has been challenged by new ideas, that states should work together to create an international community, and by international ideologies, whether religious like Islam or political like communism.

While one part of the world has declined dramatically, new powers have emerged elsewhere. In 1900, Europe, a tiny part of the world's surface when you look at it on map, dominated the world's economy and world politics. Europeans either controlled or occupied almost 80% of the world's land and European navies, civilian shipping, and cables ruled the world's seas. Ninety years later Europe is still prosperous but now shares the world's riches with the United States and the rising powers of Asia. The European empires have almost completely gone. Those changes might have happened anyway but Europe helped to destroy itself in two great wars, the first between 1914 and 1918 and the second between 1939 and 1945.

Some historians see the Second World War as a continuation of the First but we should not assume that another war was inevitable. In the twenty years from 1918 to 1939, serious attempts were made to find ways to avoid war and to settle disputes among nations peacefully. The 1920s, in particular, brought some hopeful signs. The League of Nations was established, disarmament conferences were held, and treaties were signed. On the other hand, significant minorities, dissatisfied perhaps with the outcome of the First World War or unhappy with existing structures, were prepared to risk violence to bring about change. Whether Japanese ultra-nationalists, Chinese militarists, Soviet communists, or Italian fascists, such groups posed challenges to international order. Coincidence also plays a part in history; if the Great Depression had not occurred and if the world had been better able to cope with the consequences of mass unemployment and misery, extremists might not have gained influence and power.

The Second World War deserved the name more truly than the First because it really did involve fighting world wide. There was war again in Europe, but this time there was far-flung and savage fighting in the Pacific between the western forces led by the United States and the Japanese. The Pacific conflict ended in an explosion of appalling implications when the two atom bombs were dropped on Hiroshima and Nagasaki.

A war ended in 1945, leaving behind it much of Europe and Asia in ruins, but another war began almost immediately. This new war was a curious one because the main opponents never fought each other. It was a Cold War between the United States and the Soviet Union; war because the two powers, so dominant that they were called super-powers, feared and disliked each other, cold because a hot, or shooting, war was too dangerous. For that restraint, nuclear weapons can be thanked.

But there are many ways of fighting—by proxy, through economics, science and technology, by using spies or propaganda—and the Cold War saw them all. In 1989, it came to an unexpected end, unexpected that is by the majority of the leaders and informed elites on both sides. It ended when the Soviet Union could no longer bear the burdens of its superpower status and the arms race with the United States. The Soviet Union itself collapsed and the empire it had build in the centre of Europe after 1945 vanished.

That collapse brought a brief period of hope that the world was somehow on the way to becoming a happier and more peaceful place. The Gulf War and Bosnia have destroyed that particular illusion and, yet again, the world must grapple with the issues of international order. Understanding international relations—why countries behave in certain ways, for example, or what makes a stable international order and what brings conflict—is as important as it ever was.

The international relations of this century have produced betrayal, injustice, aggression and repeated war, but they have also seen heroic efforts to build systems that might create a fairer world and prevent armed conflict. If some world leaders have welcomed the gunfire, others have struggled to prevent it. You will find here records of the attempts before 1914 to dampen conflict, the idealism of Woodrow Wilson and others who tried to build a new international co-operation after 1918, the promise of the 1920s and even the 1930s when it looked as though war could be avoided, and of the renewed attempts during the Second World War and afterwards to set up a genuinely international set of institutions to manage the world's affairs.

International relations is an enormous and in many ways a messy subject. It includes the traditional diplomatic history—the relations between heads of state, the exchange of ambassadors and the signing of agreements, but it also encompasses economic and cultural relations, the exchange of information, or its concealment, and such intangibles as shared, or hostile values. The democracies opposed Hitler's Germany and Mussolini's Italy in part at least because they found their ideologies repulsive. With the growing complexity of modern society and the spread of popular involvement in that society, international relations is also about people, about the relationships among different ethnic or national groups and about the impact of public opinion on foreign policy. The modern Olympics were supposed to be free of nationalism; they have been, almost since the day they started, another arena in which nations and peoples compete with each other.

Impersonal forces have shaped twentieth century international relations. Such factors as ideology, religion, political systems, economic changes, demography, have all helped to determine the ways in which nations have interacted. French leaders, for example, were well aware from the end of the nineteenth century that France's population was declining in numbers as that of Germany was going up; that fact contributed to French fears and concerns. But individuals matter too. Adolf Hitler made certain choices as the leader of Germany in the 1930s which led towards war and the leaders of the democracies who opposed him made their choices as well. When you read the following documents, you will discover the individuals as well as the environment in which they had to operate.

The documents have been chosen to show you the raw materials of history. As you read, try to use your knowledge of the period and of human nature to evaluate what you see on the page. Remember that people do not always tell the truth; sometimes they tell a part of it and sometimes they lie. Ask yourselves whom they are addressing; are they discussing issues freely with those they trust or are they making statements for public consumption? are they trying to win support or are they confident of their positions? Ask yourselves who is talking and, equally important, why? Hitler talked in one way when he was outlining his plans to his circle of intimates, in quite another when he was trying to bamboozle his enemies. And use the study questions; they will indicate some, but by no means all, of the major issues.

The readings in this book will acquaint you with some of the great issues which have affected international relations in this century—from the causes of the outbreak of the First World War to the end of the Cold War. Some of the questions of today—how Europe deals with a powerful Germany at its centre; what role Japan should play in Asia; how can international co-operation be encouraged—have arisen before. It helps to know what solutions came up then. And if we want to understand other peoples and other nations, we must try to know what they know and remember what they remember. Why do the Chinese distrust the West today? Why do Arabs suspect that the West will always betray them? You live and you will work in an increasingly global environment; you ought to understand what has produced the world of the late twentieth century. This is not because the past can provide blueprints for the future, but because it provides guidance and instructive precedents.

ACKNOWLEDGEMENTS

Reprinted with the permission of Simon & Schuster from *Nixon* by Stephen E. Ambrose. Copyright © 1987 by Ambrose-Tubbs, Inc.

Reprinted with the permission of Simon & Schuster from *An American Life* by Ronald Reagan. Copyright © 1990 by Ronald Reagan.

The Eagle and the Small Birds by Charlton. Copyright © 1984 by University of Chicago Press. Reprinted by permission.

Present at the Creation by Dean Acheson. Reprinted by permission of W.W. Norton & Company, Inc.

The Memoirs of Harry S. Truman, Volume 2: Years of Trial and Hope 1946-53. Reprinted by permission of Margaret Truman Daniel.

Vietnam: A History by Stanley Karnow. Copyright © 1983 WGBH Educational Foundation and Stanley Karnow. Used by permission of Viking Penguin, a division of Penguin Books USA Inc.

The Bad War by Kim Willenson, editor. Copyright © 1987 by Newsweek, Inc. Used by permission of Dutton Signet, a division of Penguin books USA Inc.

Winners and Losers by Gloria Emerson. Copyright © 1985 by Gloria Emerson. Reprinted by permission of Random House, Inc.

Song of Napalm by Bruce Weigl. Copyright © 1988 by Bruce Weigl. Used by permission of Grove/Atlantic, Inc.

Excerpts from *Conversations with Stalin* by Milovan Djilas, copyright 1962 and renewed 1990 by Harcourt Brace & Company, reprinted by permission of the publisher.

Copyright 1967 by Martin Luther King. Reprinted by arrangement with The Heirs to the Estate of Martin Luther King, Jr., c/o Writers House, Inc. as agent for the proprietor.

Khruschev Remembers by Nikita Khruschev. Copyright © 1970 by Little, Brown and Company (Inc.). By permission of Little, Brown and Company.

Thirteen Days by Robert F. Kennedy. Copyright 1971. Reprinted by permission of W.W. Norton & Company, Inc.

SECTION ONE

THE OUTBREAK OF WORLD WAR I

DOCUMENTS

CHRONOLOGY

1882	Triple Alliance (Germany, Austria-Hungary, Italy)
1895	Franco-Russian alliance
1898	start of Anglo-German naval race
1902	Triple Alliance renewed; Anglo-Japanese Treaty
1904	Anglo-French Entente (Entente Cordiale)
1904-05	Russo-Japanese War
1906	First Morocco crisis
1907	Anglo-Russian settlement of disputes
1908	Austria-Hungary annexes Bosnia-Herzegovina
1911	2nd Morocco (Agadir) crisis
1912	First Balkan War; Triple Alliance renewed
1913	Second Balkan War
1914	
June 28	assassination of Archduke Franz Ferdinand at Sarajevo in Bosnia
July 23	Austrian ultimatum to Serbia
July 28	Austria-Hungary declares war on Serbia
July 29	Germany asks for British neutrality
July 30	Austria-Hungary and Russia order general mobilization for July 31
July 31	Kaiser Wilhelm of Germany proclaims "state of imminent war"; German ultimatum to Russia
Aug. 1	German mobilization and declaration of war on Russia
Aug. 2	Britain agrees to protect north coast of France and Channel against Germany; Germany invades Luxemburg; German ultimatum to Belgium
Aug. 3	Germany declares war on France; Belgium rejects German ultimatum; Britain mobilizes army
Aug. 4	British ultimatum to Germany; Germany invades Belgium; Britain declares war on Germany
Aug. 5	Austria-Hungary declares war on Rusia; Britain decides to send force to France
Aug. 12	Britain declares war on Austria-Hungary

The causes of World War I have been argued over ever since August 1914. The following documents have been chosen not to settle the issue one way or another but to show the thinking of some of the key participants.

Document 1 THE ANGLO-GERMAN NAVAL RACE

One of the chief sources of tension in Europe before 1914 was rivalry between Germany and Britain. In 1898 Germany took the first steps to build a deep-water navy, capable of operating on the world's oceans. This led to a naval race with Great Britain, the world's leading naval power. The following comes from the preamble to the German Navy Bill of 1900, which provided for a further expansion of the German navy:

For the German Empire of today the securing of its economic development, and particularly of its world trade, is a vital question.

For this end the German Empire requires not only peace on land, but also peace at sea—not, however, a peace at any price, but a peace with honour, which takes its legitimate needs into account.

....

In order, under existing conditions, to protect Germany's maritime commerce and colonies, there is only one way: Germany must possess so strong a battlefleet, that a war with her involves, even for the most powerful naval adversary, the danger of risking his own position as a Power. For this object it is not absolutely necessary for the German battlefleet to be just as strong as that of the greatest naval Power, for a great naval Power would not as a rule be in a position to concentrate all its fighting forces against us. Even if it did succeed in meeting us with a much superior force, the defeat of a strong German fleet would nevertheless weaken our adversary so materially that in spite of any hard won victory his own position as a Power would thereafter cease to be secured by an adequate fleet...

Source: J.R.H. O'Regan, ed., The German War of 1914 *(London: Oxford University Press, 1915), p. 30.*

Document 2 KAISER WILHELM II

The activities of the German emperor, Wilhelm II, for example, his attempts to interfere with France's position in Morocco, and his frequently tactless remarks, also added to tensions. In 1900, when German troops were departing for China to help to rescue foreigners under attack from Chinese rebels known as Boxers, Wilhelm made a farewell speech:

When you meet the foe you will defeat him. No quarter will be given; no prisoners taken. Let all who fall into your hands be at your mercy. Just as the Huns a thousand years ago, under the leadership of Attila gained a reputation in virtue of which they still live in historical tradition, so may the name of Germany become known in such a manner in China that no Chinaman will ever again even dare look askance at a German.... May the blessing of God attend your flags, and may this war have the blessed result that Christianity may make its way into China.

Source: J.R.H. O'Regan, ed., The German War of 1914 *(London: Oxford University Press, 1915), pp. 30, 33.*

DOCUMENT 3

SIR EDWARD GREY ON BRITISH POLICY

France and Russia were already concerned over growing German power by the end of the 19th century and the two countries began to move closer together. Great Britain, which was traditionally averse to alliances in peacetime, began to become concerned over its own isolation. It entered into a naval alliance with Japan and started to mend fences with previous antagonists, notably the United States, France (in the Entente Cordiale), and Russia. At the same time, Britain continued to hope for an understanding with Germany. On January 1, 1906 Sir Edward Grey, the British Foreign Secretary, wrote to his ambassador in Berlin about the forthcoming conference which was to discuss the fate of Morocco.

...I think, when you speak at Berlin, our intention to keep in letter and spirit our engagements to other countries, must be emphasized. It may be in the plural so as to include the Japanese Alliance as well as the French Entente and so avoid the appearance of being specially addressed to the Morocco question.

The subject might be introduced as an instance of how very open and frank British diplomacy is. Our Alliance and Entente, the terms as well as the facts, are published to the world. This would not be so if they were directed against any other country, and as a matter of fact we have no intention or desire, nor have our partners, to use them to the detriment of third parties.

....

The danger of speaking civil words in Berlin is that they may be used or interpreted in France as implying that we shall be lukewarm in our support of the Entente at the Conference. I think it is essential to guard against this danger, even at the risk of sending a little shudder through a German audience.

The rest will be plain sailing: commercial rivalry is not resented here; we don't in the least feel that German methods are directed against British trade. German success in trade may stimulate us to fresh efforts, but will not cause political estrangement, and we want to see the commerce between the two countries grow. It is the same with the growth of the German Navy: we build ships when other Powers do, but we don't regard their building as a hostile act against ourselves: the natural motive is the general desire to protect an Empire. In fact, if we were only quite sure that Germany did not regard our public engagements as incompatible with German interests, and if she would only believe that we do not mean badly to her, recent friction would disappear.

....

But fine words butter no parsnips, and if parsnips are to be buttered it must be done at the Conference. If that ends in conclusions not adverse to the Anglo-French Entente there will be a real clearing of the sky and an assurance of peace. If not, everything said now will go for nothing, and Europe will be very uncomfortable....

Source: C.J. Lowe and M.L. Dockrill, The Mirage of Power *volume 3* The Documents *(London and Boston: Routledge & Kegan Paul, 1972), pp. 426-427.*

DOCUMENT 4 EYRE CROWE ON GERMANY

The British became increasingly pessimistic about their relations with Germany. In 1909, Eyre Crowe, a senior official in the Foreign Office, outlined his concerns:

Everything points to the fact that Germany's efforts are at present directed to the dissolution of the understanding between England, France and Russia. Germany has realized that her bullying attitude towards France failed to detach that power from England. She now seeks the same object by making up to France and holding out prospects of commercial and financial advantage, to accrue from cooperation between France and Germany. This is an insidious weapon and may well prove effective at Paris. Towards Russia this same policy of first bullying, and then cajoling, is applied. Meanwhile England is to be kept quiet by throwing out the bait of disarmament.

Source: C.J. Lowe and M.L. Dockrill, The Mirage of Power *volume 3* The Documents *(London and Boston: Routledge & Kegan Paul, 1972), pp. 430-431.*

DOCUMENT 5 "THE BLANK CHEQUE"

Another source of tension before 1914 was in the Balkans where Austria-Hungary and Russia were rivals for influence. The situation was further complicated by the ambitions of Serbia to unite all South Slavs, including those within Austria-Hungary. Serbia was infuriated when Austria-Hungary annexed Bosnia-Herzegovina in 1908. On June 28, 1914 the heir to the Austrian throne, Franz Ferdinand, was assassinated when he visited Sarajevo, the capital of Bosnia-Herzegovina. The Austrians suspected Serbian backing for the assassins. Austria-Hungary decided to deal with Serbia and to ask for Germany's support in so doing. In spite of some reservations in Germany, the government decided to back Austria fully. This decision is often known as the "blank cheque." Count Ladislaus Szögyény-Marich was the Austro-Hungarian ambassador in Berlin. On July 5 he personally brought the Austrian request for support to the Kaiser. The following is from his report to his own government:

I received an invitation to lunch with Their Majesties at noon in the Neues Palais. I gave the autograph [signed personally by the Emperor Franz Joseph of Austria-Hungary] letter and the enclosed memoir into the hands of His Majesty. In my presence the Kaiser read both with the greatest attention. The first thing he assured me was, that he had expected some serious step on our part towards Serbia, but that at the same time he must confess that the detailed statement of His Majesty made him regard a serious European complication possible and that he could give no definite answer before having taken council with he Imperial chancellor.

After lunch, when I again called attention to the seriousness of the situation, the Kaiser authorized me to inform our gracious Majesty that we might in this case, as in all others, rely upon Germany's full support. He must, as he said before, first hear what the Imperial Chancellor has to say, but he did not doubt in the least that Herr von Bethmann Hollweg would agree with him. Especially in so far as our action against Serbia was concerned. But it was his (Kaiser Wilhelm's) opinion that this action must not be delayed. Russia' attitude will no doubt be hostile, but to this he had been for years prepared, and should a war between Austria-Hungary and Russia be unavoidable, we might be convinced that Germany, our old faithful ally, would stand by our side. Russia at the present time was in no way prepared for war, and would think twice before it appealed to arms. But it will certainly set other powers on to the Triple Alliance and fuel to the fire in the Balkans.

Source: Immanuel Geiss, ed., July 1914 *(New York: Charles Scribner's Sons, 1967), pp. 76-7.*

DOCUMENT 6 THE MEETING OF THE AUSTRO-HUNGARIAN GOVERNMENT ON JULY 7, 1914

Opinion in Austria-Hungary was anti-Serbian but there were reservations in the government about the wisdom of risking war. On July 7, the Council of Ministers discussed the situation. The Foreign Minister, Count Leopold Berchtold, opened the discussion:

The Council of Ministers has been called together to advise on the measures to be taken for meeting the evils which in Bosnia and Herzegovina have resulted from the catastrophe of Sarajevo. According to his view there would be a number of internal measures which the critical state of Bosnia has made desirable; but before deciding in their favour there should be clearness whether the moment has not come when a show of force might put an end to Serbia's intrigues once and for all. A decisive stroke of this kind cannot be dealt without previous diplomatic preparation, and for this reason the German government was informed and consulted. The discussions with Germany brought about a most satisfactory result, since Kaiser Wilhelm as well as Herr von Bethmann Hollweg [German chancellor] solemnly promised the support and aid of Germany in the event of a warlike complication with Serbia. We must still take into account Italy and Rumania; he agreed with the Berlin cabinet that it would be better to act first and wait for eventual claims to compensation afterwards.

He is by no means convinced that an expedition to Serbia must necessarily involve us in a war with Russia. Russia's present policy, which is farsighted, is aiming at a league of the Balkan states including Rumania, which it would at a suitable moment play out against our monarchy. It is his belief that we must take into account that in the face of this policy our situation must become more precarious as time goes on, all the more because if we do not act, our own South Slavs and Rumanians will interpret our attitude as weakness, and would be all the more disposed to lend a willing ear to the persuasions of our neighbours across the frontier.

....

The Royal Hungarian Premier [Count Stephan Tisza]: ... fully admits that the possibility of a warlike action against Serbia seems nearer than he believed just after the crime of Sarajevo. But he would never consent to a surprise attack upon Serbia without a previous diplomatic action, such as he is afraid is being intended and he is sorry to hear has been discussed in Berlin. We should, he believes, in this case play a sorry figure in the eyes of all Europe...

It is absolutely necessary that we address demands to Serbia and if these are rejected we must make out an ultimatum. Our exactions may be hard, but not such that they cannot be complied with. If Serbia accepted them, we should have a splendid diplomatic success and our *prestige* in the Balkans would gain immensely. If our demands are refused, he would also vote for a warlike action, but he must call attention to the fact that by a war we could reduce the size of Serbia, but we could not completely annihilate it. Russia would fight to the death before allowing this and he, as Hungarian premier, could never consent to the Monarchy's annexing any part of Serbia.

It is not for Germany to decide whether we ought to go to war with Serbia just now or not. Personally he holds the belief that it is not absolutely necessary to begin a war at the present moment.

Source: Immanuel Geiss, ed., July 1914 *(New York: Charles Scribner's Sons, 1967), pp. 80-2.*

DOCUMENT 7 THE BRITISH POSITION IN JULY 1914

One of the unknown factors was the attitude of Great Britain. The Triple Entente did not bind Britain to go to war to defend France or Russia. On the other hand, the British army and navy had held secret talks with the French over possible joint actions in the event of a German attack which created a moral if not legal obligation. The British government did not have a full knowledge of what had taken place in those talks. On July 9, the German ambassador in London tried to find out from the British Foreign Secretary, Sir Edward Grey, what Britain's position was. He reported Grey's words back to Berlin:

He...could only repeat to me that secret agreements between Great Britain on the one hand and France and Russia on the other, which would entail obligations on Great Britain in case of a European war, did not exist. England wished to preserve an absolutely free hand, in order to be able to act according to her own judgment in the event of continental complications.

....

But as he did not wish to put me on the wrong track—'as I did not want to mislead you'—he at once added that his relations to the Powers referred to had none the less lost none of their earlier intimacy. So that even if there existed no agreements which imposed any obligations, he did not wish to deny that from time to time 'conversations' had taken place between the naval or military authorities on both sides, the first of them as early as the year 1906, then again during the Morocco crisis, when they had believed here, he added smiling, that we intended to attack the French. But even these conversations, about which he knew most cases nothing definite, had absolutely no aggressive intent, as English policy, now as before, was aimed toward the maintenance of peace, and would find itself in a very painful situation if a European war should break out.

Source: Immanuel Geiss, ed., July 1914 *(New York: Charles Scribner's Sons, 1967), pp. 104-5.*

DOCUMENT 8 GERMANY'S POSITION IN JULY 1914

The Germans continued to reassure the Austro-Hungarians of their full support throughout July. Germany calculated that Russia was not ready to intervene. On July 12 the Austrian ambassador in Berlin reported back to his own government:

Germany has recently found its conviction confirmed that Russia is preparing for a war with its western neighbours, and does not regard war as a possibility of the future, but positively includes it in the political calculations of the future. This is important; it intends waging war, it is preparing for it with all its might, but does not propose it for the present, or we should rather say, is not prepared for it at the present time. It is therefore anything but certain that if Serbia is engaged in a war with us, Russia would lend an armed hand; and should the Czar's empire resolve for war, it would not be ready from a military point of view, and not by any means so strong, as it will be a few years hence.

Moreover the German government believes that it has proofs that England would not take part in a war, caused by disturbances in the Balkans, even if Russia and France were involved in it. Not only have relations between England and Germany improved so far, that Germany need no longer fear direct hostilities on England's part, but England just now desires anything rather than a war...

Source: Immanuel Geiss, ed., July 1914 *(New York: Charles Scribner's Sons, 1967), pp. 110-1.*

DOCUMENT 9 GERMAN RESERVATIONS ABOUT THE AUSTRIAN ALLIANCE

Germany by 1914 had come to see the disadvantages of an alliance with a decaying Austria-Hungary but felt that German prestige and interests meant continuing to support its ally. The following is from a private letter of July 18 from the German Foreign Secretary, Gottlieb von Jagow, to the German ambassador in London:

There may also be different opinions as to whether we get all our money's worth from an alliance with that ever increasingly disintegrating composition of nations beside the Danube, but there I say with the poet—Busch, I think it was—'If you no longer like your company, look for another, if any there be.' And, unfortunately, we have not yet been able to arrive at a relationship with England that promises complete satisfaction...

Austria, which has forfeited more and more prestige as the result of their lack of vigour, hardly counts any more as a really Great Power. The Balkan crisis has weakened her position still further.

....

Austria is now going to force a showdown with Serbia, and has told us so.....we neither could nor should attempt to stay her hand. If we should do that, Austria would have the right to reproach us (and we ourselves) with having deprived her of her last chance of political rehabilitation. And then the process of her wasting away and of her internal decay would be still further accelerated. Her standing in the Balkans would be gone forever. You will undoubtedly agree with me that the absolute establishment of the Russian hegemony in the Balkans is, indirectly, not permissible, even for us. The maintenance of Austria, and in fact, of the most powerful Austria possible, is a necessity for us both for internal and external reasons. That she cannot be maintained forever, I will willingly admit. But in the meantime we may perhaps be able to arrange other combinations.

Source: Immanuel Geiss, ed., July 1914 *(New York: Charles Scribner's Sons, 1967), pp. 122-3.*

DOCUMENT 10 WILHELM II ON SERBIA

The Serbian government made every attempt to comply with the list of demands presented to it by Austria-Hungary. This compliance was received with dismay by those in Germany and Austria-Hungary who were determined on war. Wilhelm II of Germany sent a memorandum on July 28 to his Foreign Secretary urging that Serbia now be asked to accept a temporary military occupation to ensure that its promises be carried out.

...*every cause for war* falls to the ground.

Nevertheless, the piece of paper, like its contents, can be considered as little value so long as it is not translated into *deeds*. The Serbs are Orientals, therefore liars, tricksters, and masters of evasion. In order that these beautiful promises may be turned to truth and facts, a *douce [gentle] violence* must be exercised. This should be so arranged that Austria would receive a *hostage* (Belgrade [capital of Serbia]), as a guaranty for the enforcement and carrying out of the promises

....

On this basis, I am ready to *mediate for peace* with Austria. Any proposals or protests to the contrary by other nations, I should refuse regardless...

Source: Immanuel Geiss, ed., July 1914 *(New York: Charles Scribner's Sons, 1967), p. 256.*

DOCUMENT 11 THE WILLY-NICKY CORRESPONDENCE

Wilhelm II of Germany and Nicholas II of Russia were cousins. Their correspondence is often known as the Willy-Nicky letters. As war approached, they sent each other increasingly agitated cables.

29 July Nicholas to Wilhelm:

Am glad you are back. In this most serious moment I appeal to you to help me. An *ignoble* war has been declared on a *weak* country [ie Serbia]. The *indignation* in Russia, *shared fully by me*, is *enormous*. I foresee that very soon I shall be *overwhelmed* by the *pressure* brought upon me, and be *forced* to take extreme measures which will *lead to war*. To try and avoid such a calamity as a European war, I beg you in the name of our old friendship to do what you can to *stop* your *allies* from *going too far*.

29 July Wilhelm to Nicholas:

I received your telegram and share your wish that peace should be maintained. But as I told you in my first telegram, I cannot consider Austria's action against Serbia an 'ignoble' war. Austria knows by experience that Serbian promises on paper are wholly unreliable.... Austria does not want to make any territorial conquests at the expense of the Serbs. I therefore suggest that it would be quite possible for Russia to remain a spectator of the Austro-Serbian conflict without involving Europe in the most horrible war she ever witnessed.

Source: Immanuel Geiss, ed., July 1914 *(New York: Charles Scribner's Sons, 1967), pp. 260, 290.*

DOCUMENT 12 RUSSIAN MOBILIZATION

Russia felt an obligation to defend Serbia against Austria. The Serbians were fellow Slavs and Orthodox Christians; as well Russia had been interested in the Balkans for a considerable period. While Russia was prepared for a conflict with Austria-Hungary, it did not want to go to war with Germany as well. Unfortunately, the government discovered in July 1914 that its military's mobilization plans did not allow for a partial mobilization against Austria-Hungary alone but would lead to mobilization against Germany. Russia had an additional concern: the size of the country and the state of its railways meant that its mobilization took longer than either Germany's or Austria-Hungary's. On July 29 the Russian Foreign Minister, Sergei Sazonov, sent the following to Russia's ambassador in Paris:

The German ambassador today informed me of the decision of his Government to mobilize, if Russia did not stop her military preparations. Now, in point of fact, we only began these preparations in consequence of the mobilization already undertaken by Austria and owing to her evident unwillingness to accept any means of arriving at a peaceful settlement of her dispute with Serbia.

As we cannot comply with the wishes of Germany, we have no alternative but to hasten on our own military preparations and to assume that war is probably inevitable. Please inform the French Government of this, and add that we are sincerely grateful to them for the declaration which the French ambassador made to me on their behalf, to the effect that we could count fully upon the assistance of our ally, France.

Source: Immanuel Geiss, ed., July 1914 *(New York: Charles Scribner's Sons, 1967), pp. 295-6.*

DOCUMENT 13 THE GERMAN INVASION OF BELGIUM

One of the final precipitating causes of the war was the German decision, made necessary by the Schlieffen Plan, to invade Belgium and therefore break its own agreement to respect Belgian neutrality (guaranteed by all the great powers of Europe under the Treaty of London of 1839). On July 29 the German government claimed, falsely, to have evidence that French forces were preparing to advance into Belgium along the river Meuse on their way to invade Germany. The German government therefore informed the Belgian government that Germany would be obliged to enter Belgium to defend itself.

The Imperial Government [ie Germany] cannot help being concerned over the probability that Belgium, despite the best of intentions, will be unable to resist without assistance a French advance with a prospect of success so great that sufficient security against the menace to Germany may be found therein. It is for Germany a dictate of self-preservation that she anticipate the hostile attack. It would therefore fill the German Government with the deepest regret, should Belgium view as an act of hostility to herself the entrance of Germany upon Belgian soil, should she be forced by the measures of her opponents to do so in self-protection.

....

Should Belgium oppose as an enemy the German troops, and in particular throw obstacles in their way by the resistance of the Meuse fortifications, or by the destruction of railroads, roads, tunnels or other artificial structures, Germany would be obliged, to her regret, to regard the Kingdom as an enemy.

Source: Immanuel Geiss, ed., July 1914 *(New York: Charles Scribner's Sons, 1967), pp. 231-2.*

DOCUMENT 14 GERMAN ATTEMPTS TO KEEP GREAT BRITAIN NEUTRAL

On July 29 the German chancellor told the British ambassador in Berlin that Germany would respect the Netherland's neutrality but that it could not give guarantees on Belgium. He asked for British assurances that it would remain out of the coming conflict with France and expressed hope that Germany and Britain could remain friends. He also hinted that Germany would be interested in taking some of France's colonies. Sir Edward Grey, the British Foreign Secretary, commented:

The only comment that need be made on these astounding proposals is that they reflect discredit on the statesman who makes them....

It is clear that Germany is practically determined to go to war, and that the one restraining influence so far has been the fear of England joining in the defence of France and Belgium.

JULY 30: GREY TO THE BRITISH AMBASSADOR IN BERLIN

You must inform the German Chancellor that his proposal that we should bind ourselves to neutrality on such terms cannot for a moment be entertained.

He asks us in effect to engage to stand by while French colonies are taken and France is beaten so long as Germany does not take French territory as distinct form colonies.

From the material point of view such a proposal is unacceptable, for France could be so crushed as to lose their position as a Great Power and become subordinate to German policy without further territory being taken from her.

But apart from that, for us to make this bargain with Germany at the expense of France would be a disgrace from which the good name of this country would never recover.

Source: Immanuel Geiss, ed., July 1914 *(New York: Charles Scribner's Sons, 1967), pp. 301, 315.*

DOCUMENT 15 FRENCH AND GERMAN MOBILIZATION

France had been watching the growing crisis with concern. It was aware that Germany intended to strike against it in the event of a general war. By 1914 the French and German armies were roughly equal in numbers of soldiers but since France had a population only 60% that of Germany's and the French birthrate was falling, the French could see Germany pulling ahead in numbers in the near future. On the other hand, France's ally, Russia, was not expected to reach its full military strength until 1917. On balance, the French felt it was better to fight in 1914 than to wait much longer. The question for the French by July 1914 was what would Britain do? On July 30, the French ambassador in Berlin cabled René Viviani, the French prime minister and foreign minister:

...the military authorities [ie the German ones] are very anxious that mobilization should be ordered, because every delay makes Germany lose some of her advantages. Nevertheless up to the present the haste of the General Staff which sees war in mobilization, had been successfully prevented.

...

What matters is to make public mobilization measures in France only after they have been definitely decided upon in Germany, so that British public opinion, which plays such an important role in what is happening, cannot attribute to us any initiative that led to war.

Source: Immanuel Geiss, ed., July 1914 *(New York: Charles Scribner's Sons, 1967), p. 313.*

DOCUMENT 16 RUSSIA'S MOBILIZATION

Russia began partial mobilization against Austria-Hungary, while hoping to avoid a conflict with Germany. On July 31, Wilhelm cabled to his cousin Nicholas.

I now received authentic news of serious preparations for war on my eastern frontier. Responsibility for the safety of my Empire forces preventive measures of defence upon me. In my endeavours to maintain the peace of the world I have gone to the utmost limit possible. The responsibility for the disaster which is now threatening the whole civilized world will not be laid at my door. In this moment it still lies in your power to avert it.

....

My friendship for you and your Empire, transmitted to me by my grandfather on his deathbed, has always been sacred to me and I have honestly often backed up Russia when she was in serious trouble...

Source: Immanuel Geiss, ed., July 1914 *(New York: Charles Scribner's Sons, 1967), p. 324.*

DOCUMENT 17 FRANCE'S DECLARATION OF WAR

On August 4, the President of France, Raymond Poincaré spoke to the French Parliament. The deputies rose to their feet as he began to speak:

France has just been made the object of a violent and premeditated attack, which is an insolent defiance of the law of nations...

For more than forty years [ie since the Franco-Prussian war] the French, in sincere love of peace, have buried at the bottom of their heart the desire for legitimate reparation.

They have given to the world the example of a great nation which, definitely raised from defeat by the exercise of will, patience and labour, has only used its renewed and rejuvenated strength in the interest of progress and for the good of humanity.

....

At the hour when the struggle is beginning, she has the right, in justice to herself, of solemnly declaring that she has made, up to the last moment, supreme efforts to avert the war now about to break out, the crushing responsibility for which the German Empire will have to bear before history. (*Unanimous and repeated applause.*)

....

She will be heroically defended by all her sons; nothing will break their sacred union before the enemy; today they are joined together as brothers in a common indignation against the aggressor, and in a common patriotic faith (*loud and prolonged applause and cries of 'Vive la France'*).

DOCUMENT 18 EUROPE AT WAR

Sir Edward Grey spoke to a friend in London on August 3 as they watched the lamplighters with the gas lamps in the park outside:

"The lamps are going out all over Europe; we shall not see them lit again in our lifetime."

Source: Viscount Grey, [Sir Edward], Twenty-Five Years, 1892-1916, *vol.* 2 *(New York: Frederick A. Stokes Company, 1925), p. 20.*

STUDY QUESTIONS FOR SECTION ONE: THE OUTBREAK OF WORLD WAR I

1. Why were Europeans expecting war by 1914?

2. What was the alliance system?

3. Why did the war start in the Balkans?

4. Could any country have done anything to stop the slide towards a general war?

5. Does Germany bear the greatest responsibility for the outbreak of the war?

SECTION TWO

PEACEMAKING

DOCUMENTS

The victorious allies met in Paris in January 1919 for what was intended to be a preliminary peace conference to work out peace terms to be presented to the defeated nations at a full scale peace conference. For various reasons—the length of time it took to get agreement among the allies, as well as the strong public hostility to Germany in particular—the preliminary conference ended up being the only peace conference. Germany and the other defeated nations, Austria, Hungary, Bulgaria and Turkey, were summoned to Paris and given their peace terms on a virtual take-it-or-leave-it basis.

Nations present included the Big Four—the British Empire, France, Italy, and the United States—as well as Japan which was sometimes counted as another major power. The British Dominions—Canada, Australia, New Zealand, and South Africa—and India attended as part of the British Empire Delegation. In addition, the smaller allies from Serbia to China, were present as were representatives of newly independent countries such as Poland. The Russians, although Russia had been allied to the winning side, were not represented, mainly because of the difficulties of dealing with the new Bolshevik government. Large numbers of delegations, from the Zionists to the Armenians, came to Paris to put in their demands.

In the end five major treaties were drawn up in Paris. Each is named after the suburb in which it was signed: the Treaty of Versailles with Germany (June 1919), the Treaty of St. Germain with Austria (September 1919), the Treaty of Neuilly with Bulgaria (November 1919), the Treaty of Trianon with Hungary (June 1920), and the Treaty of Sèvres with Turkey (August 1920).

DOCUMENT 1 THE FOURTEEN POINTS

President Woodrow Wilson referred to American war aims and the basis on which peace should be made on several occasions after the United States entered the War in April 1917. His speech on January 8, 1918 enunciated what came to be known as the Fourteen Points. When the German government began to ask for an armistice it said, in a Note of October 12, 1918 "The German Government has accepted the terms laid down by President Wilson in his address of January 8 and in his subsequent addresses on the foundation of a permanent peace of justice. Consequently its object in entering into discussions would be only to agree upon practical details of the application of these terms." The issue of whether Wilson's statements, especially the 14 Points, were the basis and the guarantee upon which Germany surrendered was to be one of the most disputed aspects of Germany's surrender and the making of the peace which followed.

We entered this war because violations of right had occurred which touched us to the quick and made the life of our own people impossible unless they were corrected and the world secured once for all against their recurrence. What we demand in this war, therefore, is nothing peculiar to ourselves. It is that the world be made safe for every peace-loving nation which, like our own, wishes to live its own free life, determine its own institutions, be assured of justice and fair dealing by the other peoples of the world, as against force and selfish aggression. All the peoples of the world are in effect partners in this interest, and for our own part we see very clearly that unless justice be done to others it will not be done to us.

The programme of the world's peace, therefore, is our programme, and that programme, the only possible programme, as we see it, is this:

One. Open covenants of peace, openly arrived at...

Two. Absolute freedom of navigation upon the seas outside territorial waters alike in peace and war....

Three. The removal, so far as possible, of all economic barriers...

Four. ...national armaments will be reduced to the lowest point consistent with domestic safety

Five. A free, open-minded, and absolutely impartial adjustment of all colonial claims based upon a strict observance of the principle that in determining all such questions of sovereignty the interests of the populations concerned must have equal weight with the equitable claims of the Government whose title is to be determined.

Six. The evacuation of all Russian territory, and such a settlement of all questions affecting Russia as will secure the best and freest co-operation of the other nations of the world in obtaining for her an unhampered and unembarrassed opportunity for the independent determination of her own political development and national policy....

Seven. Belgium...must be evacuated and restored...

Eight. All French territory should be freed and the invaded portions restored, and the wrong done to France by Prussia in 1871 in the matter of Alsace-Lorraine, which has unsettled the peace of the world for nearly fifty years, should be righted...

Nine. A readjustment of the frontiers of Italy should be effected along clearly recognizable lines of nationality.

Ten. The peoples of Austria-Hungary... should be accorded the freest opportunity of autonomous development.

Eleven. Rumania, Serbia, and Montenegro should be evacuated, occupied territories restored, Serbia accorded free and secure access to the sea...

Twelve. The Turkish portions of the present Ottoman Empire should be assured a secure sovereignty, but the other nationalities which are now under Turkish rule should be assured...an absolutely unmolested opportunity of autonomous development...

Thirteen. An independent Polish State should be erected which should include the territories inhabited by indisputably Polish populations, which should be assured a free and secure access to the sea...

Fourteen. A general association of nations must be formed under specific covenants for the purpose of affording mutual guarantees of political independence and territorial integrity to great and small states.

Source: The Papers of Woodrow Wilson, *ed. A.S. Link et al (Princeton: Princeton University Press, 1966-) vol. XLV, pp. 534-539.*

DOCUMENT 2

INTERVENTION IN RUSSIA

One of the difficult issues facing the Allies in Paris was how to deal with Russia, which had been an ally in 1914 but which had dropped out of the war in 1917 and, under its new Bolshevik government, had made a separate peace with Germany. Allied opinion was divided with David Lloyd George, the British prime minister, arguing for inviting representatives of the new Russian government to Paris, and the French prime minister, Georges Clemenceau vehemently opposed. President Wilson of the United States, who had frequently expressed his sympathy for the Russian people, proposed as a compromise sending an allied delegation to meet the Bolsheviks near Istanbul. In the end nothing came of the scheme partly because the Bolsheviks made demands the Allies would not accept. The following discussion on Wilson's proposal for a meeting took place among the great powers on January 17, 1919.

President Wilson asked to be permitted to urge one aspect of the case. As M. Sonnino [Italian foreign minister] had implied, they were all repelled by Bolshevism, and for that reason they had placed armed men in opposition to them. One of the things that was clear in the Russian situation was that by opposing Bolshevism with arms they were in reality serving the cause of Bolshevism. The Allies were making it possible for the Bolsheviks to argue that Imperialistic and Capitalistic Governments were endeavouring to exploit the country and to give the land back to the landlords, and so bring about a reaction. If it could be shown that this was not true and that the Allies were prepared to deal with the rulers of Russia, much of the moral force of this argument would disappear.

....

M. Clemenceau [Prime Minister of France] said that, in principle, he did not favour conversation with the Bolsheviks; not because they were criminals, but because we would be raising them to our level by saying that they were worthy of entering into conversation with us. The Bolshevik danger was very great at the present moment. Bolshevism was spreading. It had invaded the Baltic Provinces and Poland, and that very morning they had received very bad news regarding its spread to Budapest and Vienna. Italy, also, was in danger. The danger was probably greater there than in France. If Bolshevism, after spreading to Germany, were to traverse Austria and Hungary and so reach Italy, Europe would be faced with a very great danger. Therefore, something must be done against Bolshevism.

....

M. Sonnino. His idea was to collect together all the anti-Bolshevik parties and help them to make a strong Government, provided they pledged themselves not to serve the forces of reaction and especially not to touch the land question, thereby depriving the Bolsheviks of their strongest argument. Should they take these pledges, he would be prepared to help them.

Mr. Lloyd George enquired how this help would be given.

M. Sonnino replied that help would be given with soldiers to a reasonable degree or by supplying arms, food, and money...

Mr. Lloyd George said he wished to put one or two practical questions to M. Sonnino. The British Empire now had some 15,000 to 20,000 men in Russia....some 150,000 additional men would be required, in order to keep the anti-Bolshevik Governments from dissolution....Now Canada had decided to withdraw her troops, because the Canadian soldiers would not agree to stay and fight against the Russians. Similar trouble had also occurred amongst other Allied troops. And he felt certain that, if the British tried to send any more troops there, there would be mutiny.

M. Sonnino suggested that volunteers might be called for.

Mr. Lloyd George, continuing, said that it would be impossible to raise 150,000 men in that way. He asked, however, what contributions America, Italy and France would make towards the raising of this army.

President Wilson and M. Clemenceau each said none.

M. Orlando [Italian prime minister] agreed that Italy could make no further contributions.

Source: Papers Relating to the Foreign Relations of the United States (hereafter cited as FRUS) 1919: The Paris Peace Conference, *(Washington: United States Government Printing Office, 1942-47), vol 3, 648-651.*

DOCUMENT 3 THE RHINELAND

The French position at the Peace Conference as far as Germany was concerned was quite straightforward: France wanted Germany so weak that it would never again be in a position to threaten French territory and French security. France's initial demands included German territory, notably the Rhineland, to the west of the Rhine river. On March 31, 1919 the chief of the French General Staff, Marshall Ferdinand Foch, made this appeal to the Allied leaders:

To give up the barrier of the RHINE is to admit the following unthinkable monstrosity: that, although she be beaten, GERMANY, all covered with blood and crime, GERMANY, who is responsible for the death of millions of human beings, GERMANY, wanted to destroy our country and turn it into a heap of ruins, GERMANY, who has undertaken to dominate the world by sheer force, would be, by our voluntary withdrawal from the RHINE, maintained in such a position that she could renew her undertakings just as if she had been victorious.

I instantly beg the Allied and Associated Governments, who in the most critical hours of the War entrusted me with the leadership of their Armies and the welfare of the common cause, to consider that, tomorrow just as today, that welfare can only be ensured in any lasting manner, by making the RHINE our military frontier, and by holding it with Allied forces.

Source: David Lloyd George, The Truth about the Peace Treaties *(London: Victor Gollancz, 1938), vol 1, p. 423.*

DOCUMENT 4 THE ANGLO-AMERICAN GUARANTEE TO FRANCE

When the French demand for the Rhineland was rejected by Britain and France at Paris, France received by way of reassurance the following guarantee on May 6, 1919 from the United States and Great Britain. The guarantee never became operational because the United States Senate rejected the peace settlement.

In addition to the securities afforded in the Treaty of Peace, the President of the United States has pledged himself to propose to the Senate of the United States and the Prime Minister of Great Britain has pledged himself to propose to the Parliament of Great Britain an engagement subject to approval of the Council of the League of Nations to come immediately to the assistance of France in the case of unprovoked attack by Germany.

Source: Papers Relating to the FRUS 1919: The Paris Peace Conference, *(Washington: United States Government Printing Office, 1942-47), vol 3, 379.*

DOCUMENT 5 THE "WAR-GUILT CLAUSE"

This was inserted into the Treaty of Versailles, in part, to provide the legal basis for assessing reparations from Germany. Because of disagreement among the victors over how much Germany could and should pay, the amount of reparations owing was not fixed in the Treaty itself. That fact and indeed the whole issue of reparations caused much trouble in international relations in the 1920s and was going to be a factor in the hostility of many Germans towards the Treaty of Versailles and in the rise of the Nazi Party to power.

Article 231, Treaty of Versailles. The Allied and Associated Governments affirm and Germany accepts the responsibility of Germany and her allies for causing all the loss and damage to which the Allied and Associated Governments and their nationals have been subjected as a consequence of the war imposed upon them by the aggression of Germany and her allies.

Source: Department of State, The Treaty of Versailles and After *(Washington: United States Government Printing Office, 1947), p. 413.*

DOCUMENT 6 GERMAN DISARMAMENT

The disarmament clauses in the Treaty of Versailles provided for a severely limited army, navy and air force for Germany.

In order to render possible the initiation of a general limitation of the armaments of all nations, Germany undertakes strictly to observe the military, naval and air clauses which follow.

Article 160. (1) By a date which must not be later than March 31, 1920, the German army must not comprise more than seven divisions of infantry and three divisions of cavalry. After that date the total number of effectives in the Army of the States constituting Germany must not exceed one hundred thousand men, including officers and establishments of depots. The Army shall be devoted exclusively to the maintenance of order within the territory and to the control of the frontiers.

Article 171. ...The manufacture and the importation into Germany of armoured cars, tanks and all similar constructions for use in war are also prohibited.

Article 177. Educational establishments, the universities, societies of discharged soldiers, shooting or touring clubs, and, generally speaking, associations of every description, whatever be the age of their members, must not occupy themselves with any military matters. In particular, they will be forbidden to instruct or exercise their members, or to allow them to be instructed or exercised, in the profession or use of arms.

Article 191. The construction or acquisition of any submarine, even for commercial purposes, shall be forbidden in Germany.

Article 198. The armed forces of Germany must not include any military or naval air forces.

Source: Department of State, The Treaty of Versailles and After *(Washington: United States Government Printing Office, 1947), pp. 309, 319, 329, 331-2, 351.*

DOCUMENT 7 THE GERMAN REACTION TO THE TREATY OF VERSAILLES

German public opinion was horrified by the harshness of the peace terms presented to the German delegation on April 29, 1919. Although the German government tried to negotiate over the treaty, the Allies insisted that Germany accept the treaty as a whole or face the consequences. After a political crisis in Germany, the government, following advice from senior army officials that resistance would be impossible, voted to accept the terms, and sent the following note to the Allies on June 23, 1919.

The Government of the German republic has seen with consternation from the last communication of the Allied and Associated Governments that the latter are resolved to wrest from Germany by sheer force even the acceptance of those conditions of peace which, though devoid of material significance, pursue the object of taking away its honour from the German people. The honour of the German people will remain untouched by any act of violence. The German people, after the frightful sufferings of the last few years, lack all means of defending its honour by external action. Yielding to overpowering force, but without on that account abandoning its views in regard to the unheard-of injustice of the conditions of the peace, the Government of the German Republic therefore declares that it is ready to accept and sign the conditions of peace imposed by the Allied and Associated Governments.

Source: Papers Relating to the FRUS 1919: The Paris Peace Conference, *(Washington: United States Government Printing Office, 1942-47), vol 6, p. 644.*

DOCUMENT 8 GENERAL SMUTS CRITICIZES THE PEACE SETTLEMENT

General Smuts, the great South African statesman and one of the strongest proponents of the League of Nations, was highly critical of the terms being offered to Germany. He wrote several private letters to David Lloyd George, the British Prime Minister, urging him to use his influence with the French and the Americans to moderate the peace. On March 26, 1919, for example, he wrote:

My dear Prime Minister,

Since my return to Paris last Sunday I have tried to get into touch with the present state of our peace preparations. May I trouble you with some of the reflections stirred in me by what I have learnt? I fear it won't be pleasant reading to you, but my criticism is well-meant, and may prove helpful to you.

I am seriously afraid that the peace to which we are working is an impossible peace, conceived on a wrong basis: that it will not be accepted by Germany, and even if accepted, that it will prove utterly unstable, and only serve to promote the anarchy which is rapidly overtaking Europe....

To my mind certain points seem quite clear and elementary.

1. We cannot destroy Germany without destroying Europe
2. We cannot save Europe without the co-operation of Germany.

Yet we are now preparing a peace which must destroy Germany, and yet we think that we shall save Europe by so doing! The fact is, the Germans are, have been, and will continue to be the *dominant factor* on the Continent of Europe, and no permanent peace is possible which is not based on that fact.

Source: Lloyd George Papers, House of Lords Records Office (London, England), F/45/9/29.

General Smuts issued the following comment on the Treaty of Versailles right after it was signed.

I have signed the Peace Treaty, not because I consider it a satisfactory document, but because it is imperatively necessary to close the war; because the world needs peace above all, and nothing could be more fatal than the continuance of the state of suspense between war and peace. The six months since the Armistice was signed have, perhaps, been as upsetting, unsettling, and ruinous to Europe as the previous four years of war. I look upon the Peace Treaty as the close of those two chapters of war and armistice, and only on that ground do I agree to it.

....

In this Treaty, however, two achievements of far-reaching importance for this world are definitely recorded. The one is the destruction of

Prussian militarism; the other is the institution of the League of Nations. *I am confident that the League of Nations will yet prove the path of escape for Europe out of the ruin brought about by this war.*

Source: H.W.V. Temperley, ed., A History of the Peace Conference of Paris *(London, Toronto, New York: Oxford University Press, 1920), vol III, Appendix III, part 1, pp. 74-5.*

STUDY QUESTIONS FOR SECTION TWO: PEACEMAKING

1. What demands and expectations did the Big Four of Great Britain, France, Italy and the United States bring to the Paris Peace Conference?

2. Why was Russia absent from the Peace Conference and what was the significance of that absence?

3. What were the major issues that had to be settled in Paris in 1919?

4. What were the strengths and weaknesses of the peace settlements in Europe?

SECTION THREE

EUROPE 1919-1939

DOCUMENTS

CHRONOLOGY

1919	Treaties of Versailles (Germany), St. German (Austria), Neuilly (Bulgaria) signed
1920	United States Senate rejects Treaty of Versailles; Treaties of Trianon (Hungary) and Sèvres (Turkey) signed
1922	Washington Naval Conference agreements on Naval Limitation and China; Treaty of Rapallo between Russia and Germany; Mussolini takes power in Italy
1923	Ruhr crisis; German passive resistance Treaty of Lausanne (Turkey)
1924	Dawes Plan
1925	Locarno Treaties
1926	Germany enters League of Nations
1928	Briand-Kellogg Pact
1929	Young Plan Wall Street crash—Great Depression starts
1931	Japanese invasion of Manchuria
1932	Japan recognizes puppet state of Manchukuo
1933	
Jan.	Hitler becomes Chancellor of Germany
Mar.	Japan leaves League of Nations
Oct.	Germany leaves League of Nations and Disarmament Conference
1934	Germany and Poland sign 10-year nonaggression pact Russia enters League of Nations
1935	Germany repudiates military clauses in Treaty of Versailles Franco-Soviet Treaty of Mutual Assistance Franco-Czechoslovak Treaty of Mutual Assistance Anglo-German naval agreement
Oct.	Mussolini invades Ethiopia (Abyssinian crisis)
1936	
Mar.	Germany denounces Locarno Treaty; German troops remilitarize Rhineland
July	Spanish Civil War starts
Oct.	Berlin-Rome Axis proclaimed
Nov.	Japan and Germany sign Anti-Comintern Pact
1937	
Jan.	Italy signs Anti-Comintern Pact
May	Neville Chamberlain British Prime Minister
July	Japan invades main part of China
Oct.	President Roosevelt's quarantine speech
1938	
Mar.	German troops take over Austria (Anschluss)
Apr.	Sudeten German leaders demand independence from Czechoslovakia
Sep.	Munich Conference
Oct.	German troops occupy Sudetenland
1939	
Mar.	German troops occupy rest of Czech lands; Slovakia becomes puppet state under German control
Apr.	Hitler denounces nonaggression pact with Poland
May	Germany and Italy sign Pact of Steel
Aug. 23	Nazi-Soviet nonaggression pact
Sep. 1	German troops invade Poland
Sep. 3	Britain and France declare war on Germany

DOCUMENT 1 THE BRIAND-KELLOGG PACT

For a brief period, in the 1920s, relations among the European powers improved. The League of Nations started work and achieved some modest success. Under Gustav Stresemann, Germany came back into the international order. Even the Soviet Union established normal trading and diplomatic relations with some of its neighbors. The Washington Naval Conference and the Locarno agreements suggested that nations were prepared to settle their differences peacefully. In 1929, the Briand-Kellogg Pact (named after the French and American foreign ministers) was signed by numerous countries.

The President of the German Reich, the President of the United States of America, His Majesty the King of the Belgians, the President of the French Republic, His Majesty the King of Great Britain, Ireland and the British Dominions beyond the Seas, Emperor of India, His Majesty the King of Italy, His Majesty the Emperor of Japan, the President of the Republic of Poland, the President of the Czechoslovakia republic,

Deeply sensible of their solemn duty to promote the welfare of mankind;

Persuaded that the time has come when a frank renunciation of war as an instrument of national policy should be made to the end that the peaceful and friendly relations now existing between their peoples may be perpetuated;

Convinced that all changes in their relations with one another should be sought only by pacific means and be the result of a peaceful and orderly process, and that any signatory Power which shall hereafter seek to promote its national interests by resort to war should be denied the benefits furnished by this Treaty;

Hopeful that, encouraged by their example, all the other nations of the world will join in this humane endeavor and by adhering to the present Treaty as soon as it comes into force bring their peoples within the scope of its beneficent provisions, thus uniting the civilized nations of the world in a common renunciation of war as an instrument of their national policy;

Have decided to conclude a Treaty....

Article 1.

The High Contracting Parties solemnly declare in the names of their respective peoples that they condemn recourse to war for the solution of international controversies, and renounce it as an instrument of national policy in their relations with one another.

Article 2.

The High Contracting Parties agree that the settlement or solution of all disputes or conflicts of whatever nature or of whatever origin they may be, which may arise among them, shall never be sought except by pacific means.

Source: W.C. Langsam, ed., Documents and Readings in the History of Europe since 1918 *(Chicago, Philadelphia, New York: J. B. Lippincott Company, 1969) pp. 220-1.*

DOCUMENT 2 THE COMINTERN AND WORLD REVOLUTION

By the late 1920s, the Soviet Union, under Joseph Stalin, was concentrating on building socialism within its borders and was taking a less active role in promoting world revolution. Other nations, though, continued to regard it with suspicion. The language used by the Soviets, and in particular by the Communist International (or Comintern) which was based in Moscow did not help matters. The following comes from a Comintern manifesto of 1928:

To the Workers of the World! To all Workers and Peasants! To all Oppressed Colonial Peoples! To the Soldiers and Sailors of the Capitalist Armies and Navies!

Comrades, Fellow Workers!

The Sixth Congress of the Communist International, the representative of the revolutionary workers all over the world, of all nations, peoples and races, appeals to you from Moscow, the red capital of the new world, to prepare yourselves for a struggle against the ever more insolent forces of capitalism.

The master of the world, capital, which exploits the labour power of the workers in the most brutal fashion, which sucks out their strength, which turns the proletariat into a unit of capitalist technique, which wears out its proletarian slaves in the process of production, which places the most wonderful discoveries of science in the service of the golden calf, which introduces ever more complicated and splendid machines, which introduces to an ever increasing extent the conveyor and flings millions of workers on to the streets, which gives them stones instead of bread, capital is now marching into the struggle against the rights and freedom of the working class. It is pressing the standard of living of the workers down ever lower, raising the bloody sword of the white terror and preparing for a new world war under the cloak of lying and bombastic phrases of world peace.

Imperialism has once again placed the question of war upon the agenda. From day to day the competition between the great powers and their finance-capitalist cliques is sharpening. Their attacks upon the colonies are becoming ever more brutal, their attempts to encircle the tremendous body of the Union of Soviet Socialist Republics ever more determined.

The Communist International appeals to all toilers, and in particular to the industrial workers, to take up the struggle for every inch of ground that has been won, to fight against the offensive of capitalism, to fight against the ruthless exploitation of capitalism, to fight against the enslavement of the proletariat, to fight against the policy of the imperialists and against imperialist war.

Source: W.C. Langsam, ed., Documents and Readings in the History of Europe since 1918 *(Chicago, Philadelphia, New York: J. B. Lippincott Company, 1969) pp. 840-1.*

DOCUMENT 3

THE ITALIAN INVASION OF ETHIOPIA

The rise of fascist movements, with their intense nationalism, threatened Europe's stability in the interwar years. The first success for fascism came in Italy where Mussolini took power in October 1922. In spite of Italy's weaknesses, he was determined to build a second Roman Empire. In 1935 Italy invaded one of the few independent parts of Africa, Ethiopia (or Abyssinia). Mussolini successfully defied the League of Nations, thus weakening it further, and encouraging other aggressors. In a speech of October 2, 1935, he justified his actions:

Mussolini's arrogant defiance of the League of Nations' decisions on Ethiopia is perhaps most clearly stated in this call to military action.

Speech by Signor Mussolini on the Eve of the Invasion of Ethiopia, October 2, 1935

Blackshirts of the revolution, men and women of Italy, Italians scattered throughout the world, across the mountains and across the oceans, listen:

A solemn hour is about to strike in the history of the fatherland. Twenty million Italians are at this moment gathered in the squares throughout the whole of Italy. It is the most gigantic demonstration which the history of mankind records. Twenty millions, a single heart, a single will, a single decision. This manifestation is to signify that the identity between Italy and Fascism is perfect, absolute, and unchangeable. Only brains weakened by puerile illusions or benumbed in a crass ignorance can think the contrary, because they do not know what this Fascist Italy of 1935 is. For many months the wheel of destiny, under the impulse of our calm determination, has been making towards the goal. In these last hours the rhythm has become more speedy and cannot now be arrested.

Not only is an army marching towards its objectives, but 40,000,000 Italians are marching in unison with this army, all united because there is an attempt to commit against them the blackest of all injustices, to rob them of a place in the sun. When in 1915 Italy united its lot with those of the Allies, how many shouts of admiration and how many promises! But after the common victory, to which Italy had brought the supreme contribution of 670,000 dead, 400,000 disabled, 1,000,000 wounded, when it came to sitting around the table of the mean peace, to us were left only the crumbs from the sumptuous colonial booty of others. During 20 years we have been patient while there tightened round us ever more rigidly the ring which wanted to suffocate our overflowing vitality. With Ethiopia we have been patient for 40 years. Now, enough!

At the League of Nations, instead of recognizing the just rights of Italy, they dared to speak of sanctions.

....

Let nobody delude himself that he can deflect us. A people which is proud of its name and of its future cannot adopt a different attitude. But let it be said once again in the most categorical manner, as a sacred pledge which I take at this moment before all the Italians who are listening to me, that we will do everything possible to avoid a colonial conflict assuming the character and bearing of a European conflict. This may be the wish of those who see in a new war revenge for fallen temples, but it cannot be our wish.

Never more than in this historic epoch has the Italian people revealed the force of its spirit and the power of its character. And it is against this people to which humanity owes the greatest of its conquests, it is against this people of heroes, poets, artists, navigators, and administrators, that they dare to speak of sanctions.

Italy, proletarian and Fascist Italy, Italy of Vittorio Veneto and of the Revolution, to your feet! To your feet!

Let the cry of your firm and unshakable decision reach the sky and be a comfort to the soldiers who are about to fight in Africa, and let this be a spur to them and a warning to enemies in all parts of the world, a cry of justice and cry of victory.

Source: Stephen Fischer-Galati, ed., Twentieth Century Europe: a documentary history *(Philadelphia and New York: J.B. Lippincott Company, 1967), pp. 195-7.*

The Speech by Mussolini is reprinted by permission from The Times *(London) October 2, 1935.*

DOCUMENT 4 NEVILLE CHAMBERLAIN AND APPEASEMENT

The response of the democracies to Hitler was mixed. While they regarded Germany under his leadership as a potential threat to stability in Europe, they also believed that Germans had legitimate grievances about the peace settlement after World War I. Leaders of nations such as Britain and France were also conscious of the huge losses their countries had incurred during that war and were anxious if possible to prevent another war. Another factor often entered into their thinking and that was fear of Soviet Communism which, especially for those on the right, was perceived as a worse threat than German Nazism. For all these reasons, men such as Neville Chamberlain, the British Prime Minister from 1937-1940, followed a policy of what came to be called "appeasement"—responding to Hitler's demands where they seemed reasonable in the hopes of containing Germany within a peaceful European system. In a speech in London in November 1937, Chamberlain outlined his approach to international relations.

...Perhaps I may put my subject in the form of a question. What sort of future are we trying to create for ourselves and for our children? Is it to be better or worse than that which we have inherited? Are we trying to make a world in which the peoples that inhabit it shall be able to live out their lives in peace of mind and in the enjoyment of a constantly rising standard of all that makes life worth living, of health and comfort, or recreation, and of culture? Or are we preparing for ourselves a future which is to be one perpetual nightmare, filled with the constant dread of the horrors of war, forced to bury ourselves below ground and to spend all our substance upon the weapons of destruction?

One has only to state these two alternatives to be sure that human nature, which is the same all the world over, must reject the nightmare with all its might and cling to the only prospect which can give happiness. And for any Government deliberately to deny to their people what must be their plainest and simplest right would be to betray their trust and to call down upon their heads the condemnation of all mankind.

I do not believe that such a Government anywhere exists among civilised peoples. I am convinced that the aim of every statesman worthy the name, to whatever country he belongs, must be the happiness of the people for whom and to whom he is responsible, and in that faith I am sure that a way can, and will, be found to free the world from the curse of armaments and the fears that give rise to them and to open up a happier and a wiser future for mankind.

Source: New York Times, April 2, 1937 [cited in Joachim Remak, The Origins of the Second World War, *(New Jersey: Prentice-Hall, 1976), pp. 64-65].*

DOCUMENT 5 HITLER'S PLANS FOR EUROPE IN 1937

In 1937 Hitler had a meeting with his senior officials in which he outlined his plans for Germany. The record of the meeting, known as the Hossbach Memorandum after the man who kept it, is accepted as authentic.

Minutes of the Conference in the Reich Chancellery, Berlin, November 5, 1937, from 4.15 to 8.30 pm.

Present: The Führer and Chancellor [ie Hitler]; Colonel General Baron von Fritsch, Commander in Chief, Army; Admiral Dr. H.C. Raeder, Commander in Chief, Navy; Colonel General Goering, Commander in Chief, Luftwaffe [air force]; Baron von Neurath, Foreign Minister; Colonel Hossbach.

The Führer began by stating that the subject of the present conference was of such importance that its discussion would, in other countries, certainly be a matter for a full Cabinet meeting, but he—the Führer—had rejected the idea of making it a subject of discussion before the wider circle of the Reich Cabinet just because of the importance of the matter. His exposition to follow was the fruit of thorough deliberation and the experiences of his 4 1/2 years in power....he asked, in the interests of a long-term German policy, that his exposition be regarded, in the event of his death, as his last will and testament.

The Führer then continued:

The aim of German policy was to make secure and preserve the racial community and to enlarge it. It was therefore a question of space....

German policy had to reckon with two hate-inspired antagonists, Britain and France to whom a German colossus in the centre of Europe was a thorn in the flesh, and both countries were opposed to any further strengthening of Germany's position either in Europe or overseas....

Germany's problem could only be solved by means of force and this was never without attendant risk....If one accepts as the basis of the following exposition the resort to force with its attendant risks, then there remain still to be answered the questions 'when' and 'how'.

[Hitler then talks about Germany's military strength, which he argues, will give Germany most advantage between 1943-45. After that other nations will have rearmed. Germany must therefore act at the latest by 1943-45.]

For the improvement of our politico-military position our first objective, in the event of our being embroiled in war, must be to overthrow Czechoslovakia and Austria simultaneously in order to remove the threat to our flank in any possible operation against the West....If the Czechs were overthrown and a common German-Hungarian frontier achieved, a neutral attitude on the part of Poland could be more certainly be counted on in the event of a Franco-German conflict. Our agreements with Poland only retained their force as long as Germany's strength remained unshaken....

On the assumption of a development of the situation leading to action on our part as planned, in the years 1943-45, the attitude of France, Britain, Italy, Poland, and Russia could probably be estimated as follows:

Actually, the Führer believed that almost certainly Britain, and probably France as well, had already tacitly written off the Czechs and were reconciled to the fact that this question would be cleared up in due course by Germany. Difficulties connected with the Empire, and the prospect of being once more entangled in a protracted European war, were decisive considerations for Britain against participation in a war against Germany. Britain's attitude would certainly not be without influence on that of France.

....

Italy was not expected to object to the elimination of the Czechs, but it was impossible at the moment to estimate what her attitude on the Austrian question would be; that depended essentially upon whether the Duce [ie Mussolini] were still alive.

Source: Anthony Adamthwaite, The Making of the Second World War *(London: Allen and Unwin, 1979), pp. 167-8.*

DOCUMENT 6 THE VIEWS OF THE FRENCH FOREIGN MINISTER IN 1938

After the Anschluss with Austria, Hitler turned his attention to Czechoslovakia, demanding that westernmost parts—the Sudetenland—where there were almost 3 million Germans living, be given to Germany. The British, who were starting to rearm, did not feel prepared for a major European war and the French, who had a treaty with Czechoslovakia which obliged France to come to its defence, felt similarly reluctant. The following is from a letter to the French President, Eduoard Daladier, from his Foreign Minister, Georges Bonnet.

Paris, September 24, 1938

My dear President,

We have reached a decisive hour when each must speak their mind clearly...

At no time in our diplomatic history since 1918 will France's position be weaker if she declares war on Germany....

In effect France ... will have to sustain, alone, on land, the shock of the German and Italian armies combined, without counting Japan who, in the Far East, will doubtless attack French Indo-China.

On the first day you will have against France, Germany and Italy. You will have two frontiers to defend and perhaps three, with Spain.

On what help could France count now?

She cannot count on Poland...now completely committed to Germany.

She cannot count any more on .... the Little Entente [Czechoslovakia, Rumania, Yugoslavia]. Neither Rumania nor Yugoslavia are willing to stand by us.

There remains the Soviet Union. Questioned by us, the Soviet Government has said that it could only help Czechoslovakia if we ourselves begin to apply the pact....

The United States Government has told us that it can give us neither a man nor a sou [the smallest unit of French currency]....

Great Britain's help, so important at sea, will however be almost non-existent on land during the first months...

I do not think that France is in a state to commit herself voluntarily to such a difficult struggle. I think that France who did not fight over the demilitarised Rhineland zone, nor over German rearmament, nor over Austria...must wait...until she has rebuilt her strength, her alliances...her air force...

For five months, night and day, in the course of our warm collaboration, we have struggled for peace. I beg you to continue on this course.

It is the only way to save the country.

Source: Anthony Adamthwaite, The Making of the Second World War *(London: Allen and Unwin, 1979), pp. 192-3.*

DOCUMENT 7 THE MUNICH AGREEMENT

As Hitler's demands for the Sudeten part of Czechoslovakia grew and as Nazi propaganda became more strident, many Europeans feared that war was unavoidable. On September 27, at the height of the crisis, Neville Chamberlain broadcast to the British people:

How horrible, fantastic, incredible it is that we should be digging trenches and trying on gas masks here because of a quarrel in a far-away country between people of whom we know nothing.

....

You know that I have done all that one man can to compose this quarrel. After my visits to Germany, I have realised vividly how Herr Hitler feels that he must champion other Germans, and his indignation that grievances have not been met before this. He told me privately, and last night he repeated publicly, that after this Sudeten German question is settled, that is the end of Germany's territorial claims in Europe.

Source: Neville Chamberlain, In Search of Peace *(New York: G.B. Putnam's Sons, 1939), pp.173-5 [cited in Joachim Remak,* The Origins of the Second World War, *(New Jersey: Prentice-Hall, 1976), p. 71].*

At the Munich Conference in September 1938, Hitler received virtually everything he had demanded (namely the Sudetenland with its German speaking inhabitants) with the concurrence of Italy, Britain, and France. The Munich Agreement is often seen as the high point of the policy of appeasement.

Germany, the United Kingdom, France and Italy, taking into consideration the agreement which has already been reached in principle for the cession to Germany of the Sudeten German territory, have agreed on the following terms and conditions governing the said cession and the measures consequent thereon, and by this agreement they each hold themselves responsible for the steps necessary to secure its fulfillment:

1. The evacuation will begin on October 1st.
2. The United Kingdom, France and Italy agree that the evacuation of the territory shall be completed by October 10th, without any existing installations having been destroyed, and that the Czechoslovak Government will be held responsible for carrying out the evacuation without damage to the said installations.

....

4. The occupation by stages of the predominantly German territory by German troops will begin in October 1st...

Annex to the Agreement

His Majesty's Government in the United Kingdom and the French Government have entered into the above agreement on the basis that they stand by the offer, contained in paragraph 6 of the Anglo-French proposals of September 19th, relating to an international guarantee of the new boundaries of the Czechoslovak State against unprovoked aggression.

When the question of the Polish and Hungarian minorities in Czechoslovakia has been settled, Germany and Italy for their part will give a guarantee to Czechoslovakia.

Signed Adolf Hitler
Neville Chamberlain
Ed. Daladier
Benito Mussolini

Munich, September 29, 1938

Source: Keith Eubank, ed., The Road to World War II: A Documentary History *(New York: Crowell, 1973), pp. 181-4.*

DOCUMENT 8 "PEACE IN OUR TIME"

Neville Chamberlain, the British prime minister, had hopes that the Munich Agreement might lead to a better relationship between Germany and Britain. After a conversation with Hitler, in the German leader's flat in Munich, Chamberlain asked Hitler to sign a general statement indicating their desire for better relations. It was this piece of paper which he said he hoped would bring "peace in our time".

We, the German Führer and Chancellor and the British Prime Minister, have had a further meeting today and are agreed in recognising that the question of Anglo-German relations is of the first importance for the two countries and for Europe.

We regard the agreement signed last night and the Anglo-German Naval Agreement [signed in 1935] as symbolic of the desire of our two peoples never to go to war with one another again...

Source: Keith Eubank, ed., The Road to World War II: A Documentary History *(New York: Crowell, 1973), p. 193.*

DOCUMENT 9 FRANCE AND BRITAIN

After Munich, the French grew increasingly pessimistic about the will of their ally, Britain, to resist Germany. In February 1939, for example, an American diplomat reported on a conversation he had had with the French President, Daladier.

...Daladier lunched with me alone today and we discussed a number of subjects.

....

Goering [the head of the German air force and a close friend of Hitler's] lately had been communicating with him a rather surprising manner. Goering had said to him personally and had followed it up: 'Why should France continue to tie herself to a decayed old nation like England—a rouged old maid trying to pretend she is still young and vigorous and capable of being a satisfactory partner to anyone'. Goering had then proposed that France should join Germany in finishing off England and that the British Empire should be divided between France and Germany.

Daladier said he had replied that this sounded very pleasant but the moment the British Empire was finished France would be the next morsel for Germany and that France could not be detached from England by any such proposal.

....

Daladier was of the opinion that Chamberlain [the British prime minister] in Rome had promised the Italians that he would use his good offices to obtain concessions from France to Italy. He said that the British had denied emphatically that this was the case but that he did not believe the British...Daladier said that he fully expected to be betrayed by the British and added that this was the customary fate of allies of the British.

Daladier went on to say that he considered Chamberlain a dessicated stick; the King a moron; and the Queen an excessively ambitious woman who would be ready to sacrifice every other country in the world in order that she might remain Queen Elizabeth of England. He added that he considered Eden [British foreign minister] a young idiot and did not know for discussion one single Englishman for whose intellectual equipment and character he had respect. He felt that England had become so feeble and senile that the British would give away every possession of their friends rather than stand up to Germany and Italy.

Source: Anthony Adamthwaite, The Making of the Second World War, *(London: Allen and Unwin, 1979), pp. 206-7.*

DOCUMENT 10 THE BRITISH GUARANTEE TO POLAND

When Hitler invaded the remnants of Czechoslovakia in March 1939, there was a decisive shift in public and official opinion in Britain in the direction of greater hostility towards Nazi Germany. In that month, the British government gave a promise of support to Poland, something it had not been prepared to do for Czechoslovakia in 1938. On March 31, 1939 the prime minister Neville Chamberlain spoke to the House of Commons.

As I said this morning His Majesty's Government has no official confirmation of the rumours of any projected attack on Poland and it must not therefore be taken as accepting them as true.

I am glad to take this opportunity of stating again the general policy of His Majesty's Government. They have constantly advocated the adjustment, by way of free negotiation between the parties concerned, of any differences that may arise between them. They consider that this is the natural and proper course where differences exist. In their opinion there should be no question incapable of solution by peaceful means and they would see no substitution of force or threats of force for the method of negotiation.

As the House is aware, certain consultations are now proceeding with other Governments [those of Greece and Rumania to whom Britain was also going to offer a guarantee]. In order to make perfectly clear the position of His Majesty's Government in the meantime before those consultations are concluded, I now have to inform the House that during that period in the event of any action which clearly threatened Polish independence, and which the Polish Government accordingly considered it vital to resist with their national forces, His Majesty's Government would feel themselves bound at once to lend the Polish Government all support in their power. They have given the Polish Government an assurance to this effect.

I may add that the French Government has authorised me to make it plain that it stands in the same position in this matter as does His Majesty's Government.

Source: Parliamentary Debates. House of Commons, *Fifth Series, vol. 345, p. 2415 [cited in Joachim Remak,* The Origins of the Second World War, *(New Jersey: Prentice-Hall, 1976), p. 102].*

DOCUMENT 11 THE NAZI-SOVIET PACT

The final act before the war started was the signing of the Non-Aggression Treaty between Nazi Germany and the Soviet Union (also known as the Nazi-Soviet Pact or the Ribbentrop-Molotov Pact, after the two foreign ministers involved). The agreement of the two to set aside their differences, at least temporarily, was the end for Poland which could no longer play one off against the other.

The Government of the German Reich and the Government of the Union of Soviet Socialist Republics, desirous of strengthening the cause of peace between Germany and the USSR, and proceeding from the fundamental provisions of the Neutrality Agreement concluded in April 1926 between Germany and the USSR, have reached the following agreement:

Article 1

Both High Contracting Parties obligate themselves to desist from any act of violence, any aggressive action, and any attack on each other, either individually or jointly with other powers.

Article 2

Should one of the High Contracting Parties become the object of belligerent action by a third power, the other High Contracting Party shall in no manner lend its support to this third power.

Article 3

The Governments of the two High Contracting Parties shall in the future maintain continual contact with one another for the purpose of consultation in order to exchange information on problems affecting their common interests....

In addition to the public clauses, the Treaty had a series of secret ones which essentially carved up the territory lying between Germany and the Soviet Union. The existence of the secret clauses was known by the end of World War II but the Soviet Union continued to deny that it had made any such deal until the late 1980s when Gorbachev's regime brought a number of previously buried matters into the open.

On the occasion of the signature of the Nonaggression pact...the undersigned plenipotentiaries of each of the two parties discussed in strictly confidential conversations the question of the boundary of their respective spheres of influence in Eastern Europe. These conversations led to the following conclusions:

1. In the event of a territorial and political rearrangement in the areas belonging to the Baltic States (Finland, Estonia, Latvia, Lithuania) the northern boundary of Lithuania shall represent the boundary of the spheres of influence of Germany and the USSR....

2. In the event of a territorial and political rearrangement in the areas belonging to the Polish state the spheres of influence of Germany and the USSR shall be bounded approximately by the rivers Narew, Vistula and San. The question of whether the interests of both parties make desirable the maintenance of an independent Polish state and how such a state should be bounded can only be definitely determined in the course of further political developments. In any event both Governments will resolve this question by means of a friendly agreement.

3. With regard to South eastern Europe attention is called by the Soviet side to its interest in Bessarabia [part of Rumania at the time]. The German side declares its complete political disinterestedness in these areas.

4. This protocol shall be treated by both sides as strictly secret.

Moscow, August 23, 1939

For the Government of the German Reich: V. Ribbentrop

Plenipotentiary of the Government of the USSR: V. Molotov

Source: Keith Eubank, ed., The Road to World War II: A Documentary History *(New York: Crowell, 1973), pp. 255-257.*

STUDY QUESTIONS FOR SECTION THREE: EUROPE 1919-1939

1. What factors contributed to instability in international relations between 1918 and 1935?

2. What was the policy of appeasement? Could it have worked?

3. How much responsibility do Hitler and Mussolini bear for the outbreak of the war?

4. What role did the Soviet Union play in international relations in the 1930s?

SECTION FOUR

ASIA 1919–1941

DOCUMENTS

CHRONOLOGY

1853-54 Japan "opens up" to international trade and diplomacy
1868 "Meiji Restoration" and a new imperial government is established
1894-95 Sino-Japanese War
1902 Anglo-Japanese Alliance
1904-05 Russo-Japanese War
1914-18 Japan fights as an Allied Power in WWI
1915
Jan. Japan's "Twenty-One Demands" against China
1918-19 Japan at the Paris Peace Conference — joins the League of Nations
1921-22 Japan at the Washington Conference on disarmament
1931
Sep. "Mukden Incident" and Japan invades Manchuria
1931-33 League of Nations' Lytton Commission investigates invasion and labels Japan the "aggressor"
1933
Feb. Japan withdraws from the League of Nations
1936
Nov. Japan signs "Anti-Comintern Pact" with Germany
1937
July "Marco Polo Bridge Incident" and Japan invades China
1939
Sep. war breaks out in Europe
1940
Aug. Japan announces its plans for a "new order" in East Asia based on the "Co-Prosperity Sphere"
Sep. Japan demands access/concessions in Indochina from France
USA places iron and steel on growing list of trade restrictions with Japan
Japan concludes the "Tripartite Pact" with Italy and Germany
1941
Apr. Japan signs non-aggression treaty with USSR
July Japan sends troops into Indochina
Aug. USA places total embargo on Japan and freezes its assets in America
Dec. Japan launches simultaneous surprise attacks on American and British positions throughout Asia and the Pacific
1941-45 Japan at war with the Allied forces throughout Asia and the Pacific

Was Japan solely responsible for the outbreak of war in Asia and the Pacific? How did it go from being an ally of the West to being an enemy? The following documents are designed to shed some light on these questions and the complex developments that led Japan to Pearl Harbour and beyond.

Japan was dissatisfied with the "new order" emerging after World War One. It had been included among the victorious powers, but felt that it was not treated as an equal. During 1921-22, the major powers conducted "arms control" negotiations specifically designed to limit the construction of stronger navies. The resulting Washington Conference produced an agreement which was strongly endorsed by the United States, but with which many Japanese were unhappy. Meanwhile, British foreign policy found itself at a crossroads:

DOCUMENT 1

THE BRITISH VIEW IN THE 1920S

Great Britain and Japan had a naval alliance and a policy of cooperation in Asia which dated back to 1902. Japan fought on the Allied side in World War I and was present at the Paris Peace Conference. By the early 1920s, however, the British found themselves in a dilemma; while they wished to keep on good terms with Japan, they also wanted to conciliate the United States. Unfortunately, there was a growing naval and political rivalry between the United States and Japan in the Pacific. In addition, important members of the British Empire, notably Canada and Australia, were opposed to the Japanese alliance. The British saw a general naval disarmament as a way out of their dilemma and a way of avoiding a costly naval building programme which they could not afford. On November 11, 1921, the British Foreign Secretary, Arthur Balfour, wrote to the Prime Minister David Lloyd George.

It is clear... that if satisfactory and durable results are to be achieved in regard to naval disarmament... an agreement must also be reached in regard to certain political problems which have arisen in China and the Pacific. First and foremost among these latter problems is that of the Anglo-Japanese Alliance. Evidence continues to reach me... that adherence to the Alliance in its present form will be very unpopular in the United States of America, and will render the conclusion of a satisfactory and enduring arrangement for the limitation of armaments extremely difficult to negotiate. Further it is undeniable that, with the collapse of the Russian Empire and the elimination of Germany from the Pacific, the conditions which brought the Anglo-Japanese Alliance into existence have disappeared for the time being... On the other hand, we are bound to give the utmost consideration to the feelings of an ally who has loyally stood by his engagements and rendered us valuable support in the late War, and we cannot contemplate any action calculated to alienate, much less to outrage, Japanese sentiment... In order to harmonize these partially conflicting elements in the problem, I have devised a formula... between the British Empire, the United States of America and Japan, dealing with the preservation of peace and the maintenance of the status quo... The object of the scheme is:

a. To enable the Americans to be parties to a tripartite arrangement without committing themselves to military operations:

b. To bring the existing Anglo-Japanese Alliance to an end without hurting the feelings of our Ally:

c. To leave it open to us to renew a defensive alliance with Japan if she should be again threatened by Germany or Russia:

d. To frame a treaty which will reassure our Australasian Dominions.

e. To make it impossible for American critics to suggest that our Treaty with Japan would require us to stand aside in the case of a quarrel between them and Japan, whatever the cause of the quarrel might be.

Source: Documents on British Foreign Policy (hereafter cited as DBFP), First Series, XIV, No. 415 - as quoted in Anthony Adamthwaite, The Lost Peace: International Relations in Europe, 1918–1939 *(New York: St. Martins Press, 1981) pp. 41-42.*

DOCUMENT 2 THE WASHINGTON CONFERENCE, 1921-22

At the end of 1921 the Washington Disarmament Conference met to discuss security issues in the Pacific. Among other things, it produced three agreements: the naval disarmament treaty which set limits on the size of navies in the Pacific, the 4-power treaty guaranteeing the status quo, and the 9-power treaty guaranteeing the integrity of China. In addition, the Anglo-Japanese naval alliance was ended. In spite of some reservations, Japan decided that it had more to gain from co-operation than from isolation. Admiral Kato Tomosaboru, a delegate to the conference, wrote from Washington to Japanese Navy Vice-Minister on December 27, 1921:

I concluded that we could not in any circumstances oppose the American proposals on principle. If we were to oppose them, Japan would pay dearly for it later... security is not the exclusive preserve of soldiers and war is not something which can be made by soldiers only. It is difficult to achieve one's objectives if one does not operate on the basis of total mobilization of the state... Frankly, one has to admit that, if one has no money one cannot make war... We cannot find any country apart from the United States which can supply us with a loan... so there is no other course open to us but to avoid war with her... Though Britain has not the power any longer to expand her great navy, she would certainly do something. Although American public opinion is opposed to expansion of armaments, America has the power, if she once feels the need, to expand as much as she wants... the United States would not ignore Japan's new building without herself making a fresh plan. Japan must make up her mind that the United States would do this... she could not cope with further American naval expansion... Thus, the gap between American and Japanese naval strength would widen more and more and we could do nothing to narrow it. Japan would therefore be seriously threatened...

Source: Ian Nish, Japanese Foreign Policy 1869–1942, *(London: Routledge and Kegan Paul, 1977). pp. 289–291.*

In 1931, Japan invaded Manchuria. The international community condemned the action, but in the midst of a world-wide economic depression, no one was prepared to do anything about it. In fact, given Japan's position among the powers, many Western politicians went out of their way to ignore or legitimize Japan's attack. However, many were also well aware that Japan represented a significant threat to the status quo in Asia. Consider these differing views on the Manchurian crisis:

DOCUMENT 3 THE BRITISH FOREIGN SECRETARY, JOHN SIMON, NOVEMBER 21, 1931

There is a widespread feeling, which I believe to be justified, that although Japan has undoubtedly acted in a way contrary to the principles of the Covenant by taking the law into her own hands, she has a real grievance against China and the merits of the matter are complicated by a further consideration. This is not a case in which the armed forces of one country have crossed the frontiers of another in circumstances where they had no previous right to be on the other's soil... she was compelled by the failure of China to provide reasonable protection for Japanese lives and property in Manchuria in the face of attacks of Chinese bandits...

Source: DBFP Second Series, VIII, No. 76 - as quoted in Adamthwaite, p.124

DOCUMENT 4 — SIR JOHN PRATT, THE FOREIGN OFFICER ADVISER IN CHINA, FEBRUARY 1932

If Japan continues unchecked the British will have to retire altogether from the Far East. If it is decided that we must check Japan certain preliminary measures could be adopted — such as a rupture of diplomatic and economic relations — but in the end Japan can only be checked by force. Ultimately we will be faced with the alternatives of going to war with Japan or retiring from the Far East. A retirement from the Far East might be the prelude to a retirement from India.

[With respect to that memo, even Sir John Simon himself noted];

1. If Japan continues unchecked and increasingly, as she indeed seems bent on doing, our position and vast interests in the far East will never recover. This may well spread to the Middle East. The Japanese victory in 1904 was the beginning of trouble here.
2. We are incapable of checking Japan in any way if she really means business and has sized up, as she certainly has done.
3. Therefore we must eventually be done for in the Far East, unless
4. The United States are eventually prepared to use force.
5. It is universally assumed here that the US will never use force.
6. I do not agree that this is necessarily so. The same was said of the US in the Great War. Eventually she was kicked in by the Germans. The Japanese may end up kicking in the US too, if they go on long enough kicking as they are now.
7. The Japanese are more afraid of the US than of us, and for obvious reasons. At present, however, they share our low view of American fighting spirit.
8. By ourselves we must eventually swallow any and every humiliation on the Far East. If there is some limit to American submissiveness, this is not necessarily so...

Source: DBFP, Second Series, IX, No. 238 - as quoted in Adamthwaite, The Lost Peace, International Relations in Europe 1918-1939 *(New York: St. Martins Press, 1981) p. 126.*

DOCUMENT 5 — THE CHINESE REACTION

The Chinese had been worried about Japanese expansion since the end of the 19th century. Japan had already acquired territory—Taiwan and Korea—which the Chinese felt was theirs. During World War I, Japan had seized German possessions in China and had also tried to force the Chinese government to accept the 21 Demands, which would have turned China into a protectorate of Japan. Japan's move into Manchuria was therefore greeted with alarm by many Chinese. The Nationalist

Government, which had established its control in China by 1928, was reluctant to confront Japan; its leaders were aware of China's weakness and they also were intent on eliminating the Chinese Communists. In May 8, 1933, Chiang Kai-shek, the Chinese Nationalist leader, spoke to his troops at Nanchang:

Most of you have been in Kiangsi fighting the Communist bandits for three years... During this difficult, bloody struggle, more than ten thousand of our brave men have perished... Taking advantage of this situation, the Japanese imperialists have continued to advance and persist in their aggression. Today we are facing dangers from within as well as without. Domestically the brutal, violent bandits are burning and killing every day, and across the sea come the Japanese imperialists who take over one piece of our territory after another. These imperialists will not be satisfied until they exterminate China as a nation... They, like other imperialists, relish other people's misfortunes and bully those who are too weak to resist. They attack us because we have this bandit rebellion that prevents our country from being unified. In other words, it is this internal rebellion that invites aggression from abroad... The only way of saving our country, from an objective and strategic point of view, is to follow an ancient adage that "internal pacification must take precedence over external war". When the country is pacified and the goal of unification has been achieved, it will not be too difficult a task to resist successfully Japanese aggression. The total population of Japan is only sixty million, and the total number of men she can put on the battlefield will not exceed six million, as compared to the total population of four hundred million for China and a much larger number of men we can arm. In terms of natural resources, territorial size, historical heritage, and individual creativity, Japan is also inferior to China... The Japanese aggression comes from without and can be compared to a disease of the skin, while the bandit rebellion, working from within, is really a disease of the heart. We must cure a disease of the heart before proceeding with the cure for a disease of the skin, because the heart disease, if not cured, will kill the patient, while the skin disease will not... We must know that only by crushing the bandit rebellion can we... assure our country's everlasting existence. I cannot find any task more honourable than this one.

Source: Chang Ch'i-yun (ed.), Works of President Chang *(Taipei; Research Institute of National Defense, 1968), Vol. I, pp. 622-26 - as quoted in Dun J. Li,* Modern China From Mandarin to Commissar *(New York: Charles Scribner, 1978), pp. 256-257.*

Throughout the 1920's and early 1930's complex international developments and changes in Japanese politics and society shaped dissatisfaction into an anti-Western and ultra-nationalist philosophy. In turn, radical nationalists and the military gradually took power away from Japan's parliamentary-style government. Documents 6 to 10 illustrate the changes in Japanese foreign policy throughout the 1930s, and the considerable difference between its real and professed objectives:

DOCUMENT 6

FOREIGN MINISTER UCHIDA TO THE SECRETARY-GENERAL OF THE LEAGUE OF NATIONS, (MARCH 27, 1933)

It is and has always been the conviction of the Japanese Government that, in order to render possible the maintenance of peace in various regions of the world, it is necessary in existing circumstances to allow the operation of the Covenant of the League to vary in accordance with the actual conditions prevailing in each of those regions... Acting on this conviction, the Japanese Government, ever since the Sino-Japanese dispute... have repeatedly emphasized and insisted upon the absolute necessity of taking into consideration the fact that China is not an organized state; that its internal conditions and external relations are characterized by extreme confusion and complexity and by many abnormal and exceptional features; and that, accordingly, the general principles and usages of international law which govern the ordinary relations between nations are found to be considerably modified in their operation so far as China is concerned, resulting in the quite normal and unique international practices which actually prevail in that country. The report adopted by the Assembly... entirely misapprehending the spirit of Japan, pervaded as it is by no other desire than the maintenance of peace in the Orient, contains gross errors both in the ascertainment of facts and in the conclusions deduced. In asserting that the action of the Japanese army... did not fall within the just limits of self-defence, the report assigned no reasons and came to an arbitrary conclusion... ignoring... the incident — for all of which the full responsibility is incumbent upon China — the report creates a source of fresh conflict in the political arena of the Orient... The conclusion must be that... the majority of the League have attached greater importance to upholding inapplicable formulas than to the real need of assuring peace, and higher value to the vindication of academic theses than to the eradication of the sources of future conflict. For these reasons, and because of the profound differences of opinion existing between Japan and the majority of the League... The Japanese Government, believing that, in these circumstances, there remains no room for further cooperation, hereby gives notice...of the intention of Japan to withdraw form the League of Nations.

Source: Ian Nish, Japanese Foreign Policy 1869-1942, pp. 299-300.

DOCUMENT 7

SPEECH BY DEPUTY FOREIGN MINISTER SHIGEMITSU MAMARU, AUGUST 1, 1935

Maintenance of peace was defined as the principal goal of world politics right after the World War. Peace was to be maintained through the mechanisms of the League and the Pact of Paris, but this was a superficial peace, merely another name for the status quo... Nations most committed to upholding the status quo are the victors, particularly those endowed with large territory and abundant resources... As it is customary for capitalists to insist on pressing the status quo, so it is with respect to international affairs. These countries have acquired all that they could and then speak of maintaining the status quo. Such an assertion is losing validity today... The idea that the maintenance of the status quo equals peace is becoming more and more difficult to accept.

Source: Katsumi Usui, "Japanese Approaches to China in the 1930s: Two Alternatives", in Akira Iriye and Warren Cohen American, Chinese and Japanese Perspectives on Wartime Asia, 1931-49. *(Wilmington (De.): Scholarly Resources, 1990), p. 101.*

DOCUMENT 8 MEMORANDUM FROM MATSUMURO KORYO, CHIEF OF THE JAPANESE INTELLIGENCE SERVICE IN CHINA, (JANUARY 3, 1936)

As Japan's industrial capacity has grown enormously in recent years, a large market is required to absorb the increasing volume of her manufactured products. The Europeans and the Americans have erected high tariff walls to restrict imports from Japan and subject her goods to discrimination... {Japan} realizes that only through a long, difficult struggle can she obtain territories large enough to satisfy her need for the supply of raw materials and the market for her finished products. She also realizes that only by close collaboration of her economic and military forces can she attain this dual goal... The population density of Japan is large and her birthrate is high. She cannot solve her population problem without the expansion of her industry... Only in the continuous, successful search for new raw materials and new markets can she guarantee her everlasting prosperity. According of the Empire's continental policy, Japan, after occupying Manchuria, must proceed with the occupation of Mongolia... But Mongolia is a vast prairie and desert, and whatever natural resources there are require future exploration and development and certainly cannot meet our demand at this moment... Besides, the Soviet Union is watching Mongolia like a hawk... All factors considered, it seems that the logical choice for Japan's next expansion is the easily obtainable North China... North China will be the best of our new colonies... The recent increase of Japanese troops in North China, besides its military implications, has as its main purpose the intensification of Nippon phobia among the Chinese... The past shows that we can always get what we want by intimidation or threat, without having to use military forces... It is most pleasing to Japan that Chinese officials, being so afraid of Japan, will not dare anything against Japanese wishes... Self-centred attitudes and total selfishness among the Chinese are the best assets we Japanese have. We can easily win a victory without having to fight a battle; the Chinese will grant us all kinds of concessions if we simply utter a word... Most Chinese are individualistic, and their loyalty and concern rarely go beyond the small group to which they belong. They have no concept of citizenship... Our strategy in China is therefore clear. We shall crush those Chinese who have exhibited strong leadership and support those who are extremely selfish... It is a unique characteristic of the Chinese that they can never love their country for more than five minutes. In fact, they do not even know what the word "country" means. Most Chinese officials are as greedy as they are stupid... As the Chinese begin to complain more about their own government and lose hope in it as a result of its inability to protect them against the immoral and illegal activities of our *ronins* they slowly change their attitude toward the Imperial Army of Japan from that of resentment and hatred to that of admiration and fear... It is always easy to find an excuse to start a war once Japan has made up its mind. The Chinese practice of not giving us any excuse by making concessions, prompted by a Nippon phobia of an advanced degree, is really laughable... At this moment, we have succeeded in placing many of our men, disguised as experts and technicians, in the various branches of the government of North China... They are bound to be extremely effective...

Source: Research Institute of China's Foreign Relations, Sino-Japanese Relations Before and After the Loukouchiao Incident *(Taipei, 1966), pp. 134-43 - as quoted in Li, pp. 258-270.*

DOCUMENT 9 FOREIGN MINISTRY PAPER, "FUNDAMENTALS OF NATIONAL POLICY", (AUGUST 7, 1936)

The basis of national policy is the need to consolidate national development internally and increase our prestige internationally through fairness and justice. Japan as the force for stability in east Asia in name and in fact must ensure the peace of the area and contribute to the well-being of men throughout the world, thereby living up to the ideals of the founding of our nation. Considering Japan's situation at home and abroad, the basic policies which she must adopt are to secure her position on the east Asian continent both diplomatically and militarily. The fundamental principles are as follows:

1. Japan must endeavour to eliminate the aggressive policies of the Powers in east Asia and share with people there cordial relations which are founded on the principles of co-existence and co-prosperity. This will be a manifestation of the spirit of the Imperial Way and a guiding light which we must use in pursuing our foreign policy.
2. Japan must complete her defence and armament programmes in order to guarantee her security and progress. Only thus can her position as a force for stability in east Asia be accomplished in name and fact.
3. The basis of our continental policy must be to cope with the threat from the Soviet Union in the north... and, meanwhile, to plan our economic expansion by creating a strong coalition between Japan, Manchukuo and China against Britain and the United States. In bringing this about, we must bear in mind the need for cordial relations with other Powers.
4. We plan social and economic developments in the South Seas... and contemplate the extension of our power by modest and peaceful means, avoiding clashes with other Powers...

Adopting these fundamentals as our criteria, we must reconcile our internal and external policies and bring our administration into line with present-day needs in the following ways:

1. In tackling Japan's security and armaments, the army must aim at dealing with the forces which Soviet Russia can deploy in the far east and increasing its garrisons in Kwantung and Korea so as to strike the first blow in the event of war...
2. The navy must aim at building up forces adequate to maintain ascendancy in the west Pacific against the American fleet.

With a view to the harmonious application of these fundamental policies, our foreign policy must be coordinated and amended. In order to enable beneficial and smooth progress be made over diplomatic activities, the military should try to help through private channels, without assuming any public role...

Source: Ian Nish, Japanese Foreign Policy 1869-1942, *pp. 301-303.*

DOCUMENT 10 SPEECH BY FOREIGN MINISTRY OFFICIAL, AND LATER FOREIGN MINISTER, YOSUKE MATSUOKA, (JANUARY 1937)

Japan is expanding. And what country in its expansion era has ever failed to be trying to its neighbours? Ask the American Indian or the Mexican how excruciatingly trying the young United States used to be once upon a time.

Source: John Toland, The Rising Sun; The Decline and Fall of the Japanese Empire 1936-45, Volume One *(New York: Random House Publishers, 1970), pp. 59-60.*

For the most part, the U.S. had retreated from the political and diplomatic stage after World War One. Many Americans were adamant about remaining "isolationist" during the 1920's and 1930's, especially when developments in Europe looked to be leading to another war. President Franklin D. Roosevelt had to deal with this belief, as well as the Great Depression, when he came to power after the 1932 election:

DOCUMENT 11 "THE QUARANTINE SPEECH"

In the summer of 1937 Japan invaded the mainland of China, thus starting a war which was going to last until the end of World War Two. The League of Nations condemned Japan's aggression. Although it was not a member of the League, the United States participated in the League's deliberations. In October 1937, President Roosevelt made a much-debated speech in Chicago.

There is a solidarity and interdependence about the modern world, both technically and morally, which makes it impossible for any nation to isolate itself from economic and political upheavals in the the rest of the world... The peace, the freedom, and the security of 90 percent of the world are being jeopardized by the remaining ten percent, who are threatening a breakdown of international order and law. Surely the ninety percent who want to live in peace under law and according to moral standards that have received universal acceptance can and must find some way to make their will prevail... It seems to be unfortunately true that the epidemic of world lawlessness is spreading. When an epidemic of physical disease starts to spread the community approves and joins in a quarantine of the patients in order to protect the health of the community against the spread of the disease... War is a contagion, whether it be declared or undeclared. It can engulf States and peoples remote from the original scenes of hostilities. We are determined to keep out of war, yet we cannot insure ourselves against the disastrous effects of war and the dangers of involvement. We are adopting such measures as will minimize our risk of involvement, but we cannot have complete protection in a world of disorder in which confidence and security have broken down... There must be positive endeavours to preserve peace. America hates war. America hopes for peace. Therefore, America actively engages in the search for peace.

Source: Stephen Heald (ed.), Documents on International Affairs, 1937 *(London: Royal Institute of International Affairs, 1939), pp. 590-591.*

DOCUMENT 12

SPEECH BY FOREIGN MINISTRY DEPUTY KAWAI TATSUO (OCTOBER, 1937)

While President Roosevelt did not name specific nations in his 'quarantine' speech, it was clear that he had in mind Germany, Italy and Japan. The Japanese considered the speech an emphatic statement of U.S. foreign policy towards them, as this speech makes clear:

The essence of good politics is not to assure that the dissatisfied should simply be left in the condition that causes them dissatisfaction. This principle applied to international as well as to domestic politics. The population of Japan has doubled in the last 50 years, yet Japan's attempts to find outlets for its expanding population have been rebuffed. The U.S., for example, has persistently violated all humane precepts by barring Japanese immigrants. This is a source of great regret to Japan. Today's world is divided into haves and have-not nations. Voices are raised in protest against the unequal distribution of resources and raw materials. Should the inequality remain uncorrected and the have nations continue to refuse to yield some of the vested interests to have not nations, what solution is there except war?

Source: Dorothy Borg and Shangei O. Kamato (eds.), Pearl Harbour As History: Japanese-American Relations 1937-1941 *(New York: Columbia University Press, 1993), p. 139.*

DOCUMENT 13

THE WORLD'S RESPONSE TO THE INVASION OF CHINA

European and American attention was primarily focused on the Great Depression and developments in Europe. Although there was considerable international protest and condemnation, once again there was little done to deter the Japanese. Japan's *Kwantung* Army was far superior to either the Communist or Nationalist forces in China, and its advance was swift and effective. Both the British and Americans began to reconsider their policy towards Japan and the state of their Pacific defenses. An American diplomat at the Brussels Conference on the Sino-Japanese dispute sent the following telegram to Secretary of State, Cordell Hull, on November 14, 1937:

...[the French Foreign Minister Yvon Delbos] is convinced entirely that it is futile to expect that normal pressure will have any appreciable effect upon Japan; that Japan is relying upon force and is impervious to reason; and that since Japan has spurned every effort towards conciliation the Conference must soon decide what further pressure the principle powers can and will exert. [British Foreign Secretary Anthony] Eden seems to believe that there is still some chance that some way may be found to bring Japan into some sort of a negotiation... I thought that they were unduly afraid of what Japan might do as she has her hands full and would be foolish to bring on herself trouble with some other power... I feel that unless we are prepared to participate in some positive steps in case Japan does not within the near future enter into some discussion looking toward a peaceful settlement, most countries will lose their nerve and fold their hands... There are indications that Japan is nervous over this conference and is maneuvering in various ways to undermine it; and she is believed to have been making veiled threats to practically all of the powers except Great Britain and ourselves. What concerns me somewhat is that while Japan is now nervous for fear we may agree upon something positive, if we go on much longer without any evidence of intention to do anything more than preach she will soon become firmly convinced that she can pursue her course without any danger of interference.

Source: FRUS, *volume IV, 1937, pp. 183-185.*

DOCUMENT 14 COMMENTS BY THE FIRST LORD OF THE ADMIRALTY, WINSTON CHURCHILL, IN NOVEMBER 1938

If Malay Peninsula has been starved for the sake of Libya and Russia... no one is more responsible than I, and I would do exactly the same again... Singapore is a fortress surrounded with 15 inch guns, and garrisoned by nearly 20,000 men. It could be taken after a siege of an army of at least 50,000 men, who would have to be landed in the marshes and jungle of the isthmus which connects it with the mainland. As Singapore is as far from Japan as Southampton from New York, the operation of moving a Japanese army with all its warships and sustaining it with men and munitions during a siege would be incredible. Moreover, such a siege, which should be at least 4 or 5 months, would be liable to be interrupted if at any time Great Britain chose to send a superior fleet to the scene. It is not considered possible that the Japanese, who are a prudent people and reserve their strength for the command of the Yellow Seas and China, in which they are fully occupied, would embark upon such an absurd enterprise.

Source: Saki Dockrill, "Introduction: One Step Forward; A Reappraisal of the 'Pacific War'", in Saki Dockrill (ed), From Pearl Harbour to Hiroshima *(New York: MacMillan Press, 1994), p. 5.*

DOCUMENT 15 EXCERPT FROM AN ARTICLE BY WALTER LIPPMAN, (JANUARY 1940)

World War II had started in September 1939. Although there was relatively little fighting before 1940, Americans were deeply concerned about the situation in Europe and about the possibilities for further Japanese aggression in Asia. Walter Lippman was one of the most distinguished American journalists of his time. He was a "liberal internationalist".

The Western nations must now do what hitherto they lacked the will and imagination to do: they must identify their cause with the freedom and security of the people of the East, putting away the "white man's burden" and purging themselves of the taint of an obsolete and ultimately unworkable white man's imperialism. In this drastic reorientation of war policy, the leadership of the western nations must be taken by the U.S.

Source: Gary R. Hess, "The Emergence of U.S. Influence in South-East Asia", in Iriye and Cohen American, Chinese and Japanese Perspectives on Wartime Asia, 1931-49, *pp. 195-196.*

DOCUMENT 16 FRANKLIN DELANO ROOSEVELT TO HIS SECRETARY OF THE INTERIOR, HAROLD ICKES, (JULY 1, 1941)

By the end of 1940, Hitler's Germany had overrun most of Europe. This had indirectly benefitted his ally, Japan, which started to put pressure on French and Dutch possessions in Asia. On June 22, 1941 he attacked the Soviet Union which created a dilemma for Japan.

The Japs are having a real drag-down and knock-out fight against themselves... trying to decide which way they are going to jump; attack Russia, attack the South Seas, or whether they will sit on the fence and be more friendly with us. No one knows what the decision will be but... it is terribly important for the control of the Atlantic for us to keep peace in the Pacific. I simply have not got enough Navy to go around and every little episode in the Pacific means fewer ships in the Atlantic.

Source: Robert Dallek, FDR and American Foreign Policy 1932-1945 *(Oxford: Oxford University Press, 1979), pp. 273-274.*

By late 1938, Japanese foreign policy essentially revolved around the war in China. Diplomacy with the US and Great Britain was determined to a large degree by the Imperial Army's objectives. This was even more the case when war broke out in Europe in September 1939, focusing American and British attentions there. Documents 17 to 21 deal with this marriage between foreign and military policy, and the dire consequences such a union had in drawing Japan into the Second World War;

DOCUMENT 17 "THE ARMY'S HOPES REGARDING CURRENT FOREIGN POLICIES", (JULY 3, 1938)

I. General Foreign Policy

Policy

1. By strengthening the anti-Comintern axis and disposing of the China Incident decisively, to win de facto recognition by the Powers of our China Policy and persuade them to cooperate in the construction of a new China accord with our wishes...

Details

1. Diplomatic efforts should concentrate on the following:

a. Strengthening the anti-Comintern axis.

b. Adopting positive measures to persuade the Soviet Union not to participate in the China Incident...

c. Inducing Britain to abandon its policy of supporting Chiang Kai-shek.

d. Persuading the United States at the very least to retain a neutral attitude, if possible to adopt a pro-Japanese attitude, and especially to strengthen friendly economic relations...

II. Operations to Strengthen the Anti-Comintern Axis

Policy

1. To strengthen political relations between Japan, Germany and Italy.

Details

1. The Policy for the strengthening of political relations between Japan, Germany and Italy

should be as follows: Separate, secret agreements should be concluded with Germany, expanding the spirit of the Anti-Comintern Pact so as to convert it into an anti-Soviet military alliance; and with Italy, so that it can serve mainly for the purpose of blocking Britain...

Source: Adamthwaite, The Lost Peace: International Relations in Europe, 1918-1939 *(New York: St. Martins Press, 1981), pp. 41-42.*

DOCUMENT 18 MEMORANDUM BY JAPANESE PREMIER KONOYE FUMIMARO, (DECEMBER 22, 1938)

The Government of Japan has decided upon the following: On the one hand, we shall continue our military operations until the anti-Japanese government of China, namely the Kuomintang... is totally and completely destroyed. On the other hand, we shall cooperate with farsighted Chinese in our effort to establish a New Order in East Asia... Since China, Japan and Manchukuo will have a common future in the establishment of a New Order in East Asia wherein they will share the same goal of maintaining friendly relations, combatting communism, and cooperating fully in economic matters, the first step China must take is to eliminate its narrow, small, and prejudicial point of view and give up her idiotic policy of opposing Japan and complaining about Manchukuo... As Communist influence in East Asia is intolerable to Japan, Japan feels that China, in recognition of the anti-Communist spirit as incorporated in the tripartite pact between Japan, Germany, and Italy, must conclude a similar anti-Communist pact with Japan. To achieve this common goal of anti-communism, Japan demands that China must allow her to station troops in China for the purpose of fighting against the Communists... Japan has no intention of establishing hegemony in China; nor does she demand that China restrict the economic interests of third powers in China... Foreigners must understand that the purpose of Japan's military operations is neither territorial aggrandizement nor the extraction of military reparations. The purpose... is to make certain that China will assume her obligations as a member of the New Order in East Asia. If China is willing to assume these obligations, Japan, on her part, will not only respect China's sovereignty as a nation but also agree to consider such issues as Japan's extraterritorial rights in China, the return by Japan of her concessions in China, and other matters, the resolution of which will assure China's full independence.

Source: Wu T'ieh-t'ing, The War of Resistance Against Japan *(Hong Kong: Hsien Tai Publishing, 1970), pp. 133-34 - as quoted in Li, pp. 272-273.*

DOCUMENT 19 SPEECH IN RESPONSE TO FUMIMARO BY CHIANG KAI-SHEK, (DECEMBER 26, 1938)

Our war of resistance has now entered a new stage... The morale of our fighting men is extremely high, and their determination to continue the struggle has never been firmer... the war and the national unity behind this determination have prompted the enemy to employ all kinds of intimidation and enticement, in addition to outright military pressure, to weaken our will... its premier, as well as its army, navy, and diplomatic spokesmen, have made absurd and contradictory statements... not only to deceive Japanese people at home and foreign powers abroad but also to confuse, stupefy, and intimidate the Chinese people. What Konoye says... is full of the same worn-out cliches that we have heard many times before... The purpose of this statement, like that of many others made previously by other Japanese leaders, is to annex China and to dominate all of East Asia — a first step to Japan's conquest of the world. The statement is an open admission of Japan's diabolic design and reveals clearly that she intends to exterminate us not only as a political entity but as a people as well... This war has revealed two things which no one can fail to recognize. It has shown, first, how low Japan can sink, morally and spiritually, and second, how determined we are to shoulder the burden of justice, not only for our own survival but for the good of humanity as well... The great powers in the world that have the obligation to insure the sanctity of treaties and also the ability to bring some light to this part of the world are merely looking on as bystanders... Our war of resistance against Japan is a war between good and evil, right and wrong, and law and lawlessness. It is a war between human justice and beastly power... Though standing alone today, we believe that sooner or later world justice will wake up from its slumber and that all men of good will, in due course, will join us in this struggle. Meanwhile we shall stand firm and fight on. The longer we fight, the stronger we become. We have our objective, and we shall achieve it. The victory will be ours.

Source: Chang Ch'i-yun (ed.), The Works of President Chiang, *Vol. I, pp. 1083-1089 - as quoted in Li, pp. 273-280.*

DOCUMENT 20 LETTER FROM FOREIGN MINISTER ARITA HACHIRO TO JAPANESE AMBASSADORS IN GERMANY AND ITALY, ON THE SIGNING OF A TRIPARTITE PACT, (JANUARY 25, 1939)

... it was decided that the strengthening of the Anti-Comintern Pact should be based on the principle that the new treaty would be merely an extension of the pact... and that the new treaty was not to be directed against countries such as Britain and France unless the Soviet Union were involved. In order for the Empire of Japan to establish its position as a stable power in East Asia and in order to carry out smoothly Japan's conception of its New Order in East Asia, it is extremely important that Japan avoid involvement in European problems not directly relevant to Japan, and that Japan avoid such situations as would result in making enemies of nations such as Britain and the United States. Therefore, it has been decided that the strengthening of cooperation between Japan, Germany and Italy should remain limited for a time to anticommunism and that conclusion of a full treaty of alliance would be inadvisable for the empire... It goes without saying that the importance of this kind of treaty is not in what is written in the documents but rather in the closer political relations between the allied states that will be promoted by the conclusion of the treaty. Already the Anti-Comintern Pact has enabled all three countries — Japan, Germany, and Italy — to influence third countries politically and to check them considerably. Therefore, it is my firm belief that although outwardly the present treaty is to be strengthened only concerning anticommunism, in actual practice it can exert considerable political pressure on Britain and France. It is not difficult to imagine that Germany and Italy will hesitate to consent to a draft that camouflages the new agreement as an anti-Comintern pact, for by giving the treaty the appearance of an alliance, they seem to be thinking of using it for their diplomatic manoeuvring in Europe...

Source: James W. Morley (ed.), Deterrent Diplomacy: Japan, Germany and the USSR, 1935-40 *(New York: Columbia University Press, 1976), pp. 273-282 - as quoted in Adamthwaite, p. 214.*

DOCUMENT 21 ADMIRAL YAMAMOTO REPORTING TO THE JAPANESE HIGH COMMAND (DECEMBER 1940)

We can give you a wild show for six months to a year, but if the war drags on to two or three years, I cannot be confident of the outcome. If we don't succeed with the surprise attack all we can do is say our luck was bad.

Source: Ikuhiko Hata, "Admiral Yamamoto and the Navy", in Saki Dockrill (ed) From Pearl Harbour to Hiroshima, *p. 65.*

STUDY QUESTIONS FOR SECTION FOUR: ASIA 1919–1941

1. Why were the Paris peace negotiations and the world order after World War One criticized in Japan?

2. What was the Manchurian crisis? Can it be seen as a step towards the world war?

3. Why and in what ways did Japanese foreign policy change from the 1920s to the 1930s?

4. Why did the United States become involved in opposing Japanese expansion in Asia?

5. Explain Japan's decision to attack the United States in 1941.

SECTION FIVE

THE ORIGINS OF THE COLD WAR

DOCUMENTS

CHRONOLOGY

1943 German defeat at Stalingrad
Teheran conference with Churchill, Roosevelt and Stalin

1944 Normandy landings
Churchill-Stalin meeting in Moscow

1945
Feb. Yalta Conference
Apr. Roosevelt dies; Truman becomes US president
May Germany surrenders
July Potsdam Conference starts
Aug. Japan surrenders
Sep. Igor Gouzenko reveals Soviet spy ring
Oct. United Nations founded

1946 Greek civil war
Chinese civil war
Churchill's "Iron Curtain" speech

1947
Jan. Bizonia created in Germany
Mar. Truman doctrine announced
June Marshall Plan announced
Oct. Cominform (Communist Information) founded

1948
Feb. Prague coup
Mar. Brussels Treaty
June Berlin blockade starts; Yugoslavia expelled from Cominform

1949
Apr. NATO established
May Berlin blockade ends; Federal Republic of Germany (West Germany) established
Aug. Soviet Union explodes first atomic bomb
Oct. Chinese Communists proclaim People's Republic; German Democratic Republic (East Germany) established

1950
June North Korea invades South Korea; Truman approves NSC-68
Sep. West German rearmament

DOCUMENT 1

THE YALTA CONFERENCE

The February 1945 war time conference at Yalta was the last time Stalin, Roosevelt and Churchill all met. Among the difficult issues was the fate of Poland. The Soviets wanted a friendly government and so backed their candidates—the Polish communists of the Lublin government. The Western Allies tried to insist that the Polish government in exile—the London government—and the Polish people themselves should have a say in choosing their rulers. On February 3, the three discussed Poland:

Marshal Stalin then gave the following summary of his views on the Polish question: Mr. Churchill had said that for Great Britain the Polish question was one of honor and that he understood, but for the Russians it was a question both of honor and security. It was one of honor because Russia had many past grievances against Poland and desired to see them eliminated. It was a question of strategic security not only because Poland was a bordering country but because throughout history Poland had been the corridor for attack on Russia. We have to mention that during the last thirty years Germany twice has passed through this corridor. The reason for this was that Poland was weak. Russia wants a strong, independent and democratic Poland. Since it was impossible by the force of Russian armies alone to close from the outside this corridor, it could be done only by Poland's own forces. It was very important, therefore, to have Poland independent, strong and democratic. It is not only a question of honor for Russia, but one of life and death.

As to the question of the Polish government, Mr. Churchill has said it would be good to create a Polish government here. I am afraid that was a slip of the tongue, for without participation of the Poles it is impossible to create a Polish government. I am called a dictator and not a democrat, but I have enough democratic feeling to refuse to create a Polish government without the Poles being consulted—the question can only be settled with the consent of the Poles.

As a military man I demand from a country liberated by the Red Army that there be no civil war in the rear. The men in the Red Army are indifferent to the type of government as long as it will maintain order and they will not be shot in the back. The Warsaw, or Lublin, government has not badly fulfilled this task. There are, however, agents of the London government who claim to be agents of the underground forces of resistance. I must say that no good and much evil comes from these forces. Up to the present time they have killed 212 of our military men. They attack our supply bases to obtain arms. Although it has been proclaimed that all radio stations must be registered and obtain permission to operate, agents of the London government are violating these regulations. We have arrested some of them and if they continue to disturb our rear we will shoot them as military law requires. When I compare what the agents of the Lublin government have done and what the agents of the London government have done I see the first are good and the second bad.

Source: FRUS. The Conferences at Malta and Yalta 1945 *(Washington: United States Government Printing Office, 1955), pp. 669, 670.*

On February 7, there was further discussion of Poland, this time of the proposal to move its boundaries some 200 miles to the west, thus incorporating a big chunk of Germany and millions of German into Poland. Winston Churchill, the British Prime Minister, speaks first:

He would always support the movement of Polish frontiers to the west since he felt they should receive compensation, but not more than they can handle. He said it would be a pity to stuff the Polish goose so full of German food that it got indigestion. He said he felt that there was a considerable body of British public opinion that would be shocked if it were proposed to move large numbers of Germans, and although he personally would not be shocked he knew that the view existed in England. He said he felt if it were confined to East Prussia, six million Germans probably could be handled quite aside from moral grounds, but the addition of the line west of the Neisse would create quite a problem in this respect.

MARSHAL STALIN remarked that most Germans in those areas had already run away from the Red Army.

THE PRIME MINISTER said this, of course, simplified the problem, and in regard to the question of space in Germany for these deported persons he felt that the fact that Germany had had six to seven million casualties in this war and would probably have a million more would simplify this problem.

MARSHAL STALIN replied that the Germans might well have one or possibly two million more casualties.

THE PRIME MINISTER said that he wasn't afraid of the problem of transfer of populations provided that it was proportioned to the capacity of the Poles to handle it and the capability of the Germans to receive them. He felt, however, that it needs study, not only in principle but as a practical matter. He said he had one other comment. In the Soviet proposal some references should be made to other democratic leaders from within Poland itself.

Source: FRUS. The Conferences at Malta and Yalta 1945 *(Washington: United States Government Printing Office, 1955), pp. 717.*

DOCUMENT 2 POLAND AT YALTA

Roosevelt and Churchill were later been accused of abandoning Poland and indeed the whole of Eastern Europe to Soviet control through their failure to confront the Soviets directly at Yalta and to insist on a democratic Poland. Alger Hiss (himself later accused—inconclusively—of being a Soviet spy) was part of the American delegation.

I've been asked, "Why the hell didn't we just say: You can't have Poland, because pretty clearly this meant Russian control", and my answer has always been that we were quite aware that the only way to disagree over Poland was to shatter the Alliance, that we certainly could not fight the Russians militarily at that stage, and that they already possessed half, maybe two-thirds, of Poland militarily. So that the question asked in retrospect now is very different from the question asked then.

Source: Michael Charlton, The Eagle and the Small Birds *(Chicago: University of Chicago Press, 1984), p. 50.*

DOCUMENT 3 SOVIET SUSPICIONS

The Soviets harboured deep suspicions of their Western Allies even during the Second World War. The Soviets criticized the slowness of the Allies to open a Second Front against the Germans, notably by landing on the French coast, even suggesting that the British and the Americans intended to make a separate peace with Hitler. Nikita Khrushchev, part of Stalin's inner circle, and later leader of the Soviet Union, wrote his reminiscences after his fall from power.

It's difficult to judge what the intentions of the Allies were toward the end of the war. I wouldn't exclude the possibility that they desired to place a still greater burden on the shoulders of the Soviet Union and to bleed us even more. Or perhaps it's as they explained; they weren't sufficiently prepared for a landing. Their arms production wasn't sufficiently developed. They needed more time and so on. Both explanations were probably true, but I think they were mostly dictated by their desire to bleed us dry so that they could come in at the last stages and determine the fate of the world. They wanted to take advantage of the results of the war and impose their will not only on their enemy, Germany, but on their ally, the USSR, as well. I can easily imagine how this thought played a significant role in their thinking.

To look at it from a class position, it was in the Allies interest to rely on the Soviet Union as a wartime ally, despite the fact that our country was founded on Socialist principles. We had to unite our forces against a common enemy. None of us could have won the war single-handed. But while exerting our collective efforts against the common enemy, each of us remained on his own class position. The Western Allies were certainly not interested in strengthening us. England and America, from their class positions, knew they had to help us to an extent, but they still wanted the Soviet Union to be considerably weaker after the war so that they could dictate their will to us.

For our part, we knew that it would be useful to become considerably stronger at the end of the war in order for our voice to carry more weight in the settlement of international questions.

Source: Strobe Talbott, ed., Khrushchev Remembers *(Boston and Toronto: Little, Brown and Company, 1970), pp. 223-4.*

DOCUMENT 4 CONVERSATIONS WITH STALIN

Milovan Djilas was a Yugoslav Communist who had several meetings with Stalin in the 1940s both in his office in the Kremlin and at his country retreat outside Moscow. In his *Conversations with Stalin*, he has left a rare record of the Soviet dictator. One meeting took place in June 1944, just before the Allied landings in Normandy; Stalin discussed Churchill, the British prime minister, and Roosevelt, the American president.

Perhaps you think that just because we are the Allies of the English that we have forgotten who they are and who Churchill is. They find nothing sweeter than to trick their allies. During the

First World War they constantly tricked the Russians and the French. And Churchill? Churchill is the kind who, if you don't watch him, will slip a kopeck out of your pocket! And Roosevelt? Roosevelt is not like that. He dips in his hand only for bigger coins. But Churchill? Churchill—even for a kopeck.

Source: Milovan Djilas [Dilas], Conversations with Stalin *(New York: Harcourt, Brace & World, 1962), p. 73.*

DOCUMENT 5 THE CULT OF STALIN

Although Djilas initially regarded Stalin and the Soviet leadership with awe and deep respect, he began to have doubts about them the more he saw them. He later painted this picture:

Turned into a deity, Stalin became so powerful that in time he ceased to pay attention to the changing needs and desires of those who had exalted him.

An ungainly dwarf of a man passed through gilded and marbled imperial halls, and a path opened before him, radiant admiring glances followed him, while the ears of courtiers strained to catch his every word. And he, sure of himself and his works, obviously paid no attention to all this. His country was in ruins, hungry, exhausted. But his armies and his marshals, heavy with fat and medals and drunk with vodka and victory, had already trampled half of Europe under foot, and he was convinced they would trample over the other half in the next round. He knew that he was one of the cruelest, most despotic personalities in human history. But this did not worry him one bit, for he was convinced that he was executing the judgment of history.

Source: Milovan Djilas, Conversations with Stalin *(New York: Harcourt, Brace & World, 1962), p. 106.*

DOCUMENT 6 THE SOVIETS AND EASTERN EUROPE

At the end of the war, the Soviets were in a very strong position in Eastern Europe. That did not prevent Stalin from fearing that the Western Allies intended to try to roll back Soviet gains. He took a deep personal interest in the affairs of the new Soviet satellites. Nikita Khrushchev remembers the situation in 1947:

One reason for Stalin's obsession with Eastern Europe was that the Cold War had already set in. Churchill had given his famous speech in Fulton [where he used the phrase "the iron curtain"] urging the imperialistic forces of the world to mobilize against the Soviet Union. Our relations with England, France, the USA, and the other countries who had co-operated with us in crushing Hitlerite Germany were, for all intents and purposes, ruined.

America was conducting its foreign policy from a position of strength. The Americans had the atomic bomb, and they knew we didn't. For the atomic bomb to be in our enemy's hands was bad enough. To make matters worse, the President at the time was Truman, who had neither an ounce of statesmanship nor a flexible mind and who was hostile and spiteful toward the Soviet Union. I can't imagine how anyone every considered Truman worthy of the Vice-Presidency, much less the Presidency. The whole world knows from the newspapers how he slapped a journalist who criticized his daughter for being a poor singer. That incident alone told us something about Truman's statesmanship, to say nothing of his suitability for so important a post as Presidency of the United States. America's air force at the time was the best in the world both in quality and in quantity of its planes. The American "flying fortress" and "super-fortresses" had played a big part in winning the war against Germany and Japan, and they were still unmatched by any other planes in the world. I would even say that America was invincible, and the Americans flaunted this fact by sending their planes all over Europe, violating borders and even flying over the territory of the Soviet Union itself, not to mention a country like Czechoslovakia.

Source: Strobe Talbott, ed., Khrushchev Remembers *(Boston and Toronto: Little, Brown and Company, 1970), pp. 361-2.*

DOCUMENT 7 YUGOSLAV-SOVIET RELATIONS

The Soviets wanted control over the countries of Eastern Europe for security, but they also treated them as colonial possessions, to be exploited and managed. In January 1948, when relations were worsening between the Soviet Union and Yugoslavia, the Yugoslav Communist, Milovan Djilas, was sent on a mission to Moscow. On the way, it stopped in the new Soviet satellite of Rumania.

Though we were only passing through Rumania, we found reason for our criticism everywhere. First, as to the relations between the Soviet Union and the other East European countries: these countries were still being held under actual occupation, and their wealth was being extracted in various ways, most frequently through joint-stock companies in which the Russians barely invested anything except German capital, which they had simply declared a prize of war. Trade with these countries was not conducted as elsewhere in the world, but on the basis of special arrangements according to which the Soviet Government bought at lower and sold at higher than world prices. Only Yugoslavia was an exception. We all knew that. And the spectacle of misery as well as the consciousness of impotence and subservience among the Rumanian authorities could only heighten our indignation.

We were most taken aback by the arrogant attitude of the Soviet representatives. I remember how horrified we were at the words of the Soviet commander in Iasi [a Rumanian town]: 'Oh, this dirty Rumanian Iasi! And these Rumanian corn-pone eaters!' ... Especially in that mild winter, Iasi was truly a sprawling backwater of a Balkan town... Yet we knew that Soviet towns looked hardly better, if not indeed worse. It was this attitude of a "superior" race and the conceit of a great power which angered us the most.

Source: Milovan Djilas [Dilas], Conversations with Stalin *(New York: Harcourt, Brace & World, 1962) pp. 139-140.*

DOCUMENT 8 SALAMI SOCIALISM

One of the factors which turned much Western opinion against the Soviet Union was the methods which the Soviets and their henchmen used to install pro-Soviet communist governments throughout Eastern Europe. Zoltan Vas, interviewed in 1984, was an important Hungarian Communist. He describes the "salami tactics" he and his colleagues used in the 1940s:

We had democratic parties—the Smallholders' Party, the Social Democratic Party, and about twenty other different kinds of parties. We could not finish them all off at the same time. So we started with the weakest ones. We applied such enormous pressure on them—partly through arrests, since we controlled the police, and partly through economic and all other kinds of pressure—that they were forced to dissolve voluntarily. In other words we 'liquidated' them. Take for example, the Smallholders' Party, which was the biggest party in Hungary. We organized a Communist-influenced left wing inside the party; then we threw all kinds of accusations at their leaders. We accused their most popular leader, Bela Kovacs, the Secretary-General of their party, of being a traitor to the cause of the Hungarian people.

....

He proved so popular that we could not ... take him to court because of his popularity. There was no court in Hungary that would have convicted Bela Kovacs. Then we turned to the Soviet army, requesting that they would arrest him. They snatched him from Hungary, accusing him of "spying on the Soviet army" for "the imperialists". He was sentenced to ten years, and he spent ten years in the Soviet Union.

Source: Michael Charlton, The Eagle and the Small Birds *(Chicago: University of Chicago Press, 1984), p. 64.*

DOCUMENT 9 DEAN ACHESON

Western statesmen became convinced in the years after the end of World War 2 that the Soviet Union was determined to extend its influence as far as it could. Dean Acheson joined the American Department of State in 1941 and became Secretary of State in 1949 in the Truman administration. In his memoirs, he gives his view of Soviet intentions in the years after 1945.

Stalin's offensive against the United States and the West, announced in his speech of February 9, 1946 [in which he argued that the existence of a hostile, capitalist West meant that international peace was impossible], had begun in Poland in 1945 and would reach its crescendo in Korea and the "hate America" campaign of the early 1950s. This was the start of the "cold war" and was to condition the rest of my official life. The offensive was mounted on territory most favorable to the interior lines of the Soviets, where their military power was superior, and on political issues in international discussions, where stubborn and skillful opposition to American proposals could be successful with little cost. Geographically, therefore, the attack was concentrated along Russia's borders in Eastern Europe and the Middle East, where the Soviets' physical position was strongest and that of the United States weakest. Politically it centered against efforts to create a United Nations military force and the United States plan to put atomic energy under effective international control. Blocking tactics in the United Nations were made easy by Soviet possession of the veto. The creation of Soviet satellites succeeded only where the Red Army was present to reinforce it. When the attempt moved beyond the Soviet-occupied areas of Eastern Europe to West Germany, the Balkans, and the Middle East, the United States Government gave fair warning that, if necessary, it was prepared to meet Soviet force with American force, rather than with mere protests and resolutions in the United Nations.

Source: Dean Acheson, Present at the Creation *(New York: W.W. Norton & Company), p. 194.*

DOCUMENT 10 "THE SOURCES OF SOVIET CONDUCT"

One of the most influential voices in shaping American policy towards the Soviet Union was George Kennan, a senior State Department official who had served in the American embassy in wartime Moscow. In the July 1947 issue of *Foreign Affairs* he published, under the pseudonym "X", an article called "The Sources of Soviet Conduct" in which he argued that the Soviet Union, with its Marxist ideology, assumed that capitalism and communism were bound to be antagonistic. Furthermore, the Kremlin (the Soviet Government) assumed that communism would eventually triumph.

Thus the Kremlin has no compunction about retreating in the face of superior force. And being under the compulsion of no timetable, it does not get panicky under the necessity for such retreat. Its political action is a fluid stream which moves constantly, wherever it is permitted to move, toward a given goal. Its main concern is to make sure that it has filled every nook and cranny available to it in the basin of world power.

....

In these circumstances it is clear that the main element of any United States policy toward the Soviet Union must be that of a long-term, patient but firm and vigilant containment of Russian expansive tendencies. It is important to note, however, that such a policy has nothing to do with outward histrionics: with threats or blustering or superfluous gestures of outward 'toughness'. While the Kremlin is basically flexible in its reaction to political realities, it is by no means unamenable to considerations of prestige. Like almost any other government, it can be placed by tactless and threatening gestures in a position where it cannot afford to yield even though this might be dictated by its sense of realism.

....

In the light of the above, it will be clearly seen that the Soviet pressure against the free institutions of the western world is something that can be contained by the adroit and vigilant application of counter-force at a series of constantly shifting geographical and political points, corresponding to the shifts and manoeuvres of Soviet policy, but which cannot be charmed or talked out of existence.

Source: Foreign Affairs *XXV (July 1947), pp. 574-576.*

DOCUMENT 11 THE TRUMAN DOCTRINE

In the winter of 1946-47, the situation in both Greece and Turkey was causing concern to the West. In Greece a vicious civil war between the royalist government, on the one hand, and the communists on the other, had broken out. Britain gave what help it could to the Greek government, while the communists had support from Greece's neighbours of Albania and Yugoslavia, both of which now had communist governments. The weak Turkish government was under pressure from the Soviet Union, both to give up territory along the two nations' common border and to allow Soviet warships to pass through the Dardanelles en route from the Black Sea to the Mediterranean. Again, Britain tried to give assistance to the Turks, but in February 1947 it was forced to tell the United States that it intended to withdraw from its role as protector of both Greece and Turkey within 38 days. The United States, realizing that it could not stand by while the eastern end of the Mediterranean fell under Soviet influence, decided to take on the role Britain was abandoning. President Truman went to Congress on March 12, 1947 and asked for approval to give Greece $250 million and Turkey $150 million in preliminary aid. The words he used were the origin of the Truman Doctrine:

I am fully aware of the broad implications involved if the United States extends assistance to Greece and Turkey, and I shall discuss these implications with you at this time.

One of the primary objectives of the foreign policy of the United States is the creation of conditions in which we and other nations will be able to work out a way of life free from coercion. This was a fundamental issue in the war with Germany and Japan. Our victory was won over countries which sought to impose their will, and their way of life upon other nations.

.....

The peoples of a number of countries of the world have recently had totalitarian regimes forced upon them against their will. The Government of the United States has made frequent protests against coercion and intimidation, in violation of the Yalta agreements, in Poland, Rumania, and Bulgaria. I must also state that in a number of other countries there have been similar developments.

At the present moment in world history nearly every nation must choose between alternative ways of life. The choice is too often not a free one.

One way of life is based upon the will of the majority, and is distinguished by free institutions, representative government, free elections, guaranties of individual liberty, freedom of speech and religion, and freedom from political oppression.

The second way of life is based upon the will of a minority forcibly imposed upon the majority. It relies upon terror and oppression, a controlled press and radio, fixed elections, and the suppression of personal freedoms.

I believe that it must be the policy of the United States to support free peoples who are resisting attempted subjugation by armed minorities or by outside pressure.

I believe that we must assist free peoples to work out their own destinies in their own way.

I believe that our help should be primarily through economic and financial aid which is essential to economic stability and orderly political processes.

Source: Congressional Record Eightieth Congress. First Session, p. 1981.

DOCUMENT 12 THE MARSHALL PLAN

Both the United States and the governments of Western Europe were increasingly concerned in the years after 1945 that the economic weakness of Europe and the misery of its people would aid the spread of communism and Soviet influence. On June 5, 1947, after considerable discussion both in the American administration and among the Western powers, the American Secretary of State, General George Marshall spoke at Harvard, outlining what came to be the European Recovery Program or Marshall Plan.

The truth of the matter is that Europe's requirements for the next three or four years of foreign food and other essential products—principally from America — are so much greater than her present ability to pay that she must have substantial additional help, or face economic, social and political deterioration of a very grave character.

Our policy is directed not against any country or doctrine but against hunger, poverty, desperation and chaos. Its purpose should be the revival of a working economy in the world so as to permit the emergence of political and social conditions in which free institutions can exist. Such assistance, I am convinced, must not be on a piecemeal basis as various crises develop. Any assistance that this government may render in the future should provide a cure rather than a palliative. Any government that is willing to assist in the task of recovery will find full co-operation, I am sure, on the part of the United States Government. Any government which manoeuvres to block the recovery of other countries cannot expect help from us. Furthermore, governments, political parties, or groups which seek to perpetuate human misery in order to profit therefrom politically or otherwise will encounter the opposition of the United States.

Source: Department of State Bulletin, *15 June 1947, pp. 1159-60.*

DOCUMENT 13 THE CZECH COUP

The forcible overthrow of the Benes government by the Czech Communists in February 1948 marked the end of the last relatively independent, non-Communist regime in the Soviet bloc and marks the completion of the "iron curtain". The death of the foreign minister, Jan Masaryk, still remains a mystery. Edward Taborsky was private secretary to President Benes and knew Masaryk well. He was interviewed in 1984.

I think probably the final outcome, when they finally reveal everything (although many things will probably be lost meanwhile), will probably conclude by saying that Masaryk was disposed of by the Soviet Secret Police. There is some evidence for it. There was disorder in Masaryk's room. The argument is that, had he wanted to commit suicide, he would have taken pills and certainly would not have jumped from a window in his bathroom which was so hard to get access to. I talked to Dr. Klinger, who was his personal physician, and he brought some evidence about this. He noted for instance that Masaryk's clothing was soiled—which is an indication that he was in fear of his life, and might have had some struggle. There were plenty of cigarettes in his room which seemed to have been smoked not only by Masaryk but by other people....

Source: Michael Charlton, The Eagle and the Small Birds *(Chicago: University of Chicago Press, 1984), p. 76.*

DOCUMENT 14 THE BERLIN BLOCKADE

As the Cold War intensified, the situation of West Berlin, located within Soviet-occupied Germany, became increasingly difficult. On April 1, 1948 the Soviets, citing "technical difficulties", cut road and rail communications with the West. The West was forced to rely on an airlift to supply the needs of West Berlin. President Truman, as he recalls in his memoirs, discussed the situation with General Lucius Clay, the American commander in Germany:

The Russians were obviously determined to force us out of Berlin. They had suffered setbacks recently in Italy, in France, and in Finland. Their strongest satellite, Yugoslavia, had suddenly developed a taste for independent action, and the European Recovery Program was beginning to succeed. The blockade of Berlin was international Communism's counter-attack. The Kremlin had chosen perhaps the most sensitive objective in Europe — Berlin, the old capital of Germany, which was and is a symbol to the Germans. If we failed to maintain our position there, Communism would gain great strength among the Germans. Our position in Berlin was precarious. If we wished to remain there, we would have to make a show of strength. But there was always the risk that Russian reaction might lead to war. We had to face the possibility that Russia might deliberately choose to make Berlin the pretext for war, but a more immediate danger was the risk that a trigger-happy Russian pilot or hot-headed Communist tank commander might create an incident that could ignite the powder keg.

General Clay came to the White House on July 23, 1948, to attend the meeting that day of the National Security Council, and I asked him to report on the situation in Germany.

Here, in substance, is what he said : The abandonment of Berlin would have a disastrous effect upon our plans for Western Germany. It would also slow down European recovery, the success of which depends upon more production, particularly from Western Germany. The Germans in general were more concerned than the Allies about the possibility of our leaving Berlin. We should be prepared to go to any lengths to find a peaceful solution to the situation, but we had to remain in Berlin.

The attitude of the German people, Clay added, was in some respects unbelievable. The party leaders in Berlin who made up the City Magistrate with headquarters in the Soviet zone had absolutely refused to accept Soviet control. The people of Berlin were determined to stand firm even if it required undergoing additional hardships.

He reported that the air lift had been averaging about 2,400 to 2,500 tons per day, which was more than enough to handle food requirements but was inadequate to include the necessary amounts of coal. The minimum required to sustain Berlin without extreme hardship was estimated to be 4,500 tons per day. For the summer 3,500 tons per day might suffice, but additional tonnage would be required during the winter.

I then asked General Clay what risks would be involved if we tried to supply Berlin by means of armed convoys. The general said he thought the initial reaction of the Russians would be to set up road blocks. Our engineers would be able to clear such obstacles, provided there was no Russian interference, but the next step the Russians would take, General Clay thought, would be to meet the convoys with armed force.

Robert Lovett, who was in attendance with Secretary Marshall, asked Clay if he thought that the Russians might try to block our airplanes with fighter patrols or by other methods. General Clay said he felt that the Russians would not attack our planes unless they had made the decision to go to war.

I asked General Clay if there were any indications known to him that the Russians would go to war. He said he did not think so. What they seemed to aim at was to score a major victory by forcing us out of Berlin, either now or after fall and winter weather forced us to curtail the air lift, without, however, extending the conflict.

We discussed the kind of assistance that we might expect from our Allies if the conflict became more intense. I stated it as my judgment that if we moved out of Berlin, we would be losing everything we were fighting for. The main question was : How could we remain in Berlin without risking all-out war?

Source: Harry S. Truman, The Memoirs of Harry S. Truman, *volume* 2 Years of Trial and Hope 1946-53 *(New York: Hodder and Stoughton, 1966), pp. 131, 132-3.*

DOCUMENT 15 THE UNITED NATIONS

The United Nations was founded at the San Francisco Conference in October 1945. Although it carried on many of the functions of the League of Nations, it was designed to be a stronger organization. The Security Council, with five permanent members (the US, the Soviet Union, Britain, France,and China), had considerable powers. Each permanent member, however, could exercise a veto over decisions.

Charter of the United Nations*

WE THE PEOPLE OF THE UNITED NATIONS determined

to save succeeding generations from the scourge of war, which twice in our lifetime has brought untold sorrow to mankind, and to reaffirm faith in fundamental human rights, in the dignity and worth of the human person, in the equal rights of men and women and of nations large and small, and

to establish conditions under which justice and respect for the obligations arising from treaties and other sources of international law can be maintained, and

to promote social progress and better standards of life in larger freedom,

and for these ends

to practice tolerance and live together in peace with one another as good neighbours, and

to unite our strength to maintain international peace and security, and

to ensure, by the acceptance of principles and the institution of methods, that armed force shall not be used, save in the common interest, and

to employ international machinery for the promotion of the economic and social advancement of all peoples,

have resolved to combine our efforts

to accomplish these aims.

Accordingly, our respective Governments, through representatives assembled in the city of San Francisco, who have exhibited their full powers found to be in good and due form, have agreed to the present Charter of the United Nations and do hereby establish an international organization to be known as the United Nations.

CHAPTER I
PURPOSES AND PRINCIPLES
ARTICLE 1

The Purposes of the United Nations are:

1. To maintain international peace and security, and to that end: to take effective collective measures for the prevention and removal of threats to the peace, and for the suppression of acts of aggression or other breaches of the peace, and to bring about by peaceful means, and in conformity with the principles of justice and international law, adjustment or settlement of international disputes or situations which might lead to a breach of the peace;

2. To develop friendly relations among nations based on respect for the principle of equal rights and self-determination of peoples, and to take other appropriate measures to strengthen universal peace;

3. To achieve international co-operation in solving international problems of an economic, social, cultural, or humanitarian character, and in promoting and encouraging respect for human rights and for fundamental freedoms for all without distinction as to race, sex, language, or religion; and

4. To be a centre for harmonizing the actions of nations in the attainment of these common ends.

CHAPTER VII
ACTION WITH RESPECT TO THE THREATS TO THE PEACE, BREACHES OF THE PEACE, AND ACTS OF AGGRESSION
ARTICLE 39

The Security Council shall determine the existence of any threat to the peace, breach of the peace, or act of aggression and shall make recommendations, or decide what measures shall be taken in accordance with Articles 41 and 42, to maintain or restore international peace and security.

ARTICLE 40

In order to prevent an aggravation of the situation, the Security Council may, before making the recommendations or deciding upon the measures provided for in Article 39, call upon the parties concerned to comply with such provisional measures as it deems necessary or desirable. Such provisional measures shall be without prejudice to the rights, claims, or position of the parties concerned. The Security Council shall duly take account of failure to comply with such provisional measures.

ARTICLE 41

The Security Council may decide what measures not involving the use of armed force are to be employed to give effect to its decisions, and it may call upon the Members of the United Nations to apply such measures. These may include complete or partial interruption of economic relations and of rail, sea, air, postal, telegraphic, radio, and other means of communication, and the severance of diplomatic relations.

ARTICLE 42

Should the Security Council consider what measures provided for in Article 41 would be inadequate or have proved to be inadequate, it may take such action by air, sea, or land forces as may be necessary to maintain or restore international peace and security. Such action may include demonstrations, blockade, and other operations by air, sea, or land forces of Members of the United Nations.

Source: T.B. Millar, ed., Current International Treaties *(London: Croom Helm, 1984), pp. 94-96.*

---

* *There are now whole libraries of United Nations' literature, both its own documentation and books of comment and analysis. For essential documentation the reader is directed to the latest edition of* Everyman's United Nations, *and to P.J.G. Kapteyn and others (eds.),* International Organization and Integration: Annoted Basic Documents and Descriptive Direction of International Organizations and Arrangements, *Martinus Nijhoff, The Hague, 2nd edition, 1981.*
Con. 26/6/45. EIF. 24/10/45

STUDY QUESTIONS FOR SECTION FIVE: THE ORIGINS OF THE COLD WAR

1. What were the main sources of tension between the Soviet Union and its allies during the Second World War?

2. What were the interests and goals of each superpower in the late 1940s?

3. What was the purpose of the Marshall Plan?

4. What was the significance of the Berlin blockade?

SECTION SIX

FROM THE KOREAN WAR TO THE CUBAN MISSILE CRISIS

DOCUMENTS

CHRONOLOGY

1950		China occupies Tibet
	June	Korean War starts
	Sep.	MacArthur lands at Inchon
	Nov.	Chinese attack across the Yalu River
1952		test of first American hydrogen bomb
1953		test of first Soviet hydrogen bomb
	Jan.	Eisenhower administration
	Mar.	Stalin dies
	July	Korean armistice
	Sep.	Khrushchev emerging as Soviet leader
1954		Algerian war of independence starts West Germany joins NATO
	Apr.	Geneva Conference on Asia starts
	May	French defeat at Dienbienphu in Vietnam
1955		Warsaw Pact unrest in Poland
	Apr.	Bandung Conference of non-aligned nations
	May	end of Soviet occupation of Austria
	July	Geneva summit
1956		
	Feb.	20th Congress of the Communist Party of the Soviet Union
	Oct.	Suez adventure; Hungarian uprising
1957		Eisenhower doctrine offering aid against Communist aggression
1957		Treaties of Rome establishing European Economic Community and Euratom launching of Sputnik
1958		crisis in Lebanon start of Berlin crisis Great Leap Forward starts in China
	Sep.	Quemoy and Matsu shelled; General Charles De Gaulle establishes 5th Republic in France
1959		
	Jan.	Castro in power in Cuba
	Sep.	Khrushchev visits United States
1960		Congo crisis starts
	May	U-2 Affair; Paris summit
1961		Sino-Soviet split open Kennedy administration
	Jan.	US breaks diplomatic relations with Cuba
	Apr.	Bay of Pigs
	June	Kennedy-Khrushchev summit in Vienna
	Aug.	Berlin Wall built
	Sep.	Belgrade Conference of non-aligned nations
1962		India-China war
	Oct.	Cuban missile crisis

DOCUMENT 1

DEAN ACHESON AND THE 'DEFENSIVE PERIMETER'

6 months before Korean War!

Ever since the start of the Korean War there has been a controversy over the signals which the United States sent out concerning its possible policies there. Certainly, some public statements by American leaders in 1949 and the early part of 1950 indicated that Korea was not necessarily a major strategic concern of the United States. Dean Acheson, the Secretary of State in the Truman Administration, made the following speech to the National Press Club in Washington on January 12, 1950.

What is the situation in regard to the military security of the Pacific area, and what is our policy in regard to it?

In the first place, the defeat and disarmament of Japan has placed upon the United States the necessity of assuming the military defense of Japan so long as that is required, both in the interest of our security and in the interests of the security of the entire Pacific area, and, in all honor, in the interest of Japanese security. We have American—and there are Australian—troops in Japan. I am not in a position to speak for the Australians but I can assure you that there is not intention of any sort of abandoning or weakening the defenses of Japan and that whatever arrangements are to be made either through permanent settlement or otherwise, that defense must and shall be maintained.

This defensive perimeter runs along the Aleutians to Japan and then goes to the Ryukyus. We hold important defense positions in the Ryukyu Islands, and those we will continue to hold....

The defensive perimeter runs from the Ryukyus to the Philippine Islands. Our relations, our defensive relations with the Philippines are contained in agreements between us... it is hardly necessary for me to say an attack on the Philippines could not and would not be tolerated by the United States. But I hasten to add that no one perceives the imminence of any such attack.

So far as the military security of other areas in the Pacific is concerned, it must be clear that no person can guarantee these areas against military attack....

Should such an attack occur—one hesitates to say where such an armed attack could come from—the initial reliance must be on the people attacked to resist it and then upon the commitments of the entire civilized world under the Charter of the United Nations...

Source: Department of State, Bulletin, *XXII (January 23, 1950), pp. 115-6 [cited in H.L. Trefusse,* The Cold War: a book of documents *(New York: Capricorn Books, 1966), pp. 53-4].*

DOCUMENT 2

THE AMERICAN REACTION TO THE INVASION OF SOUTH KOREA

When the Korean War started on June 25, 1950 Dean Acheson, the American Secretary of State, was in Washington. He tried to assess the significance of the news.

One possibility was that the attack would be called off; the other, that it would not be. For some months, as tensions had mounted again after the Berlin blockade, we had run exercises on danger spots for renewed Soviet probing of our determination. Korea was on the list but not among the favorites. Berlin, Turkey, Greece, Iran—all seemed spots where the balance of convenient operation dipped in favor of the Soviets. ...What was likely to happen next and how should we determine our response? It seemed certain that the attack had been mounted, supplied, and instigated by the Soviet Union and that it would not be stopped by anything short of force. If Korean forces proved unequal to the job, as seemed probable, only American military intervention could do it. Troops from other sources would be helpful politically and psychologically but unimportant militarily....

Plainly, this attack did not amount to a *casus belli* [cause for war] against the Soviet Union. Equally plainly, it was an open, undisguised challenge to our internationally accepted position as the protector of South Korea, an area of great importance to the security of American-occupied Japan. To back away from this challenge, in view of our capacity for meeting it, would be highly destructive of the power and prestige of the United States. By prestige I mean the shadow cast by power, which is of great deterrent importance.

Source: Dean Acheson, Present at the Creation *(New York: W.W. Norton, 1969), p. 405.*

DOCUMENT 3

THE UN SECURITY COUNCIL AND THE KOREAN WAR

On June 25, 1950 North Korean troops crossed the 38th parallel and attacked the South. The United Nations' Security Council that same day, passed a resolution calling on the North Korean troops to stop fighting immediately and withdraw north of the 38th parallel. The Soviet Union, which might have been expected to veto such a resolution, was not present; its representative had withdrawn to protest the continued presence of the Nationalist Chinese at the UN. On June 27, the Security Council passed another resolution. Again the Soviet Union was not present.

Having determined that the armed attack upon the Republic of Korea by forces from North Korea constitutes a breach of the peace;

Having called for an immediate cessation of hostilities; and

Having called upon the authorities of North Korea to withdraw forthwith their armed forces to the 38th parallel; and

Having noted from the report of the United Nations Commission for Korea that the authorities in North Korea have neither ceased hostilities nor withdrawn their armed forces to the 38th parallel, and that urgent military measures are required to restore international peace and security; and

Having noted the appeal from the Republic of Korea to the United Nations for immediate and effective steps to secure peace and security,

Recommends that the Members of the United Nations furnish such assistance to the Republic of Korea as may be necessary to repel the armed attack and to restore international peace and security in the area.

Source: American Foreign Policy, 1950-1955, *Department of State Publication No. 6446, General Foreign Policy Series 117. II, 2538-9 [cited in H.L. Trefusse,* The Cold War: a book of documents *(New York: Capricorn Books, 1966), p. 157].*

DOCUMENT 4 NSC-68

Soon after the Korean War started, President Truman approved a major policy document from the National Security Council. NSC-68 recommended a sharp increase in military spending and the development of an American thermonuclear bomb.

A continuation of present trends would result in a serious decline in the strength of the free world relative to the Soviet Union and its satellites. This unfavorable trend arises from the inadequacy of current programs and plans rather than from any error in our objectives and aims. These trends lead in the direction of isolation, not by deliberate decision but by lack of the necessary basis for a vigorous initiative in the conflict with the Soviet Union.

Our position as the center of power in the free world places a heavy responsibility upon the United States for leadership. We must organize and enlist the energies and resources of the free world in a positive program for peace which will frustrate the Kremlin design for world domination by creating a situation in the free world to which the Kremlin will be compelled to adjust. Without such a cooperative effort, led by the United States, we will have to make gradual withdrawals under pressure until we discover one day that we have sacrificed positions of vital interest.

It is imperative that this trend be reversed by a much more rapid and concerted build-up of the actual strength of both the United States and the other nations of the free world. The analysis shows that this will be costly and will involve significant domestic financial and economic adjustments.

The execution of such a build-up, however, requires that the United States have an affirmative program beyond the solely defensive one of countering the threat posed by the Soviet Union. This program must light the path to peace and order among nations in a system based on freedom and justice, as contemplated in the Charter of the United Nations. Further, it must envisage the political and economic measures with which and the military shield behind which the free world can work to frustrate the Kremlin design by the strategy of the cold war; for every consideration of devotion to our fundamental values and to our national security demands that we achieve our objectives by the strategy of the cold war, building up our military strength in order that it may not have to be used. The only sure victory lies in the frustration of the Kremlin design by the steady development of the moral and material strength of the free world and its projection into the Soviet world in such a way as to bring about an internal change in the Soviet system. Such a positive program—harmonious with our fundamental national purpose and our objectives—is necessary if we are to regain and retain the initiative and to win and hold the necessary popular support and cooperation in the United States and the rest of the free world.

This program should include a plan for negotiation with the Soviet Union, developed and agreed with our allies and which is consonant with our objectives. The United States and its allies, particularly the United Kingdom and France, should always be ready to negotiate with the Soviet Union on terms consistent with our objectives. The present world situation, however, is one which militates against successful negotiations with the Kremlin—for the terms of agreements on important pending issues would reflect present realities and would therefore be unacceptable, if not disastrous, to the United States and the rest of the free world. After a decision and a start on building up the strength of the free world has been made, it might then be desirable for the United States to take an initiative in seeking negotiations in the hope that it might facilitate the process of accommodation by the Kremlin to the new situation. Failing that, the unwillingness of the Kremlin to accept equitable terms or its bad faith in observing them would assist in consolidating popular opinion in the free world in support of the measures necessary to sustain the build-up.

In summary, we must, by means of a rapid and sustained build-up of the political, economic, and military strength of the free world, and by means of an affirmative program intended to wrest the initiative... and frustrate the Kremlin design of a world dominated by its will. Such evidence is the only means short of war which eventually may force the Kremlin to abandon its present course of action and to negotiate acceptable agreements on issues of major importance.

The whole success of the proposed program hangs ultimately on recognition by this Government, the American people, and all free peoples, that the cold war is in fact a real war in which the survival of the free world is at stake. Essential prerequisites to success are consultations with Congressional leaders designed to make the program the object of non-partisan legislative support, and a presentation to the public of a full explanation of the facts and implications of the present international situation. The prosecution of the program will require of us all the ingenuity, sacrifice, and unity demanded by the vital importance of the issue and the tenacity to persevere until our national objectives have been attained.

Source: FRUS, *1950, volume 1, pp. 290-292.*

DOCUMENT 5 — THE WARSAW PACT

By 1949 the Western nations had formed the North Atlantic Treaty Organization [NATO] for the defense of Western Europe. The Soviet Union, which already had an integrated military structure in place and large numbers of Soviet troops stationed in Eastern Europe, responded in 1955 with the Warsaw Pact Organization. The following is from the preamble of the Warsaw Treaty which was signed by the Soviet Union and all the Soviet regimes in Eastern Europe with the exception of Yugoslavia.

The Contracting Parties, reaffirming their desire for the establishment of a system of European collective security based on the participation of all European states irrespective of their social and political systems, which would make it possible to unite their efforts in safeguarding the peace of Europe; mindful, at the same time, of the situation created in Europe by the ratification of the Paris agreements, which envisage the formation a new military alignment in the shape of "Western European Union", with the participation of a remilitarized Western Germany and the integration of the latter in the North-Atlantic bloc, which increases the danger of another war and constitutes a threat to the national security of the peaceable states; being persuaded in these circumstances the peaceable European states must take the necessary measures to safeguard their security and in the interest of preserving peace in Europe; guided by the objects and principles of the Charter of the United Nations Organization; being desirous of further promoting and developing friendship, cooperation and mutual assistance in accordance with the principles of respect for the independence and sovereignty of states and of noninterference in their internal affairs, have decided to conclude the present Treaty of Friendship, Cooperation and Mutual Assistance.

Source: Robin Alison Remington, The Warsaw Pact *(Cambridge, Mass. and London: The M.I.T. Press, 1971), p. 201.*

DOCUMENT 6

KHRUSHCHEV'S SPEECH TO THE TWENTIETH PARTY CONGRESS

After Stalin's death in 1953, a short power struggle saw Nikita Khrushchev emerge as the Soviet leader. Although he was erratic and often impulsive, he did try to bring reforms within the Soviet Union and to mend fences with Soviet enemies such as Tito in Yugoslavia and even with the United States. In 1956, he astonished the Communist world by denouncing some of Stalin's crimes in a secret speech at the 20th Congress of the Communist Party of the Soviet Union. Khrushchev also called for "peaceful coexistence" with the West, arguing that the advent of atomic weapons meant that armed struggle would bring mutual annihilation. Nevertheless, he continued to hope for the eventual victory of communism over capitalism, as the following extract from his public speech at the 20th Congress makes clear.

Soon after the Second World War ended, the influence of reactionary and militarist groups began to be increasingly evident in the policy of the United States of America, Britain and France. Their desire to enforce their will on other countries by economic and political pressure, threats and military provocation prevailed. This became known as the "positions of strength" policy.

....

The international atmosphere was poisoned by war hysteria. The arms race began to assume more and more monstrous dimensions. Many big U.S. military bases designed for use against the U.S.S.R. and the People's Democracies [ie the new Soviet style regimes in Eastern Europe and Asia] were built in countries thousands of miles from the borders of the United States. "Cold war" was begun against the socialist camp. International distrust was artificially kindled, and nations set against one another. A bloody war was launched in Korea; the war in Indo-China dragged on for years.

The inspirers of the "cold war" began to establish military blocs, and many countries found themselves, against the will of their peoples, involved in restricted aggressive alignments—the North Atlantic bloc, Western European Union. SEATO (military bloc for South-East Asia) and the Baghdad pact.

The organizers of military blocs allege that they have united for defense, for protection against the "communist threat". But that is sheer hypocrisy. We know from history that when planning a redivision of the world, the imperialist powers have always lined up military blocs.

....

The arms race, the "positions of strength" policy, the lining up of aggressive blocs and the "cold war"—all this could not but aggravate the international situation and it did.

....

But other processes have also taken place in the international arena during these years, processes showing that in the world today monopolist circles are by no means controlling everything.

The steady consolidation of the forces of socialism, democracy and peace, and of the forces of the national-liberation movement is of decisive significance. The international position of the Soviet Union, the People's Republic of China, and the other socialist countries has been further strengthened during this period, and their prestige and international ties have grown immeasurably. The international camp of socialism is exerting ever-growing influence on the course of international events. (Applause.)

The forces of peace have been considerably augmented by the emergence in the world arena of a group of peace-loving European and Asian states...

....

The disintegration of the imperialist colonial system now taking place is a post-war development of history-making significance. Peoples who for centuries were kept away by the colonialists from the high road of progress followed by human society are now going through a great process of regeneration.

....

When we say that the socialist system will win in the competition between the two systems—the capitalist and the socialist—this by no means signifies that its victory will be achieved through armed interference by the socialist countries in the internal affairs of the capitalist countries. Our certainty of the victory of communism is based on the fact that the socialist mode of production possesses decisive advantages over the capitalist mode of production.

Source: Robert A. Goldwin, ed., Readings in Russsian Foreign Policy *(New York: Oxford University Press, 1959), pp. 362-9.*

DOCUMENT 7 JOHN FOSTER DULLES ON THE SOVIET THREAT

John Foster Dulles, Secretary of State in the Eisenhower Administration in the 1950s, was a determined opponent of Soviet expansion. Often portrayed as the archetypical cold-warrior, he attempted to off-set Soviet influence with a series of treaties and alliances, among them SEATO and CENTO. He also had a fondness for covert operations, among them those run by the Central Intelligence Agency which was headed by his brother Allen Dulles. Like Eisenhower, he was reluctant to spend unnecessarily on the military. He hoped to use American nuclear superiority to deter further Soviet advances; he threatened "massive retaliation". The following comes from a speech he gave to the Council on Foreign Relations on January 12, 1954.

It is now nearly a year since the Eisenhower Administration took office. During the year I have often spoken of various parts of our foreign policies. Tonight I should like to present an overall view of those polices which relate to our security.

First of all, let us recognize that many of the preceding foreign policies were good. Aid to Greece and Turkey had checked the Communist drive to the Mediterranean. The European Recovery Program [the Marshall Plan] had helped the peoples of Western Europe to pull out of the post-war morass. The Western powers were steadfast in Berlin and over come the blockade with their airlift. As a loyal member of the United Nations we had reacted with force to repel the Communist attack in Korea. When that effort exposed our military weakness, we rebuilt rapidly our military establishment. We also sought a quick buildup of armed strength in Western Europe.

These were the acts of nation which saw the danger of the Soviet Union...

....

But we need to recall that what we did was in the main emergency action, imposed on us by our enemies.

....

We need allies and collective security. Our purpose is to make these relations more effective, less costly. This can be done by placing more reliance on deterrent power, and less dependence on local defensive power.

This is accepted practice so far as local communities are concerned. We keep locks on our doors; but we do not have an armed guard in every home. We rely principally on a community security system so well equipped to punish any who break in and steal that, in fact, would-be aggressors are generally deterred. That is the modern way of getting maximum protection at a bearable cost.

What the Eisenhower Administration seeks is a similar international security system. We want, for ourselves, and the other free nations, a maximum deterrent at a bearable cost.

Local defenses will always be important. But there is no local defense which alone will contain the mighty land power of the Communist world. Local defenses must be reinforced by the further deterrent of massive retaliatory power.

Source: American Foreign Policy, 1950-1955, *Department of State Publication No. 6446, General Foreign Policy Series 117. I, 80-83 [cited in H.L. Trefusse,* The Cold War: a book of documents *(New York: Capricorn Books, 1966), pp. 170-3].*

DOCUMENT 8 PRESIDENT EISENHOWER ON THE THIRD WORLD

As decolonization moved ahead in the 1950s, many of the newly-emerging nations tried to build a non-aligned movement which would steer clear of entanglement with either of the super-powers. Nevertheless, it was difficult to avoid the Cold War; both sides offered aid, from economic to military. The following is from a speech given by President Eisenhower in May 1957.

We know, and the world knows, that the American people will fight against hostile and aggressive despotisms when their force is thrown against the barriers of freedom...But we also know that to fight is the most costly way to keep America secure and free. Even an America victorious in atomic war could scarcely escape disastrous destruction of her cities and a fearful loss of life. Victory itself could be agony.

Plainly, we must seek less tragic, less costly ways to defend ourselves. We must recognize that, whenever any country falls under the domination of communism, the strength of the free world—and that of America—is by that amount weakened and communism strengthened. If this process, through our neglect or indifference, should proceed unchecked, our continent would gradually be encircled. Our safety depends upon recognition of the fact that the Communist design for such encirclement must be stopped before it gains momentum, before it is again too late to save the peace.

This recognition dictates two tasks. We must maintain a common worldwide defense against the menace of international communism. And we must demonstrate and spread the blessings of liberty—to be cherished by those who enjoy these blessings, to be sought by those now denied them.

....

The whole design of this defense against Communist conspiracy and encirclement cannot be with guns alone. For the freedom of nations can be menaced not only by guns but by the poverty that communism can exploit.

You cannot fight poverty with guns. You cannot satisfy hunger with deadly ammunition. Economic stability and progress, essential to any nations's peace and well-being, cannot be assured merely by the firepower of artillery or the speed of jets.

And so our mutual security programs today, at a cost of some $4 billion, are designed to meet dangers in whatever form they may appear. Thus, their key purposes are three:

First: To help friendly nations equip and support armed forces for their own and our defense.

Second: To help, in a sustained effort, less advanced countries grow in the strength that can sustain freedom as their way of life.

And third: To meet emergencies and special needs affecting our own national interest.

Source: Department of State Bulletin, *June 10, 1957 [cited in Robert A. Goldwin, ed.,* Readings in American Foreign Policy *(New York: Oxford University Press, 1959), pp. 603-4].*

DOCUMENT 9 THE U-2 INCIDENT

Towards the end of the 1950s, relations between the superpowers showed signs of improvement. Khrushchev had made a number of conciliatory moves, for example, ending the Soviet occupation of Austria. In 1959 he had visited the United States, the first Soviet leader to do so since 1917. In May 1960 he and Eisenhower were scheduled to meet at a summit in Paris to discuss important issues including the German question. Shortly before the summit was to start and when Eisenhower had already arrived in Paris, the Soviet Union announced that it had shot down a high-altitude American U-2 spy plane. To the embarrassment of the Americans, who at first denied the charge, the Soviets then produced the plane's pilot, Gary Powers. The following is an extract from Khrushchev's speech to the Supreme Soviet at the beginning of May.

Comrades, I must tell you a secret. When I was making my report [his earlier one] I deliberately did not say that the pilot was alive and in good health and that we got parts of the plane. We did so deliberately because had we told everything at once, the Americans would have invented another version.

And now, just look how many silly things they have said...

....

The name of this pilot is Francis Gary Powers. He is 30 years old. He says he is a first lieutenant of the United States Air Force, where he served until 1956, that is, to the day when he went over to the Central Intelligence Agency.

Francis Powers reported, incidentally, that while serving with the American Air Force he used to get $700 a month, but when he went over to the intelligence service and started carrying out spying assignments to glean secret information, he began getting $2,500 a month. That is how capital buys lives, buys people. The flier testified that he had no dizziness, nor had his oxygen apparatus failed. He was flying along the assigned course, accurately executing his chief's orders, switching on and off the equipment over the pre-selected targets for gleaning intelligence on the Soviet Union's military and industrial establishments, and flew on until he very moment his piratical flight into this country's interior was cut short.

....

The plane was in no way equipped for "upper atmosphere research" or for taking "air samples", as official American spokesmen assert.

Not at all. This was a real military reconnaissance aircraft fitted with various instruments for collecting intelligence, and, among other things, for aerial photography...

But the installation of the infernal machine was not the only precaution taken. To cover up the tracks of the crime the pilot was told that he must not fall alive in the hands of the Soviet authorities. For this reason he was supplied with a special pin. He was to have pricked himself with this poisoned pin, resulting in instantaneous death.

What a barbarism! Here is this instrument—the latest achievement of American technology for the killing of their own people...

[Khrushchev produced a photograph; he also refers to a pistol with a silencer that Powers had.] He was given this pistol after making low bows as they do in church. And yet they call us godless atheists. Yet we have never committed such crimes against humanity and never will.

....

The pilot was also given French gold francs. I have seen those gold francs with my own eyes. And you can see them here in the photograph. They are covered with cellophane on both sides of the coins. Done in a cultured, American way. But what did the pilot need these francs for? He also had West German, Italian and other currency. Besides his own watch he was also given for his trip another two gold watches and seven gold rings for ladies. Why was all this necessary in the upper layers of the atmosphere? Or maybe, the pilot was to have flown higher still to Mars and was going to lead astray Martian ladies?

Source: The New York Times, *8 May 1960 [cited in H.L. Trefusse,* The Cold War: a book of documents *(New York: Capricorn Books, 1966), pp. 221-4].*

DOCUMENT 10 THE PARIS SUMMIT

The United States admitted responsibility for the flight but Khrushchev went on to demand an American apology and punishment for those responsible. He also withdrew his invitation to President Eisenhower to visit Russia. Although Khrushchev came to Paris, the summit was essentially finished. On May 17, Eisenhower issued a statement.

Having in mind the great importance of this Conference and the hopes that the peoples of all the world have reposed in this meeting, I concluded that in the circumstances it was best to see if at today's private meeting any possibility existed through the exercise of reason and restraint to dispose of this matter of overflights, which would have permitted the Conference to go forward.

....

Accordingly, at this mornings's private session, despite the violence and inaccuracy of Mr. Khrushchev's statements, I replied to him in the following terms:

....

In my statement of May 11 ... the position of the United States was made clear with respect to the distasteful necessity of espionage activities in a world where nations distrust each other's intentions. We pointed out that these activities had no aggressive intent but rather were to assure the safety of the United States and the free world against surprise attack... As is well known, not only the United States but most other countries are constantly the targets of elaborate and persistent espionage of the Soviet Union.

....

I have come to Paris to seek agreements with the Soviet Union which would eliminate the necessity for all forms of espionage, including overflights. I see no reason for this incident to disrupt the conference.

....

My words were seconded and supported by my Western colleagues, who also urged Mr. Khrushchev to pursue the path of reason and commonsense, and to forget propaganda.

....

Mr. Khrushchev brushed aside all arguments of reason, and not only insisted upon this ultimatum, but also insisted he was going to publish his statement in full at the time of his own choosing. It was thus made apparent that he was determined to wreck the Paris Conference.

In fact, the only conclusion that can be drawn from his behavior this morning was that he came all the way from Moscow to Paris with the sole intention of sabotaging this meeting on which so much of the hopes of the world have rested.

Source: Department of State Press Release no. 271, May 17, 1960 [cited in H.L. Trefusse, The Cold War: a book of documents *(New York: Capricorn Books, 1966), pp. 225-7].*

DOCUMENT 11 THE BAY OF PIGS

The Kennedy administration, which took office in January 1961, inherited a number of issues from its predecessor. Relations with Cuba had been broken off. Shortly after Kennedy was sworn in, the CIA presented him with a plan to invade Cuba using Cuban exiles, who were already in training camps in Central America. Kennedy and his advisors had to decide whether to cancel preparations which were quite advanced or to cancel the invasion. After a considerable debate, it was decided to let the invasion, at the bay of Pigs on the coast of Cuba, go ahead in April. The attempt was a disaster. The United States initially tried to deny that it was involved. Castro, the Cuban premier, issued a communiqué on April 20.

...the revolution has emerged victorious although it had to pay a high price in precious lives of revolutionary fighters, who faced the invaders and attacked them incessantly without a single pause...in this fashion the army which was organized in the space of many months by the imperialist Government of the United States, was destroyed in less than seventy-two hours... Part of the mercenaries tried to escape from the country in several ships, which were sunk by the revolutionary air force. The rest of the mercenary forces, after suffering many casualties—dead and injured—scattered in a swampy area from which there was no possible escape route.

A large quantity of arms, manufactured in the United States, were captured, including several Sherman heavy tanks. No complete count has yet been made of the captured weapons.

Source: New York Times, *21 April 1961 [cited in H.L. Trefusse,* The Cold War: a book of documents *(New York: Capricorn Books, 1966), pp. 255-6].*

DOCUMENT 12 SOVIET SUPPORT FOR CUBA

Even before the Bay of Pigs, the Soviet Union had begun to supply weapons to Cuba. After the invasion, the Soviet leadership had to consider what its policy should be. Khrushchev later wrote in his memoirs:

We were sure that the Americans would never reconcile themselves to the existence of Castro's Cuba. They feared, much as we hoped, that a Socialist Cuba might become a magnet that would attract other Latin American countries to Socialism. Given the continual threat of American interference in the Caribbean, what should our own policy be? This question was constantly on my mind, and I frequently discussed it with other members of the Presidium [the Soviet equivalent to a cabinet]. Everyone agreed that America would not leave Cuba alone unless we did something. We had an obligation to do everything in our power to protect Cuba's existence as a Socialist country and as a working example to the other countries of Latin America.

....

We had to establish a tangible and effective deterrent to American interference in the Caribbean. But what exactly? The logical answer was missiles. The United States had already surrounded the Soviet Union with its own bomber bases and missiles. We knew that American missiles were aimed against us in Turkey and Italy, to say nothing of West Germany.

....

I knew that first we'd have to talk to Castro and explain our strategy to him in order to get the agreement of the Cuban government. My thinking went like this: if we installed the missiles secretly and then the United States discovered the missiles were there after they were already poised and ready to strike, the Americans would think twice before trying to liquidate our installations by military means. I knew that the United States could knock out some of our installations, but not all of them. If a quarter or even a tenth of our missiles survived—even if only one or two big ones were left—we could still hit New York, and there wouldn't be much of New York left. I don't mean to say that everyone in New York would be killed—not everyone, of course, but an awful lot of people would be wiped out. I don't know how many: that's a matter for our scientists and military personnel to work out. ... But that's all beside the point. The main thing was that the installation of our missiles in Cuba would, I thought, restrain the United States from precipitous military action against Castro's government. In addition to protecting Cuba, our missiles would have equalized what the West likes to call "the balance of power". ... And it was high time America learned what it feels like to have her own land and her own people threatened. We Russians have suffered three wars over the last half century: World War I, the Civil War, and World War II. America has never had to fight a war on her own soil, at least not in the past fifty years. She's sent troops abroad to fight in the two World Wars—and made a fortune as a result. America has shed a few drops of her own blood while making billions by bleeding the rest of the world dry.

Source: Strobe Talbott, ed., Khrushchev Remembers *(Boston and Toronto: Little, Brown & Co., 1970), pp. 492-4.*

DOCUMENT 13

PRESIDENT KENNEDY'S SPEECH ON THE SOVIET MISSILES IN CUBA

The thirteen days of the Cuban Missile Crisis—from October 15 when President Kennedy was told that the presence of Soviet missiles in Cuba had been confirmed, to October 28, when Premier Khrushchev agreed to dismantle the missiles—were probably the most dangerous period of the Cold War. On October 22, 1961 President Kennedy went on television to address the American people about the Soviet missiles.

...this secret, swift, and extraordinary buildup of Communist missiles—in an area well known to have a special and historical relationship to the United States and the nations of the Western Hemisphere, in violation of Soviet assurances, and in defiance of American and hemispheric policy—this sudden, clandestine decision to station strategic weapons for the first time outside of Soviet soil—is a deliberately provocative and unjustified change in the status quo which cannot be accepted by this country, if our courage and our commitments are ever to be trusted again by either friend or foe.

The 1930s taught us a clear lesson: aggressive conduct, if allowed to go unchecked and unchallenged, ultimately leads to war

....

Acting, therefore, in the defense of our own security and of the entire Western Hemisphere, and under the authority entrusted to me by the Constitution as endorsed by the resolution of the Congress, I have directed that the following *initial* steps be taken immediately:

First: To halt this offensive buildup, a strict quarantine on all offensive military equipment under shipment to Cuba is being initiated. All ships of any kind bound for Cuba from whatever nation or port will, if found to contain cargoes of offensive weapons, be turned back. .....

Second: I have directed the continued and increased surveillance of Cuba and its military buildup... Should these offensive military preparations continue, thus increasing the threat to the hemisphere, further action will be justified. I have directed the Armed Forces to prepare for any eventualities...

Third: It shall be the policy of this Nation to regard any nuclear missile launched from Cuba against any nation in the Western Hemisphere as an attack by the Soviet Union on the United States, requiring a full retaliatory response upon the Soviet Union.

....

Seventh and finally: I call upon Chairman Khrushchev to halt and eliminate this clandestine, reckless, and provocative threat to world peace. I call upon him further to abandon this course of world domination, and to join in an historic effort to end the perilous arms race and to transform the history of man. He has an opportunity now to move the world back from the abyss of destruction—by returning to his government's own words that it had no need to station missiles outside its own territory, and by withdrawing these weapons from Cuba ...

Source: Public Papers of the Presidents of the United States: John F. Kennedy, 1962 *(Washington, 1963), pp. 806-9 [cited Lester Langley, ed.,* The United States, Cuba, and the Cold War *(Lexington, Mass: D.C. Heath and Co., 1970), pp. 48-9.*

DOCUMENT 14 THE CUBAN MISSILE CRISIS

Wednesday, October 24, 1961 was a particularly tense day during the Cuban Missile Crisis. President Kennedy had announced [see Document 11] that the United States was enforcing a quarantine around Cuba, and several Soviet ships had slowed down or turned back. One Soviet freighter continued to steam towards the quarantine line. Robert Kennedy, who was one of his brother's closest advisers during the crisis, remembers the meeting of the Executive Committee of the National Security Council that morning.

This Wednesday-morning meeting, along with that of the following Saturday, October 27, seemed the most trying, the most difficult, and the most filled with tension. The Russian ships were proceeding, they were nearing the five-hundred-mile barrier, and we either had to intercept them or announce we were withdrawing. I sat across the table from the President. This was the moment we had prepared for, which we hoped would never come. The danger and concern that we all felt hung like a cloud over us all and particularly over the President.

....

It was now a few minutes after 10:00 o'clock. Secretary McNamara announced that two Russian ships, the Gagarin and the Komiles, were within a few miles of our quarantine barrier. The interception of both ships would probably be before noon Washington time. Indeed, the expectation was that at least one of the vessels would be stopped and boarded between 10:30 and 11:00 o'clock. ... Then came the disturbing Navy report that a Russian submarine had moved into position between the two ships.

....

It had originally been planned to have a cruiser make the first interception, but, because of the increased danger, it was decided in the past few hours to send in an aircraft carrier supported by helicopters, carrying antisubmarine equipment, hovering overhead. The carrier Essex was to signal the submarine by sonar to surface and identify itself. If it refused, said Secretary McNamara, depth charges with a small explosive would be used until the submarine surfaced.

....

I think these few minutes were the time of gravest concern for the President. Was the world on the brink of a holocaust? Was it our error? A mistake? Was there something further that should have been done? Or not done? His hand went up to his face and covered his mouth. He opened and closed his fist. His face seemed drawn, in his eyes pained, almost gray. We stared at each other across the table. For a few fleeting seconds, it was almost as though no one else was there and he was no longer the President.

....

Then it was 10:25—a messenger brought in a note to John McCone. "Mr. President, we have a preliminary report which seems to indicate that some of the Russian ships have stopped dead in the water." Stopped dead in the water? Which ships? Are they checking the accuracy of the report? Is it true? I looked at the clock. 10:32. "The report is accurate, Mr. President. Six ships previously on their way to Cuba at the edge of the quarantine line have stopped or have turned back toward the Soviet Union. A representative from the Office of Naval Intelligence is on his way over with the full report." A short time later, the report came that the twenty Russian ships closest to the barrier had stopped and were dead in the water or had turned around.

Source: Robert F. Kennedy, Thirteen Days *(New York and London: W.W. Norton and Company, 1971), pp. 46-49.*

On Friday, October 26, the United States received a dramatic letter from Khrushchev in which he said that no one, including him, wanted nuclear war, and that the world must be pulled back from the precipice. Robert Kennedy, on the debate in the Executive Committee:

A great deal has been written about this message, including the allegation that at the time Khrushchev wrote it he must have been so unstable or emotional that he had become incoherent. There was no question that the letter had been written by him personally. It was very long and emotional. But it was not incoherent, and the emotion was directed at the death, destruction, and anarchy that nuclear war would bring to his people and all mankind. That, he said again and again and in many different ways, must be avoided.

Source: Robert F. Kennedy, Thirteen Days *(New York and London: W.W. Norton and Company, 1971), p. 64.*

The next day another letter arrived from Khrushchev; this one was more formal and less conciliatory. Robert Kennedy again:

On Saturday morning, October 27, I received a memorandum from J. Edgar Hoover, Director of the Federal Bureau of Investigation, that gave me a feeling of considerable disquiet. He had received information the night before that certain Soviet personnel in New York were apparently preparing to destroy all sensitive documents on the basis that the U.S. would probably be taking military action against Cuba or Soviet ships, and this would mean war. I asked myself as I drove to the White House: If the Soviets were anxious to find an answer to the crisis, why this conduct on the part of Soviet personnel? Did the Khrushchev letter really indicate a solution could be found?

....

It was therefore with some sense of foreboding that I went to the meeting of our Ex Comm. My concern was justified. A new, this time very formal, letter had arrived from Khrushchev to President Kennedy. It was obviously no longer Mr. Khrushchev personally who was writing, but the Foreign Office of the Kremlin. The letter was quite different from the letter received twelve hours before.

Source: Robert F. Kennedy, Thirteen Days *(New York and London: W.W. Norton and Company, 1971), pp. 71-2.*

That afternoon, after considerable discussion, it was decided to send a reply to the Soviets. Robert Kennedy:

I suggested, and was supported by Ted Sorensen and others, that we ignore the latest Khrushchev letter and respond to his earlier letter's proposal, as refined in the offer made to John Scali, that the Soviet missiles and offensive weapons would be removed from Cuba under UN inspection and verification if, on its side, the United States would agree with the rest of the Western Hemisphere not to invade Cuba.

Source: Robert F. Kennedy, Thirteen Days *New York and London, 1971), pp. 79-80.*

Study Questions for Section Six: From the Korean War to the Cuban missile crisis

1. Who started the Korean War?

2. What was the impact of the Korean War on the Cold War?

3. Was there a thaw in the Cold War after Stalin's death?

4. Why did Berlin become an issue between East and West in the late 1950s?

5. Why did the Soviet Union place missiles in Cuba?

6. Was there a winner in the Cuban missile crisis?

SECTION SEVEN

INDOCHINA

DOCUMENTS

CHRONOLOGY

1883 to 1940 French colonial rule

1940 to 1945 French administration under Japanese military

1945 (Aug) Vietnamese guerillas (the Vietminh) proclaim a provisional government under Ho Chi Minh; (Sep) Ho proclaims independence, but British forces return authority to the French; massive famine kills nearly two million in northern Vietnam

1946 (Mar) French-Vietminh accord recognizing Vietnam as a "free state" in French Indochina; (Nov) truce breaks down and First Indochinese War begins

1950 (Jan). the Soviet Union and Communist China recognize the North Vietnam as proclaimed by Ho; (Feb) the US and Britain recognize the French-backed Bao Dai government in the South

1953 (Oct) France grants Laos and Cambodia full independence; (Dec)Vietminh forces move into Laos to assist communists and to use border areas as sanctuaries against the French

1954 (May) French forces defeated at Dienbienphu; (Jul) Geneva Conference divides Vietnam pending elections; US aid to the government of Ngo Dien Diem in South Vietnam; US agrees to but does not sign provisions reached at Geneva; SEATO is formed

1955 (Jan) US training of the South Vietnamese army; French forces withdraw; (Jul) Diem renounces the Geneva agreements and cracks down on "radicals"; Ho "formally" agrees to Soviet and Chinese aid; (Oct) Diem proclaims the South a Republic

1958 (Jul) neutralist government in Laos falls and a US-backed regime takes over

1959 (Jan) plot linking the CIA to kill the "neutralist" Cambodian Prince Norodom Sihanouk; (May) North Vietnamese begin moving arms into the South via the jungle "Ho Chi Minh Trail"

1960 (May) army coup in Laos restores neutralists - US backs opposition forces; (Nov) South Vietnamese army units failed coup against Diem; (Dec) North Vietnamese leaders form the "National Liberation Front" (NLF or Vietcong) for South Vietnam

1961 (Jan) civil war erupts in Laos; (May) Geneva Conference on Laos sets up neutral coalition government; (Jun) Kennedy rejects sending US troops to South but agrees to military aid for Diem

1962 (Feb) American Military Assistance Command is formed in the South, increasing advisers from 700 to 12,000; (Jul) Kennedy agrees to Geneva accords on Laos - increases US role in Vietnam

1963 (spring-summer) increased protests against Diem; (Nov) coup overthrows Diem

1964 (Aug) Gulf of Tonkin incident and Tonkin Gulf Resolution; the Second Indochinese War begins

1965 (Feb) sustained bombing of the North; (Mar) first US ground combat troops sent; (Apr) North Vietnam rejects Johnson's offer of US-backed economic development programme for peace

1967 (Sep) Nguyen Van Thieu and Nguyen Cao Ky are "elected" President and Vice-President of South Vietnam after nearly four years of intense political instability

1968 (Jan) Tet offensive; (May) US and North Vietnamese negotiators meet in Paris

1969 (Mar) secret bombings of Cambodia and "Vietnamization" begins; (Sep) Ho dies; (Oct) anti-war demonstrations in US swell

1970 (Feb) Sihanouk overthrown by US-backed forces; (Apr) US attacks against Vietcong in Cambodia; Kent State incident

1971 (Feb) South Vietnamese forces move into Laos against the Ho Chi Minh trail

1972 (Feb) Nixon goes to Communist China; (Apr) intensified bombing of North; (Dec) "Christmas Bombings" of North and breakdown of talks

1973 (Jan) cease fire agreement announced; draft in US ends; (Mar) the last US combat troops are withdrawn, ending US war

1975 (Apr) North Vietnamese forces move into Saigon; communist forces (Khmer Rouge) take over Cambodia; (May) communist forces (Pathet Lao) dominate "neutral" government in Laos

1978 (Dec) Vietnam invades Cambodia; thousands flee Vietnam and Cambodia as "boat people"; Cambodian "killing fields" revealed

1979 (Jan) Vietnamese forces install puppet regime in Cambodia; (Feb) Chinese forces invade Vietnam, starting the Third Indochinese War; (Dec) Chinese troops withdraw from Vietnam

1989 (Sep) Vietnam withdraws from Cambodia; talks in Paris continue until 1992 over Cambodia when UN moves in

1994 (Mar) US President Bill Clinton announces the end of the American embargo on Vietnam - formal diplomatic relations have still not been re-established

As a young man, Ho Chi Minh was impressed by the American emphasis on liberty and independence. He even thought of himself as the "George Washington" of Vietnam. Consequently he believed that the US would endorse the idea of Vietnamese independence after World War Two, especially considering how the Vietminh fought with the Allies against Japan. Ho was not alone in this expectation. However, as uncertainty about the post-World War Two order mounted, opinions on the situation in Indochina were divided and more complex.

DOCUMENT 1 MEMO BY US PRESIDENT FRANKLIN ROOSEVELT TO SECRETARY OF STATE CORDELL HULL - JANUARY 24, 1944

...I had, for over a year, expressed the opinion that Indo-China should not go back to France but that it should be administered by an international trusteeship. France has had the country — thirty million inhabitants — for nearly one hundred years, and the people are worse off than they were at the beginning.... Each case must, of course, stand on its own feet, but the case of Indo-China is perfectly clear. France has milked it for one hundred years. The people of Indo-China are entitled to something better than that.

Source: United States, Department of State, FRUS, 1944 *(Vol. III) (Washington: Government Printing Office, 1965-67), p. 773.*

DOCUMENT 2 "DECLARATION OF INDEPENDENCE OF THE DEMOCRATIC REPUBLIC OF VIETNAM" - SEPTEMBER 2, 1945

We hold truths that all men are created equal, that they are endowed by their Creator with certain unalienable rights, among these are Life, Liberty and the pursuit of Happiness... Every man is born equal and enjoys free and equal rights... These are undeniable truths. Yet, during and throughout the last eighty years, the French imperialists, abusing the principles of "Freedom, equality and fraternity", have violated the integrity of our ancestral land and oppressed our countrymen. Their deeds run counter to the ideals of humanity and justice... They have denied us every freedom. They have enforced upon us inhuman laws... They have built more prisons than schools... They have drowned our revolutions in blood... They have shamelessly exploited our people, driven them into the worst misery and mercilessly plundered our country... We are convinced that the Allies who have recognized the principles of equality of peoples... cannot but recognize the Independence of Viet Nam. A people which has so stubbornly opposed the French domination for more than eighty years, a people who, during these last years, so doggedly ranged itself and fought on the Allied side against fascism, such a people has the right to be free, such a people must be independent...

Source: Allan W. Cameron (ed.), Viet-Nam Crisis: A Documentary History *(Volume I: 1940-1956) (Ithaca, NY: Cornell University Press, 1971), pp. 52-54.*

Are they nationalists or communists? Are they pro-Soviet? Pro-Chinese? Pro-American? Neutralists? Isolationists? Deciding was one of the biggest problems facing foreign policy decision-makers everywhere as they examined the situation in Indochina after World War Two. By 1948 Washington was sharply opposed to a restoration of French rule in Indochina, but it was also against a complete withdrawal for fear of communist expansion in the region. Faced with this dilemma, the United States remained essentially passive, accepting French policy with which it could not agree. However, the "loss" of China to communism in 1949 made Indochina an even more pressing problem.

DOCUMENT 3

PAPER ON MILITARY AID FOR INDOCHINA BY A WORKING GROUP IN THE DEPARTMENT OF STATE - FEBRUARY 1, 1950

... Unavoidably, the United States is, together with France, committed in Indochina...The choice confronting the United States is to support the French in Indochina or face the extension of Communism over the remainder of the continental area of Southeast Asia and, possibly, farther westward. We would then be obliged to make staggering investments in those areas and in that part of Southeast Asia remaining outside Communist domination... It would seem a case of "Penny wise, Pound foolish" to deny support to the French in Indochina.

Source: FRUS, *1950, Vol. VI, pp. 711-715.*

DOCUMENT 4

CABLE FROM SECRETARY OF STATE DEAN ACHESON TO US CONSUL O'SULLIVAN IN HANOI - MAY 20, 1949

Question [whether] Ho as much nationalist as Commie is irrelevant. All Stalinists in colonial areas are nationalists.

Source: Marilyn B. Young, The Vietnam Wars 1945-1990 *(New York: HarperCollins Publishers, 1991), p. 20.*

The Vietminh fought the French for nearly eight years using guerilla warfare. Most of the fighting took place in northern Vietnam, where the guerillas were able to tie down a much larger and better equipped force. In May of 1954 a large French force was defeated at the jungle outpost of Dienbienphu, just as negotiations to end the war were underway in Geneva. This humiliation essentially marked the end of French involvement in Indochina, and the Geneva Conference confirmed it two months later. However, convinced that Ho was a communist, the United States began to consider a more active role in Southeast Asia.

DOCUMENT 5

FRENCH PARATROOPER ON THE SEIGE OF DIENBIENPHU

... It was all for nothing... In the prison camp the Viets told us they had won because they were fighting for an ideal and we were not... I told them about my paras at Dienbienphu. I told them how they fought. And they said, 'Heroism is no answer'...

Source: Bernard Fall, Hell in a Very Small Place: The Siege of Dienbienphu *(Philadelphia: J.B. Lippincott, 1967), p. 137.*

DOCUMENT 6

FINAL DECLARATION OF THE GENEVA CONFERENCE - JULY 21, 1954

1. The Conference takes note of the agreements ending hostilities in Cambodia, Laos, and Vietnam and organizing international control and the supervision of the execution of the provisions of these agreements.
2. ... expresses satisfaction at the ending of hostilities in Cambodia, Laos, and Vietnam; the Conference expresses its conviction that the execution of the provisions... will permit Cambodia, Laos, and Vietnam henceforth to play their part, in full independence and sovereignty, in the peaceful community of nations.
4. ... prohibiting the introduction into Vietnam of foreign troops and military personnel as well as of all kinds of arms and munitions...
5. ... no military base under the control of a foreign State may be established in the regrouping zones of the two parties... they will not join in any agreement with other States if this agreement includes the obligation to participate in a military alliance not in conformity with the principles of the Charter of the United Nations...
6. ... relating to Vietnam... the military demarcation line should not in any way be interpreted as constituting a political or territorial boundary...
7. ... so far as Viet-Nam is concerned, the settlement of political problems, effected on the basis of respect for the principles of independence, unity and territorial integrity, shall permit the Vietnamese people to enjoy the fundamental freedoms, guaranteed by democratic institutions established as a result of free general elections by secret ballot... held in July 1956, under the supervision of an international commission....
12. ... each member of the Geneva Conference undertakes to respect the sovereignty, the independence, the unity, and the territorial integrity of the above-mentioned states, and to refrain from any interference in their internal affairs.

Source: Peter V. Curl (ed.), Documents on American Foreign Relations, 1954 *(New York: Council on Foreign Relations, 1955), pp. 311-314.*

DOCUMENT 7 CLOSING STATEMENT BY WALTER BEDELL SMITH, US DELEGATE TO THE GENEVA CONFERENCE - JULY 21, 1954

... my Government is not prepared to join in a Declaration by the Conference such as is submitted. However, the United States makes this unilateral declaration of its position in these matters:... it will refrain from the threat or the use of force... the United States reiterates its traditional position that peoples are entitled to determine their own future and that it will not join in an agreement which would hinder this...

Source: Marvin E. Gettleman, Vietnam: History, Documents, and Opinions on a Major World Crisis *(New York: Fawcett Publications, 1965), pp. 162-168.*

DOCUMENT 8 NSC 5492/2, "REVIEW OF US POLICY IN THE FAR EAST" - AUGUST 20, 1954

Communist successes in Indochina, culminating in the agreement reached at the Geneva Conference... jeopardize the security interests of the U.S. in the Far East and increase Communist strength there... the Communists have secured possession of an advance salient in Vietnam from which military and non-military pressures can be mounted against adjacent and more remote non-Communist areas... The loss of prestige in Asia suffered by the U.S. as a backer of the French... will raise further doubts in Asia concerning U.S. leadership and the ability of the U.S. to check further expansion of Communism in Asia...By adopting an appearance of moderation at Geneva and taking credit for the cessation of hostilities in Indochina, the Communists will be in a better position to exploit their political strategy of imputing to the United States motives of extremism, belligerency, and opposition to coexistence seeking thereby to alienate the U.S. from its allies. The Communists thus have a basis for sharply accentuating their "peace propaganda" and "peace program" in Asia in an attempt to allay fears of Communist expansionist policy and to establish closer relations with the nations of free Asia...

Source: Gareth Porter, Vietnam: A History in Documents *(New York: New American Library Inc., 1979), pp. 164-165.*

Despite the agreements reached at the Geneva Conference, by the late 1950s foreign powers were very much involved in Indochina. The United States increasingly supported the regime of Ngo Dien Diem in South Vietnam, while the North under Ho was backed by the Soviets and Communist China. With the French gone, the question became whether or not the Americans would risk another potentially "hot war" against the spread of communism in Asia so soon after the Korean War. For their part, the North Vietnamese were initially cautious not to provoke the United States into an outright intervention.

DOCUMENT 9 VIETCONG LEADER ON HANOI RADIO - NOVEMBER 23, 1957

Revolution is an art. The question is not the acquiring of a good reputation for the revolutionist; the question is the success of the revolution... Revolutions must be rationally and fundamentally organized. Revolutions must be guided scientifically. We Easterners used to say; "We can kill a chicken with a knife used to cut areca nuts; but we cannot cut an areca nut with a knife used to kill chickens."... this saying means that the method of organizing and leading an uprising during a colonialist period must be suitable to the organization and resistance of the enemy who is not unfamiliar with the science of domination... this enemy has a powerful concentrated and rapid repressive machinery. Thus if an uprising is raised when the revolutionary force is not powerful enough... this uprising cannot succeed. It cannot escape certain failure, and an abortive uprising will exert a bad influence, especially on the revolutionary force itself.... If it is too windy, the captain must trim his sails so that the ship will not be upset... In other words, one must contain oneself before a temporarily powerful enemy. All these are aimed at husbanding our strength and developing it in view of the final battle, the life or death struggle.

Source: Gareth Porter, Vietnam: A History *(New York: New American Library Inc., 1979). pp. 191-192.*

DOCUMENT 10 LETTER FROM HO CHI MINH TO MIECZYSLAW MANELI, POLISH DELEGATE TO THE INTERNATIONAL CONTROL COMMISSION - FALL 1963

Neither you nor I... know the Americans well, but what we do know of them, what we have read and heard of them, suggests that they are more practical and clear-sighted than other capitalist nations. They will not put their resources into Vietnam endlessly. One day they will take pencil in hand and begin figuring. Once they really begin to analyze our ideas seriously, they will come to the conclusion that it is possible and even worthwhile to live in peace with us. Weariness, disappointment, the knowledge that they cannot achieve the goal which the French pursued to their own discredit will lead to a new sobriety, new feelings and emotions.

Source: Marilyn B. Young, The Vietnam Wars 1945-1990 *(New York: Harper Collins Publishers, 1991), p, 89.*

The Kennedy administration began as a major crisis unfolded in Laos, but even though that situation was temporarily settled by negotiations, conditions in Vietnam sharply deteriorated. The Diem regime was widely unpopular in the South as a result of its notorious corruption and brutal suppression of all opposition. The situation was so bad that by 1963 even the Americans wanted Diem gone. The important question was who would replace him? More importantly, to what extent would the United States go to prevent the further decay of the South?

DOCUMENT 11 LETTER FROM KENNEDY TO DIEM - DECEMBER 14, 1961

... Our indignation has mounted as the deliberate savagery of the Communist program of assassination, kidnapping, and wanton violence became clear... the campaign of force and terror... is supported and directed from the outside by the authorities in Hanoi. They have thus violated the provisions of the Geneva Accords designed to ensure peace in Vietnam... If the Communist authorities in North Vietnam will stop their campaign to destroy the Republic of Vietnam, the measures we are taking to assist your defense efforts will no longer be necessary...

Source: Arthur M. Schlesinger, Jr. (Gen. Ed.), The Dynamics of World Power: A Documentary History of United States Foreign Policy 1945-1973 *(Vol. IV) (New York: Chelsea House Publishers, 1973), pp. 482-483.*

DOCUMENT 12 MEMO BY ASSISTANT SECRETARY OF STATE FOR FAR EASTERN AFFAIRS ROGER HILSMAN - DECEMBER 3, 1962

... If Diem can demonstrate a continuing improvement in security conditions, he should be able to alleviate concern and boost morale within his bureaucracy and military establishment. However, if the fight against the Viet Cong goes badly... the chances of a coup against Diem could increase substantially. Moreover, the possibility of a coup attempt at any time cannot be excluded. Many officials and oppositionists feel that... the GVN is not winning the war principally because of Diem's virtual one-man rule... Diem's removal — whether by a military coup, assassination, or death from accidental or natural causes — would probably considerably strengthen the power of the military... US military and intelligence officials might well have advance notice of an impending coup and might be able to restrain the coup plotters from precipitous action. Even if unable to restrain such action, however, US officials might have greater success in averting widespread fighting and a serious power struggle which would lead to excessive bloodshed and weaken the front against the Viet Cong. The US could also be helpful in achieving agreement among the coup leaders as to who should lead the government in restoring the momentum of the government's counterinsurgency effort.

Source: Gareth Porter, Vietnam: A History in Documents *(New York: New American Library Inc., 1979), pp. 233-235.*

As decision-makers in Washington debated what course to take in Southeast Asia, dramatic and bizarre developments in Vietnam occurred which fundamentally changed American policy. Diem was removed in a coup in November 1963. Then in early August 1964, the Gulf of Tonkin incident prompted the US to bomb strategic military targets in North Vietnam. Moreover, President Johnson went to Congress for special authority in the "defense" of Southeast Asia. In many ways, the mysterious circumstances surrounding the incident became symbolic of the US experience in Vietnam.

DOCUMENTS 13

DEBATE IN THE US CONGRESS - AUGUST 6, 1964

(Senator Ernest Gruening)"... the United States has not pursued peace as it has pursued and carried out armed intervention on an ever-increasing scale. The latest episode — the attack by North Vietnam vessels on U.S. naval vessels, I consider an inevitable development of the U.S. steady escalation of our own military action...

(Senator Morse) ... if we are to talk about provocation... the United States was a provocateur by having any ships anywhere within striking distance or bombing distance... what do we think would have been the attitude of the United States if Castro had sent two Russian-supplied, armed PT boats off Key West to bombard Key West, and a Russian destroyer or Russian submarines had been 30, 40, 50 or even 75 or 100 miles from Key West at the time?... we cannot have it both ways — and we were in Tonkin Bay...

Source: Marvin E. Gettleman, Vietnam: History, Documents, and Opinions on a Major World Crisis. *(New York: Fawcett Publications, 1965). pp. 399-408.*

DOCUMENT 14

JOINT RESOLUTION OF CONGRESS: PUBLIC LAW 88-408; "THE GULF OF TONKIN RESOLUTION" - PASSED AUGUST 10, 1964

Whereas naval units of the Communist regime in Vietnam, in violation of the principles of the Charter of the United Nations and of international law, have deliberately and repeatedly attacked the United States naval vessels present in international waters, and have thereby created a serious threat to international peace; and Whereas these attacks are part of a deliberate and systematic campaign of aggression that the Communist regime in North Vietnam has been waging against it neighbours... and Whereas the United States is assisting the peoples of Southeast Asia to protect their freedom and has no territorial, military or political ambitions in that area, but desires only that these peoples should be left in peace...: Now, therefore, be it resolved by the Senate and House of Representatives of the United States of America in Congress assembled. That the Congress approves and supports the determination of the President... to take all necessary measures to repel any armed attack against the forces of the United States and to prevent further aggression... the United States is, therefore, prepared, as the President determines, to take all necessary steps, including the use of armed force, to assist any member or protocol state of the Southeast Asia Collective Defense Treaty requesting assistance in defense of its freedom... This resolution shall expire when the President shall determine that the peace and security of the area is reasonably assured... except that it may be terminated earlier by concurrent resolution of the Congress.

Source: Senator Mike Gravel (ed.), The Pentagon Papers *(Volume III) (Boston: Beacon Press, 1972), p. 722.*

Limited bombing of the North was a relatively easy operation. However, it was soon apparent that American air superiority was ineffective for the war in the South. In this regard the trouble for the Americans was in clearly identifying who the enemy was, and where they could be found. The jungle and general population helped to conceal the Vietcong, making an air war by itself useless. The question for the US then became was Vietnam worth a broader US commitment? If so, could the Americans succeed where the French had failed so dismally?

DOCUMENT 15 STATE DEPARTMENT "WHITE PAPER" - FEBRUARY 1965

South Vietnam is fighting for its life against a brutal campaign of terror and armed attack inspired, directed, supplied, and controlled by the Communist regime in Hanoi... Vietnam is *not* another Greece, where indigenous guerilla forces used friendly neighbouring territory as a sanctuary. Vietnam is *not* another Malaya, where Communist guerillas were, for the most part, physically distinguishable from the peaceful majority they sought to control. Vietnam is *not* another Philippines, where Communist guerillas were physically separated from the source of their moral and physical support. Above all, the war in Vietnam is *not* a spontaneous and local rebellion against the established government... In Vietnam a Communist government has set out deliberately to conquer a sovereign people in a neighbouring state... China and other Communist states have been the prime suppliers... This aggression violates the United Nations Charter. It is directly contrary to the Geneva Accords of 1954 and of 1962 to which North Vietnam is a party. It shatters the peace of Southeast Asia...

Source: Marvin E. Gettleman, Vietnam: History, Documents, and Opinions on a Major World Crisis *(New York: Fawcett Publication, 1965), pp. 300-331.*

DOCUMENT 16 JOHNSON AT JOHNS HOPKINS UNIVERSITY - APRIL 7, 1965

... Tonight Americans and Asians are dying for a world where each people may choose its own path to change... Why must we take this painful road?... We fight because we must fight if we are to live in a world where every country can shape its own destiny... Over this war, and all Asia, is another reality: the deepening shadow of Communist China. The rulers in Hanoi are urged on by Peking. This is a regime which has destroyed freedom in Tibet, attacked India, and been condemned by the United Nations for aggression in Korea. It is a nation which is helping the forces of violence in almost every continent. Around the globe, from Berlin to Thailand, are people whose well-being rests, in part, on the belief that they can count on us if they are attacked. To leave Vietnam to its fate would shake the confidence of all these people in the value of American commitment, the value of America's word... We will not be defeated. We will not grow tired. We will not withdraw, either openly or under the cloak of a meaningless agreement... Every night before I turn out the lights to sleep, I ask myself this question: Have I done everything that I can do to unite this country? Have I done everything I can to help unite the world, to try to bring peace and hope to all the peoples of the world? Have I done enough?... This generation of the world must choose; destroy or build, kill or aid, hate or understand... We will choose life. And in doing so we will prevail over the enemies within man, and over the natural enemies of all mankind.

Source: Marvin E. Gettleman, Vietnam: History, Documents, and Opinions on a Major World Crisis *(New York: Fawcett Publications, 1965), pp. 341-347.*

DOCUMENT 17 MEMOS FROM UNDER-SECRETARY OF STATE GEORGE BALL TO THE PRESIDENT - JUNE 8, 1965 (1) AND JULY 1, 1965 (2)

The position taken in this memorandum does not suggest that the United States should abdicate its leadership in the cold war. But any prudent military commander selects the terrain on which to stand and fight, and no great captain has ever been blamed for a tactical withdrawal. From our point of view, the terrain of South Vietnam could not be worse. Jungles and rice paddies are not designed for modern arms and, from a military point of view, this is clearly... a "rotten country". Politically, South Vietnam is a lost cause. The country is bled white from twenty years of war and the people are sick of it... Hanoi has a government and a purpose and a discipline. The "government" in Saigon is a travesty. In a very real sense, South Vietnam is a country with an army and no government. In my view, a deep commitment of United States forces in a land war in South Vietnam would be a catastrophic error. If there was ever an occasion for a tactical withdrawal, this is it...(1)... No one has demonstrated that a white ground force of whatever size can win a guerilla war —which is at the same time a civil war between Asians — in jungle terrain in the midst of a population that refuses cooperation... The alternative — no matter what we may wish it to be — is almost certainly a protracted war involving an open-ended commitment of U.S. forces, mounting U.S. casualties, no assurance of a satisfactory solution, and a serious danger of escalation at the end of the road... The decision you face now, therefore, is crucial... Our involvement will be so great that we cannot — without national humiliation — stop short of achieving our complete objectives. (2)

Source: 1. Larry Berman, Planning a Tragedy: The Americanization of the War in Vietnam *(New York: W.W. Norton and Company, 1982), pp. 86-87.*
2. Senator Mike Gravel (ed.), The Pentagon Papers *(Volume IV) (Boston: Beacon Press, 1972), pp. 615-619.*

DOCUMENT 18 NORTH VIETNAM'S PARTY CHIEF LE DUAN - JULY 6-8, 1965

We are not only determined to defeat the U.S. but must know how to defeat the U.S. in the manner most appropriate to the relation of forces between the enemy and us during each historical phase... if it switches to limited war, the U.S. still will have weaknesses which it cannot overcome. The U.S. rear area is very far away, and American soldiers are "soldiers in chains", who cannot fight like the French, cannot stand the weather conditions, and don't know the battlefield but on the contrary have many weaknesses in their opposition to people's war. If the

U.S. puts 300,000 - 400,000 troops into the South, it will have stripped away the face of its neocolonial policy and revealed the face of an old-style colonial invader... Thus, the U.S. will not be able to maintain its power with regard to influential sectors of the United States... Fighting for a prolonged period is a weakness of U.S. imperialism. The Southern revolution can fight a protracted war, while the U.S. can't, because American military, economic, and political resources must be distributed throughout the world. If it is bogged down in one place and can't withdraw, the whole effort will be violently shaken. The U.S. would lose its preeminence in influential sectors at home... Therefore although the U.S. can send 300,000 to 400,000 troops at once, why must it do it step by step? Because even if it does send many troops like that, the U.S. would still be hesitant; because that would be a passive policy full of many contradictions; because fear of protracted war, and the even stronger opposition of the American people and the world's people, and even of their allies who would also not support widening the war...

Source: Gareth Porter, Vietnam: A History in Documents *(New York: New American Library Inc., 1979), pp. 315-317.*

Johnson sent ground troops to South Vietnam in the spring of 1965, but like the French, US military planners found fighting a guerilla army very difficult. It became evident early on that the US would require a larger commitment. Consequently, Johnson was faced with the dilemma of a humiliating withdrawal or a dangerous escalation throughout his Presidency. Right from the start many people questioned the necessity and morality of the war. Anti-war protest began on college campuses, but it quickly spread throughout American society. The war was inextricably linked with dissent it caused in the US, especially when anti-war protest converged with the civil rights movements. The late 1960s proved to be painful and turbulent years for the US, as Americans wrestled with the irony of fighting and dying for "liberty and freedom" in Vietnam while many didn't have them at home.

DOCUMENT 19

NATIONAL SECURITY ADVISER MCGEORGE BUNDY ON CANCELLING HIS APPEARANCE AT "TEACH-IN" ON US POLICY- MAY 15 1965

It has been argued that debate of this kind should be avoided because it can give encouragement to the adversaries of our country. There is some ground for this argument, since it is true that Communists have little understanding of the meaning of debate in a free society. The Chinese will continue to pretend that American policy is weaker because 700 faculty members have made a protest against our policy in Vietnam. The American people know better. They know that those who are protesting are all a minority of American teachers and students... We cannot let the propaganda of... totalitarians divert us from our necessary arguments with one another any more than we can let them be misled by such debates if we can help it.

Source: Marvin E. Gettleman, Vietnam: History, Documents, and Opinoins on a Major World Crisis *(New York: Fawcett Publications, 1965), pp. 408-426.*

DOCUMENT 20 SPEECHES BY MARTIN LUTHER KING, JR., NEW YORK - MARCH 30, 1967 AND APRIL 4, 1967

... it became clear to me that the war was doing far more than devastating the hopes of the poor at home. It was sending their sons and their brothers and their husbands to fight and die in extraordinary high proportions relative to the rest of the population. We were taking the young black men who had been crippled by our society and sending them 8000 miles away to guarantee liberties in Southeast Asia which they had not found in Southwest Georgia and East Harlem. So we have been repeatedly faced with the cruel irony of watching Negro and white boys on TV screens as they kill and die together for a nation that has been unable to seat them together in the same schools. So we watch them in brutal solidarity burning the huts of a poor village...

What do peasants think as we ally ourselves with the landlords and as we refuse to put any action into our many words concerning land reform? What do they think as we test our latest weapons on them, just as the Germans tested out new medicine and new tortures in the concentration camps of Europe? Where are the roots of the independent Vietnam we claim to be building?... We must find new ways to speak for peace in Vietnam and justice throughout the developing world... If we do not act we shall surely be dragged down the long dark and shameful corridors of time reserved for those who possess power without compassion, might without morality, and strength without sight.

Source: Marilyn B. Young, The Vietnam Wars 1945–1990 *(New York: Harper Collins Publishers Inc), pp. 192, 199.*

The war was not only contentious at home, it also caused some serious moral dilemmas for those who fought it. Despite their technical superiority, the war did not go well for Americans, and the protest at home only added to the problems the average serviceman faced. American military strategy in Vietnam was and remains the topic of considerable debate, but by 1968 it was clear that the war was not as "winnable" as the Johnson administration claimed. Many asked what it would take to win, while others wondered what they were fighting for anyway.

DOCUMENT 21 CIA MEMO - MAY 12, 1967

impossible to win

Through the end of April 1967 the US air campaign against North Vietnam — Rolling Thunder — had significantly eroded the capacities of North Vietnam's limited industrial and military base. These losses, however, have not meaningfully degraded North Vietnam's material ability to continue the war in South Vietnam... North Vietnam's ability to recuperate from the air attacks has been of a high order... an effective system of dispersed storage and distribution... supplies and troops dispersed throughout the country... large infusions of military and economic aid from the USSR and Communist China... Damage frequently repaired within a matter of days, if not hours...

Source: Gareth Porter, Vietnam: A History in Documents *(New York: New American Library Inc., 1979), pp. 344-345.*

DOCUMENT 22 — LETTER HOME FROM A US SOLDIER - MARCH 27, 1967

Today a buddy of mine called.. into a hut and an old man came out of the bomb shelter. My buddy told the old man to get away from the hut and since we have to move quickly on a sweep, just threw a hand grenade into the shelter. As he pulled the pin the old man got excited and started jabbering and running toward my buddy and the hut. A GI, not understanding, stopped the old man with a football tackle just as my buddy threw the hand grenade into the shelter... [then] we heard a baby crying from inside the shelter! There was nothing we could do. After the explosion we found the mother, two children... and an almost newborn baby. That is what the old man was trying to tell us!... We looked at each other and burned the hut... The old man was just whimpering in disbelief outside the burning hut. We walked away and left him there.

Source: Marilyn B. Young, The Vietnam Wars 1945-1990 *(New York: Harper Collins Publishers, 1991), p. 195.*

DOCUMENT 23 — US AIR FORCE PILOT ON THE USE OF CHEMICAL AGENTS

We sure are pleased with those backroom boys at Dow. The original product wasn't so hot — if the gooks were quick they could scrape it off. So the boys started adding polystyrene — now it sticks like shit to a blanket. But then if the gooks jumped under water it stopped burning, so they started adding Willie Peter {or "WP" — white phosphorus} so's to make it burn better. It'll even burn under water now. And one drop is enough, it'll keep burning right down to the bone so they die anyway from phosphorus poisoning.

Source: Marilyn B. Young, The Vietnam Wars 1945-1990 *(New York: Harper Collins Publishers, 1991), p. 130.*

DOCUMENT 24 — TELEVISION ADDRESS BY JOHNSON - MARCH 31, 1968

Tonight I renew the offer I made last August — to stop the bombardment of North Vietnam. We ask that talks begin promptly, they be serious talks on the substance of peace. We assume that during those talks Hanoi will not take advantage of our restraint. We are prepared to move immediately toward peace through negotiations. So tonight, in the hope that this action will lead to early talks, I am taking the first step to deescalate the conflict. We are reducing — substantially reducing — the present level of hostilities. And we are doing so unilaterally and at once... But if peace does not come now through negotiations, it will come when Hanoi understands that our common resolve is unshakable and our common strength is invincible... Finally, my fellow Americans, let me say this: Of those to whom much is given, much is asked. I cannot say, and no man could say, that no more will be asked of us. Yet, I believe that now, no less than when the decade began, this generation of Americans is willing to "pay any price, bear any burden, meet any hardship, support any friend, oppose any foe to assure the survival and the success of liberty."... we must always be mindful of this one thing, whatever the trials and tests ahead; The ultimate strength of our country and our cause will lie not in the powerful weapons or infinite resources or boundless wealth but will lie in the unity of our people. This I believe very deeply... And in these times as in times before, it is true that a house divided against itself by the spirit of faction, of party, of region, of religion, of race, is a house that cannot stand. There is a division in the American house now. There is divisiveness among us all tonight. And holding the trust that is mine, as President of all the people, I cannot disregard the peril to the progress of the American people... With America's sons in the fields far away, with America's future under challenge right here at home, with our hopes and the world's hopes for peace in the balance every day, I do not believe that I should devote an hour or a day of my time to any personal partisan causes or to any duties other than the awesome duties of this Office — the Presidency of your country. Accordingly, I shall not seek, and I will not accept, the nomination of my party for another term as your President. But let men everywhere know, however, that a strong, a confident, and a vigilant America stands ready tonight to seek an honourable peace — and stand ready tonight to defend an honoured cause — whatever the price, whatever the burden, whatever the sacrifices that duty may require. Thank you for listening. Good night and God bless all of you.

Source: Arthur M. Schlesinger, Jr. (Gen. ed.) The Dynamics of World Power: A Documentary History of United States Foreign Policy 1945-1973 *(Volume IV) (New York: Chelsa House Publishers, 1973), pp. 538-540.*

During the 1968 Presidential campaign, Richard Nixon ran on the platform of ending America's role in the Vietnam War, coining the phrase "peace with honour". However, shortly after he won the election, it was evident that Nixon was not willing to withdraw so quickly. In fact, in many ways the Nixon administration expanded the war.

DOCUMENT 25

TV ADDRESS BY RICHARD NIXON - NOVEMBER 3, 1969

For the South Vietnamese our precipitate withdrawal would inevitably allow the Communists to repeat the massacres which followed their takeover in the North 15 years before. They then murdered more than 50,000 people and hundreds of thousands more died in slave labour camps... For the United States, this first defeat in our Nation's history would result in a collapse of confidence in American leadership, not only in Asia but throughout the world... My fellow Americans, I am sure you can recognize from what I have said that we really only have two choices open to us if we want to end this war. I can order an immediate, precipitate withdrawal of all Americans from Vietnam without regard to the effects of that action. Or, we can persist in our search for a just peace through negotiated settlement if possible, or through continued implementation of our plan for Vietnamization if necessary... I have chosen the second course. It is not the easy way. It is the right way...In speaking of the consequences of a precipitate withdrawal, I mentioned that our allies would lose confidence in America. Far more dangerous, we would lose confidence in ourselves. Oh, the immediate reaction would be a sense of relief that our men were coming home, but as we saw the consequences of what we had done, inevitable remorse and divisive recrimination would scar our spirit as a people... And now I would like to address a word if I may to the young people of this Nation who are particularly concerned, and I understand why they are concerned, about this war. I respect your idealism. I share your concern for peace. I want peace as much as you do... I know it may not be fashionable to speak of patriotism or national destiny these days. But I feel it is appropriate to do so on this occasion... And so tonight — to you, the great silent majority of my fellow Americans — I ask for your support... Let us be united for peace. Let us also be united against defeat. Because let us understand: North Vietnam cannot defeat or humiliate the United States. Only Americans can do that.

Source: Arthur M. Schlesinger, Jr. (Gen. ed.) The Dynamics of World Power: A Documentary History of United States Foreign Policy 1945-1973 *(Volume IV) (New York: Chelsa House Publishers, 1973), pp. 557-565.*

DOCUMENT 26 NIXON TO WHITE HOUSE AIDE BOB HALDEMAN - MARCH 1969

I call it the madman theory, Bob... I want the North Vietnamese to believe I've reached the point where I might do anything to stop the war. We'll just slip the word out to them that, "for God's sake, you know Nixon is obsessed about Communists. We can't restrain him when he's angry — and he has his hand on the nuclear button," — and Ho Chi Minh himself will be in Paris in two days begging for peace.

Source: H.R. Haldeman, The Ends of Power *(New York: NY Times Books, 1978), p. 83.*

DOCUMENT 27 SENATE FOREIGN RELATIONS COMMITTEE STAFF STUDY, "BOMBING AS A POLICY TOOL IN VIETNAM" - OCTOBER 12, 1972

There is no indication... that any of the major intelligence agencies believed that the bombing of the North could or would reduce the level of support for the war in the South... Rather, the agencies placed their hopes in punishing North Vietnam and in possibly breaking her will.

Source: Marilyn B. Young, The Vietnam Wars 1945-1990 *(New York: Harper Collins Publishers, 1991), p. 124.*

After the Paris Peace Accords of 1973, the United States gradually began its final withdraw from Indochina. In April 1975, North Vietnamese and Vietcong forces finally took the South. Although American troops came home, for many the war was not truly over. There were not only immediate costs in terms of human life, physical and financial devastation, but also considerable long-term and psychological trauma on both sides. For Vietnam, winning the war against the Americans proved easier than building a peace. In fact, throughout the 1970s and 1980s a unified, communist Vietnam fought continuing wars in Indochina. For those who defended American intervention in Southeast

Asia, the establishment of brutal regimes in Vietnam, Laos and Cambodia was proof that they were right. Regardless, as these countries try to recover from nearly fifty years of violence and destruction, the legacy of conflict in Indochina continues to affect international relations.

DOCUMENT 28 INTERVIEW BY JOURNALIST STANLEY KARNOW WITH VIETCONG VETERAN TRAN THI TRUYEN - HANOI 1981

The rainy season had just started, and the route was muddy. Occasional flash floods forced us to cling to trees and shrubs and keep from being washed away. The jungles were infested with leeches and other insects that swarmed all over us... The Americans had denuded the jungles with their bombs, and there was no place to hide. They would light up the area with flares, then drop bombs everywhere... Even after the bombing had stopped, I couldn't focus my eyes, and my head ached for hours... I was inexperienced, and my first sight and smell of blood and pus so nauseated me that I vomited and couldn't work. Some of the wounded had lost arms or legs. Or their bellies had been ripped open by bomb fragments, and their intestines were spilling out. Others were horribly burnt by napalm. Many, who had been lying injured in the jungle for days, were brought in with maggots crawling out of their infected wounds...

Source: Stanley Karnow, Vietnam: A History *(New York: Penguin Books, 1983), pp. 455-456.*

DOCUMENT 29 RECOLLECTION OF MAJOR GENERAL GEORGE S. PATTON III

The trouble is the goal was never clear. It changed under the Johnson administration from time to time. Our overall goal was pacification, but it didn't work because of lack of strategic direction from the United States... The national leadership, the President, did not bring the country into the total scene of the war. There was a lack of unification of the American people... the fundamental principles of war... were violated... The United States can never afford again to allow itself to be at such a vast strategic disadvantage as we were in Vietnam... We were defeated by an eighth-rate power...

Source: Kim Willenson, The Bad War: An Oral History of the Vietnam War *(New York: New American Library, 1987), pp. 78-79.*

DOCUMENT 30 RECOLLECTION OF CASPAR WEINBERGER, NIXON'S SECRETARY OF HEALTH (LATER RONALD REAGAN'S SECRETARY OF DEFENSE)

I suppose the most vivid memory I have of Vietnam was the reception of the troops coming back to San Francisco and the really terrible way they were received, with pickets and boos and all of that, because of the unpopularity of the war. The thing that struck me was the basic unfairness of taking that out on people who had participated in it, suffered very greatly, and had done a very good job and had not been supported sufficiently to win. This carried over even to the reception of the very young infants and children who were brought from the nurseries and the hospitals in the days just before the end of the Vietnam War for safer-keeping, so to speak, in the United States. And the demonstrations against these infants were because they were Vietnamese and they were a visible reminder of the war... And there was a bunch of pickets outside, booing and jeering as these little children were carried in. It was a pretty vivid recollection... It was a terrible period in our history when we had that kind of demonstration against people who had nothing whatever to do with the war except to suffer. And it was an indication of what length people would go to demonstrate their anger against that kind of war. Utterly illogical, terribly unfair, and yet there it was.

Source: Kim Willenson, The Bad War: An Oral History of the Vietnam War *(New York: New American Library, 1987), pp. 263-264.*

DOCUMENT 31 POETRY FROM THE WAR

"Song of Napalm"
by Bruce Weigl, former US Marine

But the branches are wire
And thunder is the pounding mortar,
Still I close my eyes and see the girl
Running from her village, napalm
Stuck to her dress like jelly,
Her hands reaching for the no one
Who waits in waves of heat before her

So I can keep on living,
So I can stay here beside you,
I try to imagine she runs down the road and
wings
Beat inside her until she rises
Above the stinking jungle and her pain
Eases, and your pain, and mine.

The lie works only as long as it takes to speak
And the girl runs only as far
As the napalm allows
Until her burning tendons and crackling
Muscles draw her up
Into that final position
Burning bodies so perfectly assume. Nothing
Can change that; she is burned behind my
eyes
And not your good love and not the rain-
swept air
And not the jungle green
pasture unfolding before us can deny it.

Source: Harrison E. Salisbury (ed.), Vietnam Reconsidered: Lessons from a War *(New York: Harper and Row Publishers, 1984), pp. 224-226.*

"Americans Are Not Beautiful"
by Hoang San,
a 14 year old Vietnamese girl,
Saigon - 1974

They are called *My*
Which my brother says means beautiful.
But they are not beautiful:
They have too much hair on their arms
like monkeys,
They are tall like trees without branches,
Their eyes are green like eyes of boiled pigs
In the markets during the New Year.
Their hair is blond and not black.
Their skin is pink and not brown,
Their cars frighten cyclists in the streets,
Their flying machines and their dragonflies
Drop death on people and animals
And make trees bare of their leaves.
Here, Americans are not beautiful.
"But they are, In their faraway country"
My brother says.

Source: Gloria Emerson, Winners and Losers *(New York: Random House, 1985), pp. 242-243.*

STUDY QUESTIONS FOR SECTION SEVEN: INDOCHINA

1. Explain the background to the conflict between the French and the Vietnamese after World War II.

2. Were the Vietminh nationalists or communists? Did this distinction matter from an American perspective?

3. How and why did the Americans get involved in Indochina?

4. Were the Americans defeated in Vietnam and, if so, why?

5. What was the impact of Vietnam on American foreign policy?

SECTION EIGHT

DÉTENTE

DOCUMENTS

CHRONOLOGY

1960	Sino-Soviet split becomes open
1961	Berlin Crisis
1962	Cuban Missile Crisis
1963	Nuclear Test Ban Treaty
1964	escalation of US involvement in Vietnam Khrushchev deposed; succeeded by Brezhnev 1st Chinese atomic bomb
1967	6 Days War between Israel and its Arab neighbours
1968	Tet offensive Nuclear Non-Proliferation Treaty Soviet invasion of Czechoslovakia Nixon elected president
1969	Willy Brandt becomes chancellor of West Germany Strategic Arms Limitation Talks start (SALT 1)
1970	treaties signed by West Germany with the Soviet Union and Poland
1972	Nixon visits People's Republic of China SALT 1 signed
1973	end of Vietnam war treaty between West and East Germany Watergate scandal October War (Yom Kippur War) between Israel and its Arab neighbours oil price rise
1974	Nixon resigns; succeeded by Gerald Ford
1975	Helsinki Accords of the Conference on Security and Co-operation in Europe
1979	SALT 2 treaty signed Soviet invasion of Afghanistan

DOCUMENT 1 HENRY KISSINGER'S VIEWS ON SUPER-POWER RELATIONS

Henry Kissinger, first as Nixon's National Security Adviser (1969-1973), and then as Secretary of State (1973-77), was a strong anti-Communist. He also felt that the United States had to improve its relationship both with the People's Republic of China and the Soviet Union. In July 1969 he had a long conversation with Anatoly Dobrynin, Soviet ambassador in Washington. The following comes from Dobrynin's report to his own government:

Kissinger said that he can with full responsibility declare, that in foreign policy—besides the settlement of the Vietnam question (on which he intended to dwell a little later)—President Nixon feels that the other basic area which demands his attention is Soviet-American relations. He poses his main goal in this area as the necessity of avoiding situations which could lead to direct confrontation between the USA and the USSR.

....

Nevertheless, went on Kissinger, this is only one side of the question. Nixon would like very much that during his Presidency—until 1972, or maybe even until 1976 in case he's re-elected—Soviet-American relations would enter a constructive phase, different from those relations which existed during the 'cold war' and unfortunately continue to make themselves apparent even now. Although ideological disagreements, undoubtedly, will remain, and since they are very deep will make themselves known, the President nonetheless thinks that the above-mentioned turn in relations between our countries is entirely possible and desirable...

....

Moving on further to concrete problems and regions, Kissinger said that in Europe Nixon agreed that it is not appropriate to undertake any sort of attempts to change the situation which developed there as a result of the Second World War. The USA, as is well known, in principle favors the unification of Germany, but this is still a question, taking everything into account, realistically speaking, of the very very distant future. The current administration does not intend to push or force events in this direction.

...

In the course of the conversation on European affairs Kissinger repeated that President Nixon takes into account the special interests of the Soviet Union in Eastern Europe, and does not intend to do anything there which could be evaluated in Moscow as a 'challenge' to her position in that region. This is Nixon's basic approach to this question, and it is not necessary, asserted Kissinger, to pay much attention to isolated critical public comments about some East European country, because that is only a tribute to the mood of certain sub-strata of the American population which play a role in American elections.

....

Overall from the conversation a certain impression was formed that for Nixon foreign policy problem No.1 remains the question of how to find an exit from the Vietnam War under acceptable conditions, which would guarantee him re-election as President of the USA.

....

Several words about Kissinger himself. Observing the activities of Nixon and his main foreign policy advisors (and I am now acquainted with practically all of them), it is possible to state with sufficient confidence that at the present time Kissinger has basic, in fact dominant influence on the President in the area of foreign policy.

....

Kissinger himself, though he is a smart and erudite person, is at the same time extremely vain and in conversations with me, especially during a private lunch (we have established a pretty good personal relationship), not averse to boasting about his influence. During our last conversation he, for example, without any excessive humility, announced that in all of Washington 'only two people can answer precisely at any given moment about the position of the USA on this or that question: these are President Nixon and he, Kissinger'.

Source: Woodrow Wilson International Center for Scholars, Cold War International History Project Bulletin *(Washington, D.C.), Issue 3, pp. 64-67.*

DOCUMENT 2

THE BREZHNEV DOCTRINE

The Soviet Union made it quite clear that it intended to maintain its hold over Eastern Europe. In 1968, a reforming Communist government under Alexander Dubcek came to power in Czechoslovakia and tried to implement "socialism with a human face". The Soviet Union watched the political and economic liberalization in its satellite with growing concern; in August 1968, Soviet troops invaded and installed a more conservative and hard-line regime. Brezhnev provided a justification for this step in a speech to the Polish communists in November 1968.

The socialist states stand for strict respect for the sovereignty of all countries. We emphatically oppose interference in the affairs of any states and violations of their sovereignty.

At the same time the establishment and defence of the sovereignty of states which have set out on the road of building socialism is of particular importance for us communists. The forces of imperialism and reaction are seeking to deprive the people now of this, now of that socialist country of the sovereign right they have won to ensure the prosperity of their country and the wellbeing and the happiness of the broad masses of the working people by building a society free from all oppression or exploitation. And when attacks on this right meet with the united rebuff from the socialist camp, bourgeois propagandists raise a clamour around 'defence of sovereignty' and 'non-interference'. It is clear that this is a complete fraud and utter demogogy on their part. In reality those who shout in that way are not concerned with preserving socialist sovereignty but with destroying it.

It is common knowledge that the Soviet Union has done much for the real strengthening of the sovereignty and independence of the socialist countries. The Communist Party of the Soviet Union has always advocated that each socialist country should determine the specific forms of its development along the road of socialism, taking into consideration its own specific national conditions. However, as we know, comrades, there are also common laws governing socialist construction, departure from which might lead to a departure from socialism as such.

And when internal and external forces that are hostile to socialism seek to reverse the development of any socialist country in the direction of restoring the capitalist system, when a threat to the cause of socialism in that country appears, and a threat to the security of the socialist community as a whole, that is no longer only a problem for the people of that country but also a common problem, a matter of concern for all socialist countries.

It goes without saying that such an action as military aid to a fraternal country to put an end to a threat to the socialist system is an extraordinary, an enforced step, which can be sparked off only by direct actions on the part of enemies of socialism inside the country and beyond its frontiers—actions creating a threat to the common interests of the socialist camp.

Source: Soviet News, *19 November 1968 [cited in James Mayall and Cornelia Navari, eds.,* The End of the Post-War Era *(London: Cambridge University Press, 1980) pp. 523-4].*

DOCUMENT 3 WILLY BRANDT AND OSTPOLITIK

Willy Brandt, mayor of West Berlin in the 1950s and later foreign minister and West German chancellor (1969-74), was a strong advocate of Ostpolitik or a better relationship with the East. For Brandt, that involved recognizing the post war reality through, for example, treaties with countries such as Poland and the Soviet Union. He is writing here in 1971.

Our policy on Europe must not stand against something; it must stand for something. And it must link itself vigorously to the requirements of the scientific and technical revolutions.

The beginnings of the policy of European unification after 1945 were in point of time and in their political logic partially—yet surely not only—parallel to the growing threat from the East. The initial unification in the West was conceived by many as a consequence of the Cold War. Some people thought that integration was the political rounding off of what had been the military assignment of NATO, with the sole aim of building a dam against communism. In this way, the policy on Europe carried a defensive restrictive or almost negative feeling.

The Cold War of the postwar years lies behind us, but difficult confrontations continue that cannot be overcome by illusions or by becoming prisoners of outmoded formulations of questions. I consider the policy on Europe to be stronger if it is not defined as mere anti-communism. Rather, Europe should be unified for the good of the European people and for their constructive role in the world, and the policy of European statesmen must be harmonized with the long range goal of a European peace order.

Not only the West, but also the East is becoming aware of the importance of pan-European cooperation. Slowly, and hopefully not too late, it will become clear that the cooperation and unification of Europe is not directed against anyone. Rather, in a dangerous epoch and strife-divided world, it could be an example of how nations and states, regardless of different kinds of governmental and social systems, can achieve prosperity and security by peacefully working together.

Reconciliation and cooperation, which we are striving for between West and East, have already become a fact in Western Europe and will succeed in spite of the above described difficulties. The economic and political unification of Europe is a substantive element of a worldwide peace.

....

The Federal Republic, I said as early as December 1966, before the council of NATO in Paris, will not evade discussions based on mutual confidence, aimed at a reform of NATO during the coming years. It wishes to contribute toward a policy of détente between the states of the Warsaw pact and those of the North Atlantic pact, while opposing any danger to the security of any country. The Federal Republic of Germany is no obstacle to the peaceful, secure future that is to the interest of us all. Nor shall we, in this respect, allow ourselves to be led astray by the aggressive speeches made against us by Communist leaders in their own countries, in neutral states, and in the countries of our allies.

NATO and a policy of détente are not mutually exclusive alternatives. On the contrary, the existence of NATO—that is, its political weight and its readiness to defend our territory against all attacks—has shown that a policy of tensions and crises is of no avail. The weakening of NATO would reduce the possibility of a détente and lessen its effectiveness. The military deterrent has ensured peace in Europe. It would be frivolous to encroach upon it and to risk losing what has been achieved.

Our policy of détente is not to be understood in the sense of underestimating and neglecting the vital importance of the Western alliance. On the contrary, we have warned against allowing the bilateral attitude in East-West relations to grow out of hand. In place of that, we have worked toward having the alliance as a whole take a stand with respect to new tasks.

Germany and the Soviet Union—Beginning of a Dialogue

In addition to economic and cultural relations between Germany and the Soviet Union, we hope for an improvement of the political relationship between us. Because it would not be realistic to expect an abrupt and fundamental change, we are exerting ourselves to attain an understanding step by step.

Obviously the special importance of the Soviet Union is rooted in its position as a world power, and for us, to be sure, also in its position as one of the four powers that still bear responsibility for the problem of Germany. It was no accident that in December 1966, the Soviet Union was mentioned first in the foreign affairs section of the government statement. It is no contradiction to acknowledge the Soviet Union as the leading Communist and East European power, and at the same time to take cognizance of the differentiations within the Communist world. But we are going out of our way to be fair to the role of the Soviet Union, and not to give it the impression that we are speculating on differences of opinion within the Communist camp....

In this age of transition—and against the background of the partition of Germany—it is a difficult enterprise to bring about good relations with the Soviet Union. A great deal of patience is required. We do not wish either our patience or our good will to fail. We owe that to Europe and to our own country. Our democratic Europe must and will oppose the Soviet Union if and for as long as it tries, by pressure or by other methods, to make its own ideas of state and social order an article of export and thus involve itself in other people's internal affairs. But our democratic Germany can be, and the German people would like to be a sincere friend of the Soviet Union. To this it might be added that greatness is also capable of showing greatheartedness. It is not that we are begging for this, but a Soviet Union that would respect the vital rights of the German people would not have to be afraid—and not only because it is powerful—of the German people. And we, those Germans of good will—that is, the great majority—want to see to it with equal concern that no danger of war can ever again arise on German territory.

Source: Klaus Harpprecht, Willy Brandt, Portrait and Self-Portrait *(Los Angeles: Nash Publishing, 1971), pp. 253-4, 262-3, 265.*

DOCUMENT 4 — THE TREATY BETWEEN THE TWO GERMANIES

By the end of the 1960s, relations between the two Germanies were beginning to ease. Travel for humanitarian reasons was allowed; in 1968 over two million Germans were able to visit relatives on the other side of the Wall. On November 8, 1972, the Federal Republic of Germany (West Germany) and the German Democratic Republic (East Germany) agreed to recognize each other.

24. Treaty on the Basis of Relations between the Federal Republic of Germany and the German Democratic Republic, Bonn, 8 November 1972, with Protocol, statements and letters

The High Contracting Parties,

Conscious of their responsibility for the preservation of peace,

Anxious to render a contribution to détente and security in Europe.

Aware that the inviolability of frontiers and respect for the territorial integrity and sovereignty of all States in Europe within their present frontiers are a basic condition for peace,

Recognizing that therefore the two German States have to refrain from the threat or use of force in their relations,

Proceeding from the historical facts and without prejudice to the different views of the Federal Republic of Germany and the German Democratic Republic on fundamental questions, including the national question,

Desirous to create the conditions for cooperation between the Federal Republic of Germany and the German Democratic Republic for the benefit of the people in the two German States,

Have agreed as follows:

Article 1

The Federal Republic of Germany and the German Democratic Republic shall develop normal, good-neighbourly relations with each other on the basis of equal rights.

Article 2

The Federal Republic of Germany and the German Democratic Republic will be guided by the aims and principles laid down in the United Nations Charter, especially those of the sovereign equality of all States, respect for their independence, autonomy and territorial integrity, the right of self-determination, the protection of human rights, and non-discrimination.

Article 3

In conformity with the United Nations Charter the Federal Republic of Germany and the German Democratic Republic shall settle any disputes between them exclusively by peaceful means and refrain from the threat or use of force.

They reaffirm the inviolability now and in the future of the frontier existing between them and undertake fully to respect each other's territorial integrity.

Article 4

The Federal Republic of Germany and the German Democratic Republic proceed on the assumption that neither of the two States can represent the other in the international sphere or act on its behalf.

Article 5

The Federal Republic of Germany and the German Democratic Republic shall promote peaceful relations between the European States and contribute to security and cooperation in Europe.

They shall support efforts to reduce forces and arms in Europe without allowing disadvantages to arise for the security of those concerned.

The Federal Republic of Germany and the German Democratic Republic shall support, with the aim of general and complete disarmament under effective international control, efforts serving international security to achieve armaments limitation and disarmament, especially with regard to nuclear weapons and other weapons of mass destruction.

Article 6

The Federal Republic of Germany and the German Democratic Republic proceed on the principle that the sovereign jurisdiction of each of the two States is confined to its own territory. They respect each other's independence and autonomy in their internal and external affairs.

Article 7

The Federal Republic of Germany and the German Democratic Republic declare their readiness to regulate practical and humanitarian questions in the process of the normalization of their relations. They shall conclude agreements with a view to developing and promoting on the basis of the present Treaty and for their mutual benefit cooperation in the fields of economics, science and technology, transport, judicial relations, posts and telecommunications, health, culture, sport, environmental protection, and in other fields. The details have been agreed in the Supplementary Protocol.

Article 8

The Federal Republic of Germany and the German Democratic Republic shall exchange Permanent Missions. They shall be established at the respective Government's seat.

Practical questions relating to the establishment of the Missions shall be dealt with separately.

Article 9

The Federal Republic of Germany and the German Democratic Republic agree that the present Treaty shall not affect the bilateral and multilateral international treaties and Agreements already concluded by them or relating to them.

Source: Department of State, Bulletin, *14 November 1972 [cited in James Mayall and Cornelia Navari, eds.,* The End of the Post-War Era *(London: Cambridge University Press, 1980), pp. 68-70].*

DOCUMENT 5 THE HELSINKI AGREEMENTS

One of the high points of détente was the Helsinki meeting of the Conference on Security and Co-operation in Europe in 1975. It brought together all European states (except Albania) and Canada and the United States. Overhead, as a symbol of superpower co-operation, the American Apollo and Soviet Soyuz spacecraft met. President Gerald Ford spoke to the meeting:

The American people, like the people of Europe, know well that mere assertions of good will, passing changes in the political mood of governments, laudable declarations of principles are not enough. But if we proceed with care, with commitment to real progress, there is now an opportunity to turn our people's hopes into realities.

In recent years, nations represented here have sought to ease potential conflicts. But much more remains to be done before we prematurely congratulate ourselves.

Military competition must be controlled. Political competition must be restrained. Crises must not be manipulated or exploited for unilateral advantages that could lead us again to the brink of war. The process of negotiation must be sustained, not at a snail's pace, but with demonstrated enthusiasm and visible progress.

Nowhere are the challenges and the opportunities greater and more evident than in Europe. That is why this Conference brings us all together. Conflict in Europe shakes the world. Twice in this century we have paid dearly for this lesson; at other times, we have come perilously close to calamity. We dare not forget the tragedy and the terror of those times.

Peace is not a piece of paper.

But lasting peace is at least possible today because we have learned from the experiences of the last 30 years that peace is a process requiring mutual restraint and practical arrangements.

This Conference is a part of that process—a challenge, not a conclusion. We face unresolved problems of military security in Europe; we face them with very real differences in values and in aims. But if we deal with them with careful preparation, if we focus on concrete issues, if we maintain forward movement, we have the right to expect real progress.

The era of confrontation that has divided Europe since the end of the Second World War may now be ending. There is a new perception and a shared perception of a change for the better, away from confrontation and toward new possibilities for secure and mutually beneficial cooperation. That is what we all have been saying here. I welcome and I share these hopes for the future.

Source: Presidential Documents, 11, pp. 809-14 [cited in Richard P. Stebbins and Elaine P. Adam, eds., American Foreign Relations 1975: A Documentary Record *(New York: Council on Foreign Relations/New York University Press, 1977), p. 286].*

The Final Act of the Conference, signed on August 1, 1975, dealt with three main areas or "baskets":—security, economic, and human rights issues. It has since been argued that the human rights provisions played a significant role in undermining the regimes of Eastern Europe and the Soviet Union. All signatories promised to respect the following principles:

I. Sovereign equality, respect for the rights inherent in sovereignty

The participating States will respect each other's sovereign equality and individuality as well as all the rights inherent in and encompassed by its sovereignty, including in particular the right of every State to juridical equality, to territorial integrity and to freedom and political independence. They will also respect each other's right freely to choose and develop its political, social, economic and cultural systems as well as its right to determine its laws and regulations.

Within the framework of international law, all the participating States have equal rights and duties. They will respect each other's right to define and conduct as it wishes its relations with other States in accordance with international law and in the spirit of the present Declaration. They consider that their frontiers can be changed, in accordance with international law, by peaceful means and by agreement. They also have the right to belong or not to belong to international organizations, to be or not to be a party to bilateral or multilateral treaties including the right to be or not to be a party to treaties of alliance; they also have the right to neutrality.

II. Refraining from the threat or use of force

The participating States will refrain in their mutual relations, as well as in their international relations in general, from the threat or use of force against the territorial integrity or political independence of any State, or in any other manner inconsistent with the purposes of the United Nations and with the present Declaration. No consideration may be invoked to serve to warrant resort to the threat or use of force in contravention of this principles.

Accordingly, the participating States will refrain from any acts constituting a threat of force or direct or indirect use of force against another participating State. Likewise they will refrain from any manifestation of force for the purpose of inducing another participating State to renounce the full exercise of its sovereign rights. Likewise they will also refrain in their mutual relations from any act of reprisal by force.

No such threat or use of force will be employed as a means of settling disputes, or questions likely to give rise to disputes, between them.

III. Inviolability of frontiers

The participating States regard as inviolable all one another's frontiers as well as the frontiers of all States in Europe and therefore they will refrain now and in the future from assaulting these frontiers.

Accordingly, they will also refrain from any demand for, or act of, seizure and usurpation of part or all of the territory of any participating State.

IV. Territorial integrity of States

The participating States will respect the territorial integrity of each of the participating States.

VI. Non-intervention in internal affairs

The participating States will refrain from any intervention, direct or indirect, individual or collective, in the internal or external affairs falling within the domestic jurisdiction of another participating State, regardless of their mutual relations.

They will accordingly refrain from any form of armed intervention or threat of such intervention against another participating State.

VII. Respect for human rights and fundamental freedoms, including the freedom of thought, conscience, religion or belief

The participating States will respect human rights and fundamental freedoms, including the freedom of thought, conscience, religion or belief, for all without distinction as to race, sex, language or religion.

They will promote and encourage the effective exercise of civil, political, economic, social, cultural and other rights and freedoms all of which derive from the inherent dignity of the human person and are essential for his free and full development.

Source: Department of State, Bureau of Public Affairs, Office of Media Services, Conference on Security and Co-operation in Europe: Final Act, Helsinki 1975 *(Department of State Publication 8826: Washington, 1975) [cited in Richard P. Stebbins and Elaine P. Adam, eds.,* American Foreign Relations 1975: A Documentary Record *(New York: Council on Foreign Relations/New York University Press, 1977), pp. 294-7].*

DOCUMENT 6 THE SHANGHAI COMMUNIQUÉ

In the 1970s, while relations of the People's Republic of China with the Soviet Union remained poor, those with the United States improved dramatically. Kissinger travelled to China in 1971 and in 1972 Nixon became the first American president to visit. At the end of his trip, on February 27, 1972, the two nations issued the Shanghai Communiqué:

There are essential differences between China and the United States in their social systems and foreign policies. However, the two sides agreed that countries, regardless of their social systems, should conduct their relations on the principles of respect for the sovereignty and territorial integrity of all states, non-aggression against other states, non-interference in the internal affairs of other states, equality and mutual benefit, and peaceful coexistence. International disputes should be settled on this basis, without resorting to the use or threat of force. The United States and the People's Republic of China are prepared to apply these principles to their mutual relations.

With these principles of international relations in mind the two sides stated that:

—progress toward the normalization of relations between China and the United States is in the interests of all countries;

—both wish to reduce the danger of international military conflict;

—neither should seek hegemony in the Asia-Pacific region and each is opposed to efforts by any other country or group of countries to establish such hegemony; and

—neither is prepared to negotiate on behalf of any third party or to enter into agreements or understandings with the other directed at other states.

Both sides are of the view that it would be against the interests of the peoples of the world for any major country to collude with another against other countries, or for major countries to divide up the world into spheres of interest.

The two sides reviewed the long-standing serious disputes between China and the United States. The Chinese side reaffirmed its position: The Taiwan question is the crucial question obstructing the normalization of relations between China and the United States; the Government of the People's Republic of China is the sole legal government of China; Taiwan is a province of China which has long been returned to the motherland; the liberation of Taiwan is China's internal affair in which no other country has the right to interfere; and all U.S. forces and military installations must be withdrawn from Taiwan. The Chinese Government firmly opposes any activities which aim at the creation of "one China, one Taiwan," "one China, two governments," "two Chinas," and "independent Taiwan" or advocate that "the status of Taiwan remains to be determined."

The U.S. side declared: The United States acknowledges that all Chinese on either side of the Taiwan Strait maintain there is but one China and that Taiwan is a part of China. The United States Government does not challenge that position. It reaffirms its interest in a peaceful settlement of the Taiwan question by the Chinese themselves. With this prospect in mind, it affirms the ultimate objective of the withdrawal of all U.S. forces and military installations from Taiwan. In the meantime, it will progressively reduce its forces and military installations on Taiwan as the tension in the area diminishes.

The two sides agreed that it is desirable to broaden the understanding between the two peoples. To this end, they discussed specific areas in such fields as science, technology, culture, sports and journalism, in which people-to-people contacts and exchanges would be mutually beneficial. Each side undertakes to facilitate the further development of such contacts and exchanges.

Both sides view bilateral trade as another area from which mutual benefit can be derived, and agreed that economic relations based on equality and mutual benefit are in the interest of the peoples of the two countries. They agree to facilitate the progressive development of trade between their two countries.

The two sides agreed that they will stay in contact through various channels, including the sending of a senior U.S. representative to Peking from time to time for concrete consultations to further the normalization of relations between the two countries and continue to exchange views on issues of common interest.

The two sides expressed the hope that the gains achieved during this visit would open up new prospects for the relations between the two countries. They believe that the normalization of relations between the two countries is not only in the interest of the Chinese and American peoples but also contributes to the relaxation of tension in Asia and the world.

President Nixon, Mrs. Nixon and the American party expressed their appreciation for the gracious hospitality shown them by the Government and people of the People's Republic of China.

Source: Presidential Documents, February 28, 1972, pp. 473-6 [cited in Richard P. Stebbins and Elaine P. Adam, eds., American Foreign Relations 1971: A Documentary Record *(New York: Council on Foreign Relations and New York University Press, 1976), pp. 309-10].*

STUDY QUESTIONS FOR SECTION EIGHT: DÉTENTE

1. What brought about the détente of the 1970s?

2. Compare and contrast the foreign policies of Presidents Richard Nixon and Jimmy Carter.

3. Did the United States and the Soviet Union view détente differently?

4. When and why did détente end?

SECTION NINE

THE END OF THE COLD WAR

DOCUMENTS

CHRONOLOGY

1979		Sandinista government in Nicaragua
		Margaret Thatcher prime minister in Britain
	Nov.	American hostage crisis begins in Iran
	Dec.	Soviet decision to invade Afghanistan
1981		Solidarity formed in Poland
		Francois Mitterand becomes president of France
	Jan.	Ronald Reagan sworn in as US President
	Dec.	martial law in Poland
1982		Falklands war between Britain and Argentina
	Nov.	Brezhnev dies; Andropov succeeds him
1983		Helmut Kohl becomes Chancellor of Germany
	Mar.	President Reagan announces the Strategic Defense Initiative (Star Wars)
	Aug.	KAL 007 shot down
1984		Andropov dies; Chernenko succeeds him
1985		
	Mar.	Chernenko dies; Gorbachev succeeds him
	Nov.	Geneva summit between Reagan and Gorbachev
1986		Gorbachev abandons Brezhnev doctrine
	Oct.	Rejkjavik summit between Reagan and Gorbachev
1987		Intermediate Nuclear Forces treaty between the Soviet Union and the United States
	Dec.	Washington summit between Reagan and Gorbachev
1988		Soviets withdraw from Afghanistan
	May	Moscow summit between Reagan and Gorbachev
1989		
	July	non-Communist government takes office in Poland
	Nov.	Berlin Wall falls
1991		
	Jan.	Gulf War with Iraq starts
	July	START treaty
	Aug.	attempted coup by hardliners in Soviet Union

DOCUMENT 1 THE SOVIET INVASION OF AFGHANISTAN

The Soviet invasion of Afghanistan brought about an immediate deterioration in East-West relations. President Jimmy Carter announced a series of measures against the Soviet Union, from economic sanctions to a boycott of the 1980 Moscow Olympics. Recently opened Soviet documents indicate that the Soviet leadership was in fact reluctant to invade Afghanistan, even though it was receiving increasingly desperate requests for help from the Marxist regime there. In March, 1979 the main Soviet policy-making body, the Politburo of the Communist Party, discussed the issue. Leonid Brezhnev, secretary-general of the Party, was the recognized leader of the Soviet Union, but by this stage his health was deteriorating markedly. Andrei Gromyko was its Foreign Minister, Alexei Kosygin Prime Minister, and Yuri Andropov head of the KGB. The first extract comes from a discussion on March 17.

GROMYKO: We have to discuss what we will do if the situation gets worse. Today, the situation in Afghanistan for now is unclear to many of us. Only one thing is clear—we cannot surrender Afghanistan to the enemy. We have to think how to achieve this. Maybe we won't have to introduce troops.

KOSYGIN: All of us agree—we must not surrender Afghanistan. From this point, we have to work out first of all a political document, to use all political means in order to help the Afghan leadership to strengthen itself, to provide the support which we've already planned, and to leave as a last resort the use of force...

The discussion resumed on March 18.

ANDROPOV: We know Lenin's teaching about a revolutionary situation. Whatever type of situation we are talking about in Afghanistan, it is not that type of situation. Therefore I believe that we can suppress a revolution [against Marxist Afghan government] in Afghanistan only with the aid of our bayonets, but that is for us entirely inadmissible. We cannot take such a risk...

GROMYKO: I fully support Comrade Andropov's proposal to exclude a measure as the introduction of our troops into Afghanistan. The [Afghan] army there is unreliable. Thus our army if it enters Afghanistan will be an aggressor. Against whom will it fight? Against the Afghan people first of all, and it will have to shoot at them. Comrade Andropov correctly noted that indeed the situation in Afghanistan is not ripe for a [socialist] revolution. And all that we have done in recent years with such effort in terms of a détente in international tensions, arms reductions, and much more—all that would be thrown back. Of course, this will be a nice gift for China. All the nonaligned countries will be against us. In a word, serious consequences are to be expected from such an action. There will no longer be any question of a meeting of Leonid Ilych [Brezhnev] with Carter [US president]...

The leader of Afghanistan, Nur Mohammed Taraki, came to Moscow on March 20 and was told firmly by the Soviet leaders that the Soviet Union was the firm friend of Afghanistan, that the Soviets would send economic and military aid, but that the Afghans must be "self-reliant" when it came to fighting their internal enemies. Between that visit, however, and December, the situation continued to worsen for the Taraki government in Afghanistan. Taraki was overthrown and killed by a Marxist rival in October, who in turn continued to meet resistance. Reluctantly the Soviets decided that they would have to intervene to salvage any Soviet influence. They may also have been affected by two other developments: the spread of Islamic fundamentalism from Iran which was threatening to stir up the Islamic populations along the Soviet Union's southern tier and the worsening relations with the United States. (The Senate, for example, had made no move to ratify the SALT II treaty.) No documents have yet emerged of the discussions in the Politburo but on December 6, 1979, it approved the sending of a special military intelligence unit to Afghanistan. On December 12, a small group which included Andropov and Gromyko got Brezhnev's signature on a hand-written memorandum.

Top Secret
SPECIAL FILE
Concerning the situation in "A"

1. Ratify evaluations and measures set forth by Andropov, Yu.V., Ustinov D.F. [Defence Minister], and Gromyko A.A. Authorize them to introduce amendments of non-essential character in the course of the execution of these measures....
2. Entrust comrades Andropov, Yu.V., Ustinov D.F., and Gromyko A.A. to keep the CC [Central Committee] Politburo informed on the status of the execution of the outlined measures.
[signed] L. Brezhnev

Source: Cold War International History Project, Bulletin, *Issue 4 (Fall 1994) (Washington D.C.).*

DOCUMENT 2 THE AMERICAN RESPONSE

The United States, already concerned over the unstable situation in the Middle East as a result of the fall of the Shah of Iran, was outraged by the Soviet invasion of Afghanistan. Jimmy Carter was president at the time.

The Soviets still claimed their action was in response to an appeal by the Afghan government leaders to strengthen their security forces, but there were obviously other purposes for such a large-scale operation. In the past, Soviet leaders had not hesitated to use their own troops to maintain domination over the Warsaw Pact countries or surrogate troops from Cuba and Vietnam to accomplish their ends elsewhere. However, this was the first time they had used their troops to expand their sphere of influence since they had overthrown the government of Czechoslovakia in February 1948 and established a Soviet puppet government there.

The brutality of the act was bad enough, but the threat of this Soviet invasion to the rest of the region was very clear—and had grim consequences. A successful takeover of Afghanistan would give the Soviets a deep penetration between Iran and Pakistan, and pose a threat to the rich oil fields of the Persian Gulf area and to the crucial waterways through which so much of the world's energy supplies had to pass.

Carter sent a strong message to the Soviet leader, Brezhnev, demanding that the Soviet Union back down. Brezhnev sent an ambiguous reply and Soviet troops continued to pour into Afghanistan. The US administration then had to decide on what measures to take. The following is an extract from Carter's diary for January 4, 1980.

We discussed how far we wanted to go with economic measures against the Soviet Union. I want to go the maximum degree—interrupting grain sales, high technology, canceling fishing rights, reexamining our commerce guidelines...canceling visits to the Soviet Union, restricting any sort of negotiations on culture, trade, and so forth...possibly withdrawing from the Olympics. We're asking Australia and Canada not to replace the grain we might withhold....We'll give Pakistan aid, both economic and military, working hopefully through a consortium of nations.

Source: Jimmy Carter, Keeping Faith: Memoirs of a President *(New York, 1982), pp. 471-6.*

DOCUMENT 3 PRESIDENT REAGAN ON THE SOVIET UNION

Ronald Reagan became American president in January 1981. Although he did not use the term "the evil empire" until 1983, in his first press conference, he made his view of the Soviet Union clear.

I know of no leader of the Soviet Union since the revolution, and including the present leadership, that has not more than once repeated in the various Communist congresses they hold, their determination that their goal must be the promotion of world revolution and a one-world Socialist or Communist state...the only morality they recognize is what will further their cause, meaning they reserve unto themselves the right to commit any crime, to lie, to cheat, in order to attain that.

Source: Martin Walker, The Cold War *(New York and Toronto, 1994), p. 268.*

DOCUMENT 4 STAR WARS

Early on in his administration, President Reagan was captured by the idea that the United States might be able to erect a defensive system which could destroy incoming Soviet missiles in space. The Strategic Defense Initiative (SDI) or Star Wars was announced in 1983. It was enormously costly and would probably not have worked. After the collapse of the Soviet Union, some of Reagan's advisers claimed that its only purpose had been to spend the Soviets into bankruptcy. Here is Reagan's own view.

I came into office with a decided prejudice against our tacit agreement with the Soviet Union regarding nuclear missiles. I'm talking about the MAD policy—"mutual assured destruction"...Somehow this didn't seem to me something that would send you to bed feeling safe. It was like having two westerners standing in a saloon aiming their guns at each other's head—permanently. There had to be a better way.

Early in my first term, I called a meeting of the Joint Chiefs of Staff...and said to them: Every offensive weapon ever invented by man has resulted in the creation of a defense against it; isn't it possible in this age of technology that we could invent a defensive weapon that could intercept nuclear weapons and destroy them as they emerged from their silos?

They looked at each other, then asked if they could huddle for a few moments. Very shortly, they came out of their huddle and said, "Yes, it's an idea worth exploring." My answer was, "Let's do it."

....

As the myths grew, one of them was that I had proposed the idea to produce a bargaining chip for use in getting the Soviets to reduce their weaponry. I've had to tell the Soviet leaders a hundred times that the SDI was not a bargaining chip. I've told them all along I'd share it with others willing to give up their nuclear missiles.

Source: Ronald Reagan, An American Life *(New York, 1990), p. 547-8.*

DOCUMENT 5 THE EVIL EMPIRE

The year 1983 marked a low point in Soviet-American relations. The US was planning to deploy Pershing-2 and cruise nuclear missiles in Western Europe in the fall; and the superpowers were confronting each other through their proxies in the Middle East (in Lebanon in particular), in Afghanistan, and in Nicaragua. On March 8, President Reagan spoke to a conservative religious group, the National Association of Evangelicals, attacking the Western peace movement.

If history teaches us anything, it teaches that simpleminded appeasement or wishful thinking about our adversaries is folly. It means the betrayal of our past, the squandering of our freedom. So I urge you to speak out against those who would place the United States in a position of military and moral inferiority....In your discussions of the nuclear freeze proposals, I urge you to beware the temptation of pride—the temptation of blithely declaring yourself above it all and label both sides at fault, to ignore the facts of history and the aggressive impulses of an evil Empire, to simply call the arms race a giant misunderstanding and thereby remove yourself from the struggle between right and wrong and good and evil....

I believe we shall rise to the challenge. I believe Communism is another sad, bizarre chapter in history whose last pages even now are being written.

Source: Ronald Reagan, An American Life *(New York, 1990), p. 570.*

DOCUMENT 6 THE SOVIET RESPONSE TO REAGAN

On March 27, Reagan announced the Strategic Defense Initiative (SDI) which the Soviets viewed as a violation of the 1972 Anti-Ballistic Missile Treaty. In May, the Western allies held a summit meeting in Williamsburg, Virginia at which they decided to go ahead with the missile deployment in Europe in spite of a declaration from the Soviet Union that it would see this as a provocation. On May 31, the Politburo discussed the international situation. Yuri Andropov had succeeded Brezhnev and Mikhail Gorbachev was now a member of the Politburo.

ANDROPOV: Today I've talked with a number of members of the Politburo about our government's announcement of the response connected with the deployment of American missiles "Pershing-2" and cruise missiles in the countries of Western Europe; and also concerning the resolution adopted by the countries of "Big Seven" in Williamsburg. It's important that we discuss this matter, exchange opinions, and express the suggestions that should be developed.

If you look at the events that are taking place in the Western countries, you can say that an anti-Soviet coalition is being formed out there. Of course, that's not accidental, and it's highly dangerous ....

If you analyze the reaction of the countries of the West on our declaration, then the reaction has two sides. From one side, our declaration has impressed them very much. There are indications, seen through some of the speeches of some of the western politicians that give hope to normal and productive high level talks about the decrease of the arms race and disarmament, especially of the nuclear weapons. On the other side, there are indications of absolute fulfillment of the so-called double decision of NATO, which is the placement of nuclear missiles in the countries of Western Europe.

Actions of President Reagan, who is a bearer and creator of all anti-soviet ideas, creator of all the untrue insinuations regarding our country and the other countries of the Socialist Community, deserve very critical and harsh reaction from our side.

....

Now let's see what we can do. To my disappointment we act alone. Some of us speak out, but we all do it separately. We, the countries of the Warsaw Pact and the other socialist countries that don't belong under the Warsaw Pact, have to demonstrate strong unity. But the leaders of the socialist countries are buried in their national problems. These, if you pardon my words, are just minor unimportant actions.

....

We have to open up a wider network to win public opinion, to mobilize public opinion of the Western countries of Europe and America against the location of the nuclear weapons in Europe and against a new arms race, that's being forced by the American administration. The behavior of Japan, and especially of the president Nakasone worries me. He completely took the side of the more aggressive part of the Western countries, and he completely supports Reagan's actions. Because of that we should consider some sort of compromise in our relations with Japan.

Source: Cold War International History Project, Bulletin, *Issue 4 (Fall 1994) (Washington D.C.).*

DOCUMENT 7 THE KAL 007 INCIDENT

On August 31, 1983 the unarmed Korean airliner, flight KAL 007, was shot down over Soviet airspace into which it had strayed. 269 passengers, including a US congressman and a number of Canadian citizens, were killed. The Soviet Union claimed that the plane had been on a spying mission. While there is some evidence that both American and South Korean intelligence services may have been taking advantage of the flight to gather intelligence, a later investigation by the Soviet newspaper *Isvestiya* concluded that the shooting had been a dreadful accident. At the time President Reagan and other leaders in the West, such as the British Prime Minister Margaret Thatcher, viewed it as deliberate murder. Reagan spoke to the American people just after Labour Day.

...this attack was not just against ourselves or the Republic of Korea. This was the Soviet Union against the world and the moral precepts which guide human relations among people everywhere. It was an act of barbarism, born of a society which wantonly disregards individual rights and the value of human life and seeks constantly to expand and dominate other nations.

DOCUMENT 8 GORBACHEV'S REFORMS

In 1985, Mikhail Gorbachev took over the leadership of the Soviet Union. Determined to salvage a system which he still believed in, he initiated a series of reforms within the Soviet Union. These can be grouped under three main headings: greater democracy, *perestroika* or restructuring, and *glasnost* or openness. On February 25, 1986, Gorbachev made a major speech to the 27th Congress of the Communist Party of the Soviet Union, in which he outlined what needed to be done. He also hinted that the Soviet leadership was prepared to accept different roads to communism in the countries under its control, thus opening the door to the abandonment of the Brezhnev Doctrine.

While duly appraising our achievements, the leadership of the CPSU considers it its duty to tell the Party and the people honestly and frankly about the shortcomings in our political and practical activities, the unfavourable tendencies in the economy and the social and moral sphere, and about the reasons for them. For a number of years the deeds and actions of the Party and Government bodies lagged behind the needs of the time and of life...The problems in the country's development grew more rapidly than they were being solved. The inertness and rigidity of the forms and methods of management, the decline of dynamism in our work, and increased bureaucracy—all this was doing no small damage. Signs of stagnation had begun to surface in the life of society.

....

The situation has reached a turning point not only in internal but also external affairs....The situation created by the nuclear confrontation calls for new approaches, methods and forms of relations between the different social systems, states and regions.

After a lengthy discussion of areas that need reform inside the Soviet Union, Gorbachev turns to the ways in which the Soviet Union intends to operate internationally.

Now, as never before, it is important to find ways for closer and more productive cooperation with governments, parties, and mass organizations that are genuinely concerned about the destinies of peace on earth, with all peoples in order to *build an all-embracing system of international security* [stressed in original].

We see the Fundamental Principles of this system in the following:

1. In the military sphere
   —renunciation by the nuclear powers of war—both nuclear and conventional—against each other or against third countries....
2. In the political sphere
   —strict respect in international practice for the right of each people to choose the ways and forms of its development independently....

Source: Mikhail Gorbachev, Selected Speeches and Articles *(Moscow, 1987), pp. 342-3, 432-3.*

DOCUMENT 8

ANDREI SAKHAROV'S TREATMENT

One of the areas where Gorbachev showed that he intended to break with the past was in the treatment of dissidents in the Soviet Union. Andrei Sakharov, the distinguished nuclear physicist, and his wife Yelena Bonner, had been sent into internal exile and were constantly harassed by the KGB. This had led to repeated protests and demonstrations in the West. In July 1985 Sakharov wrote to Gorbachev urging that his wife be allowed to go to the United States for medical treatment and to see her relatives. On August 29, the Politburo discussed the request.

GORBACHEV: Now a few words on another subject. At the end of July I received a letter from the not unfamiliar Sakharov. He is requesting that his wife, Bonner, be allowed to go abroad to undergo treatment and visit with relatives.

CHEBRIKOV [head of the KGB]: This is an old story. It has been going on for 20 years. During this time various situations have arisen. Appropriate measures were employed in relation to Sakharov and Bonner. But no actions were permitted which would have violated the law. This is very important and should be emphasized.

Sakharov is now 65 and Bonner is 63. Sakharov is in poor health. He's undergoing oncological tests because he has been losing weight.

Sakharov as a political figure has basically lost his image of late and has been saying nothing new. Bonner should probably be allowed to go abroad for three months......Allowing Bonner to go abroad would have the appearance of a humanitarian step.

...

According to specialists, Sakharov could continue to work in military research if he would be given a laboratory. Bonner has a strong influence on Sakharov's behaviour.

GORBACHEV: Now there's real Zionism.

CHEBRIKOV: Bonner has a 100 percent influence over him. We believe that without her his behaviour will change. He has two daughters and a son from his first marriage. They behave well and can influence their father.

....

We must resolve this question right now. If we make this decision prior to or even right after your meetings with Mitterand [French President] and Reagan, it will be seen as a concession which is undesirable.

GORBACHEV: Yes. We should make a decision.

ZIMYANIN [Politburo member]: No doubt that Bonner will be used against us in the West. ...And you can't expect any kind of decency from Bonner. She's a beast in a skirt, an imperialist plant.

GORBACHEV: What will hurt us more—to allow Bonner to go abroad or to forbid it?

Source: Cold War International History Project, Bulletin, *Issue 4 (Fall 1994) (Washington D.C.).*

DOCUMENT 10 THE FIRST REAGAN-GORBACHEV MEETING

In foreign relations, Gorbachev made a series of overtures to the United States, urging that both sides start negotiating a limit on strategic weapons such as intercontinental ballistic missiles and that both withdraw some of their weapons from Europe. The Americans responded with caution but President Reagan agreed to meet Gorbachev at a summit in Geneva in November 1985. Reagan remembers their first meeting.

On the morning of November 19, I was waiting for Gorbachev at Villa Fleur d'Eau. When I was told his car had arrived, I hurried out to the porch and walked down several steps to greet him. He was dressed in a heavy topcoat and wearing a hat; I was hatless and in a suit. Why the press made a point of the fact that he was bundled up and I wasn't, I don't know—I suppose this was only one measure of the enormous attention being paid to the summit—but for whatever reason, the reporters who were keeping score gave me credit for winning the first round at the summit because I looked more casual than he did. (I hadn't planned it that way; the next time we were outdoors, I was wearing a topcoat—I didn't want to rub it in.)

As we shook hands for the first time, I had to admit—as Margaret Thatcher and Prime Minister Brian Mulroney of Canada had predicted I would—that there was something likable about Gorbachev. There was warmth in his face and his style, not the coldness bordering on hatred I'd seen in most senior Soviet officials I'd met until then.

The two men exchanged formal statements and then the arms control experts took the floor.

...it was during this pause that I suggested to Gorbachev that the two of us walk down to the boat house for a breath of fresh air and talk. He leaped out of his chair almost before I had finished.

The fire was roaring when we got to the cottage and sat down across from each other in stuffed chairs beside the hearth. I had considered suggesting to him that we go on a first-name basis, as our group did at economic summits, but our experts had told me he wasn't likely to appreciate such a gesture of informality at our first meeting, and so I addressed him as "Mr. General Secretary."

It was during the first moments of this fireside chat that I said I thought the two of us were in a unique situation. Here we were, I said, two men who had been born in obscure rural hamlets in the middle of our respective countries, each of us poor and from humble beginnings. Now we were the leaders of our countries and probably the only two men in the world who could bring about World War III.

At the same time, I said, we were possibly the only two men in the world who might be able to bring peace to the world.

I said I thought we owed it to the world to use the opportunity that had been presented to us to work at building the kind of human trust and confidence in each other that could lead to genuine peace.

I watched as Gorbachev listened to the translation of my words, and he seemed to nod in agreement.

Source: Ronald Reagan, An American Life *(New York, 1990), pp. 635-6.*

DOCUMENT 11 THE REYKJAVIK SUMMIT

In October 1986, Reagan and Gorbachev held an impromptu summit in Iceland's capital, Reykjavik, where they came close to dismantling the nuclear arsenals on both sides. On Saturday, October 11, the two men agreed to eliminate nuclear missiles in Europe and to eliminate their long range missiles within ten years. On Sunday, they went still further, as Reagan recalled in his memoirs.

In addition to nuclear missiles, we said we would try to reduce and eventually eliminate other nuclear weapons as well, including bombers, and Gorbachev pledged his commitment to strong and mutually acceptable verification procedures.

When I said we couldn't eliminate tactical battlefield nuclear weapons in Europe because they constituted NATO's principal deterrent against an invasion by the much larger Warsaw Pact conventional forces, Gorbachev volunteered drastic reductions in their conventional forces...

George [Schulz, Secretary of State] and I couldn't believe what was happening. We were getting amazing agreements. As the day went on I felt something momentous was occurring.

Our noon deadline came and went. We ignored the clock and kept on working, the four of us and our interpreters in that room above the sea.

As evening approached, I thought to myself: Look what we have accomplished—we have negotiated the most massive weapons reductions in history. I thought we were in complete agreement and were going to achieve something remarkable.

Then, after everything had been decided, or so I thought, Gorbachev threw us a curve. With a smile on his face, he said: "This all depends, of course, on you giving up SDI."

Source: Ronald Reagan, An American Life *(New York, 1990), pp. 676-7.*

DOCUMENT 12 THE BERLIN WALL COMES DOWN

While the Rejkjavik summit did not deliver all that it promised, the momentum for arms control kept going. In the next few years, the superpowers were going to agree on the INF (intermediate nuclear forces) and the START (strategic arms reductions) treaties. At the same time, events in the Soviet Union and in its empire in Eastern Europe started to spin out of Gorbachev's control. In November, 1989, the Berlin Wall finally came down. Eric Gabriel, a young American writer, was there at the time.

That Friday, about twelve hours after East Berlin opened its border to the West, I biked to Checkpoint Charlie. This border crossing point is normally reserved for the Allies and is crowded mostly in summer, when Americans flock to East Berlin to see how ugly and gray life is under Communism.... That Friday, the streets were packed with people streaming past the East German border guards, their ID cards freshly stamped with an exit visa. Cars from East Berlin slowed to a crawl alongside the crowds of West Berliners waiting just over the white stripe painted on the asphalt, cheering every car with an East German license plate, handing cans of beer to the drivers...

The breaks in the wall, necessary because the regular border crossing points couldn't handle the flow of people waiting to enter West Berlin, seemed to signal that the evil spell of history was broken as well. People stared unbelieving, as East German cranes lifted away slabs of concrete along the Bernauerstrasse, setting them down like the monoliths of a new Stonehenge. It was along this stretch of the wall that people once flung themselves out of the windows of the adjacent buildings to escape into the West.

Source: William M. Brinton and Alan Rinzler, eds., Without Force or Lies: Voices from the Revolution of Central Europe in 1989-90 *(San Francisco, 1990), pp. 194, 196.*

STUDY QUESTIONS FOR SECTION NINE: THE END OF THE COLD WAR

1. Why did the Cold War intensify in the early 1980s?

2. What was the significance of Gorbachev for Soviet relations with the West?

3. Account for the collapse of the Soviet Union.

4. Why did the East Europeans succeed in gaining their freedom from Soviet rule in the late 1980s where they had previously failed?

5. Who won the Cold War?

SECTION TEN

DECOLONIZATION AND NON-ALIGNMENT

DOCUMENTS

CHRONOLOGY

1912	the African National Congress (ANC) is formed in South Africa
1945	the United Nations is formed with only four independent African states
1947	India, Pakistan and Burma gain independence
1948	Yugoslavia breaks from the Soviet bloc, claiming to be "non-aligned"
1951	Libya gains independence
1952	nationalist revolution in Egypt overthrows King Farouk
1954	Algerian War of independence; Geneva Conference on Indochina and independence of Laos and Cambodia with division of Vietnam
1955	Bandung Conference of Asian and African leaders/non-aligned nations
1956	Sudan, Tunisia and Morocco gain independence; Suez Crisis in Egypt
1957	Ghana, Malaysia and Indonesia gain independence
1958	conference of Independent African States and All-African People's Conference
1959	Chinese-Indian border incidents
1960	"Year of Africa" with 17 colonies gaining independence and admission to the UN; Katanga crisis in the Congo; division of African states over the Congo
1961	Belgrade Conference on non-alignment; civil war erupts in Angola
1962	Chinese-Indian border war; "neutralist" coup in Burma; Algeria gains independence; Katangese secession crushed
1963	Organization of African Unity (OAU) formed; Nelson Mandela jailed
1964	Indonesian-Malaysian conflict; civil war erupts in Mozambique and Ethiopia
1965	failed communist coup in Indonesia; U.S. troops to Vietnam; India-Pakistan conflict over Kashmir; declaration of independence by Southern Rhodesia
1966	military coups in Nigeria and Ghana
1967	Association of Southeast Asian Nations (ASEAN) formed; civil war in Nigeria
1969	Libyan invasion of Chad
1973	OAU call for a New International Economic Order" (NIEO); Arab-Israeli War
1975	Russian and Cuban intervention in Angola civil war; Libya-Chad war
1976	Marxist government is formed in Angola with renewed civil war; start of conflict over Western Sahara between Morocco, Algeria and Mauritania

1977 conflict between South Africa and communist rebels in South-West Africa
1978 Ethiopian-Somali war
1979 civil war in Uganda and overthrow of Idi Amin
1980 white minority rule ends in Rhodesia—renamed Zimbabwe
1983 military coup in Nigeria
1990 Nelson Mandela released from prison after 27 years; drought in East Africa
1991 apartheid abolished in South Africa; Siad Barre regime falls in Somalia
1993 civil war in Liberia and Somalia; conflict over elections in Nigeria
1994 election of Nelson Mandela; U.S. intervention in Somalia; civil war in Rwanda

India was the "crown jewel" of the British colonial empire. However, managing the diverse ethnic and religious make-up of the sub-continent was no easy task. When the British granted independence in 1947, they acknowledged the divisions by partitioning the predominantly Hindu India from a separate Muslim state in Pakistan. Tensions between the two have been a constant feature of international relations since that time, but despite this and the problems inherent in running the world's second most populous state, India's Prime Minister sought a unique leadership role for his country. Jawaharlal Nehru was an articulate spokesman for the developing world, and he saw in the emerging Cold War the need for a "middle" ground between the two ideological adversaries. Nehru became one of the primary leaders of neutralism during the 1950s, and with his pacifist message India served as a model for many newly emerging states during decolonization. But Nehru was also masterful at manipulating both sides of the Cold War to compete for India's favour, thus demonstrating not just moral but also pragmatic leadership.

DOCUMENT 1 PRIME MINISTER NEHRU OF INDIA'S VIEWS

A compilation of Nerhru's comments on the U.S., Cold War alignment, communism and Indian foreign policy.

(May 1950 — on the U.S.)

I must say that the Americans are either very naïve or singularly lacking in intelligence. They go through the identical routine whether it is Nehru or the Shah of Iran or Liaqat Ali...All this lessens the value of their fervent protestations and the superlatives they use. A superlative used too often ceases to have any meaning. Having been trained in a school of more restrained language and action, I am afraid I do not appreciate this kind of thing.

....

It surprises me how immature in their political thinking the Americans are! They do not even learn from their own or other people's mistakes; more especially in their dealings with Asia, they show a lack of understanding which is surprising.

(August 1955 — on communism)

My own experience of Communists has been that it is exceedingly difficult to rely on their word or on their basic integrity.... Their loyalty to their party overrides all other loyalties and, therefore, they are prepared often to function in a way which cannot be reconciled with my standards of personal behaviour... Personally I have had no animosity against the Communists at all but I have come to feel increasingly how quite out-of-date Communist parties in non-Communist countries are... they are like the Jesuits belonging to the strict Order and not over-scrupulous in their dealings with others, provided they carry out the dictates of that Order to whom they owe their basic loyalty.

(February 1950 — on the Cold War)

If there is a world war, there is no possibility of India lining up with the Soviet Union whatever else she may do. It is obvious that our relations with the United States as with the United Kingdom in political and economic matters are far closer than with other countries. We have practically no such relations with the Soviets, nor is it likely that they will develop to any great extent for obvious reasons.

(various times — on Indian policy)

We, in India, have endeavored to follow a foreign policy which we feel is not only in the interests of world peace but is particularly indicated for the countries of Asia. That policy is an independent one and of non-alignment with any power bloc.

....

It is not enough to talk of peace; one has to shape one's policy to that end. Otherwise we go straight to the atomic bomb and all its progeny.

....

When you think of India or Asia, please remember always that the primary problems of Asia and India are problems that relate to the basic necessities of life—food, clothing and housing, etc.... Once you satisfy those primary cravings of human beings, then you have a little leisure to look around and play about on the chess-board of world politics. Other desires arise then which sometimes may be described as power politics and the like. But those who want those primary cravings satisfied have no desire for anything else for the time being.

....

When we talk about Asian unity or Asian cooperation, it is something not particularly easy to think in precise terms. That is to say, Asia is too big and rather different in its various regions. The main thing that brought together the various countries of Asia in the past century was a common subjection to colonial rule by European countries.

....

Asia, largely because it has experienced the progressive termination of colonial rule, is, in a state, as you know very well, of extraordinary upheaval and ferment. The upheavals need not necessarily take place as revolutionary activities.

....

The first thing to remember is that, still in Asia, nationalism is the primary urge apart from the urge of hunger and starvation etc. It is nationalism that is the most important feeling there. Nationalism after political freedom tends to fade away to some extent and it is economic problems that come up. Where nationalism is still strong because the memory of colonialism is near, where actual freedom that is political freedom has not been obtained, nationalism remains still the strongest feeling.

....

To regard the present unsettled state of South-East Asia as a result or as part of an ideological conflict would be a dangerous error. The troubles and discontents of this part of the world and indeed of the greater part of Asia are the result of obstructed freedom and dire poverty. The remedy is to accelerate the advent of freedom and to remove poverty. If this is achieved, Asia will become a powerful factor for stability and peace. The philosophy of Asia has been and is the philosophy of peace.

....

Racial discrimination is still in evidence in some countries and there is still not enough realization of the importance of Asia in the councils of the world.

India's championship of freedom and racial equality in Asia as well as in Africa is a natural urge of the facts of geography and history. India desires no leadership or dominion or authority over any country. But we are compelled by circumstances to play our part in Asia and in the world, because we are convinced that unless these basic problems of Asia are solved, there can be no world peace.

....

When the world is full of tension and possible conflicts and people's passions are excited, it is a little difficult to look on with equanimity at a country which tries at any rate not to be entangled in this way and not to allow momentary passions to govern its actions. So it happens that other countries look with a certain amount of disapproval at a policy which perhaps they consider either an unwise policy or a weak policy or a policy of inaction or some kind of neutrality.

....

Whatever policy we were pursuing was not just merely neutral or passive or negative, but that it was a policy which flowed from our past history, from our recent past and from our national movement and from the various ideals that we have proclaimed from any point of view, whether long-term or short-term that you may apply to the circumstances existing today.

....

We wanted to follow a policy, not a negative or merely neutral policy, but a positive policy naturally helping those forces that we consider right and naturally disapproving of the things that we do not like, but fundamentally keeping apart from other countries and other alignments of powers which normally lead to major conflicts. That does not mean that we do not, in our economic life or other life, incline this way or that in respect of many matters. But it does mean, in the jargon of the day, that we do not line up with this set of forces or that and try to maintain a certain friendliness and spirit of co-operation with the other great and small countries of the world.

....

In whatever field of activity we might function, and more especially in the field of foreign policy, if India is to have any weight, she must function according to the way of her own thinking and the methods she can adopt herself. That way of thinking may be affected by other people—in fact it should be affected—because it is not an isolated thinking regardless of reality; but nevertheless the resultant must be her own way of thinking. If she chooses it to be her own way, if it is not derived from her own experience, desires, objectives and ideals, then it becomes a feeble imitation of some other way and it all becomes ineffectual and ineffective. It may be that some countries are so situated, they are so small in size, or in economic or other aspects of importance, that they cannot resist and inevitably they are swept by great forces and by the policies of great powers. India today, whatever else she may be, is neither small in extent, nor in importance, nor in potential resources, nor in the tremendous background of thought and action behind her. She may fail or succeed but whether she fails or succeeds, she does so because of her own strength or weakness, not because of other people sweeping her away.

Source: Sarvepalli Gopal, Jawaharlal Nehru: A Biography *(Volume 2, 1947-1956) (London: Jonathan Cape, 1979), pp. 63, 253, 64, 321-323, 401-408, 475-477.*

With Nehru's guidance, the first international conference of independent African and Asian nations was held at Bandung, Indonesia in April 1955. There a diverse collection of leaders representing twenty-nine developing states agreed to form a "non-aligned" movement. Although from very different backgrounds, the members agreed that the movement should promote the cause of world peace by staying out of the superpower rivalry. While this course of neutralism was plagued by division almost from its inception, the non-aligned movement nonetheless represented a significant shift in international relations. In addition to India, membership included some very important states, such as Indonesia, Yugoslavia and Egypt. In this the Bandung Conference demonstrated that the process of decolonization would have major repercussions on the Cold War. However, one of the most important aspects of the conference was the observer-status attendance by representatives from the People's Republic of China. While hardly non-aligned, Communist China's interest in the movement demonstrated its desire to take a leadership role among the developing states, and to potentially become a third superpower.

DOCUMENT 2 — EXCERPTS FROM SPEECHES BY VARIOUS LEADERS AT BANDUNG (APRIL 1955)

(President Soekarno of Indonesia)

You have not gathered together in a world of peace and unity and cooperation. Great chasms yawn between nations and groups of nations. Our unhappy world is torn and tortured, and the peoples of all countries walk in fear lest, through no fault of theirs, the dogs of war are unchained once again.

And if, in spite of all that the peoples may do, this should happen, what then? What of our newly-recovered independence then? What of our children and our parents?...

How is it possible to be disinterested about colonialism? For us, colonialism is not something far and distant. We have known it in all its ruthlessness. We have seen the immense human wastage it causes, the poverty it causes, and the heritage it leaves behind when, eventually and reluctantly, it is driven out by the inevitable march of history. My people, and the peoples of many nations of Asia and Africa know these things, for we have experienced them.

Indeed, we cannot yet say that all parts of our counties are free already. Some parts still labour under the lash. And some parts of Asia and Africa which are not represented here still suffer from the same condition.

Yes, some parts of our nations are not yet free. That is why all of us cannot yet feel that journey's end has been reached. No people can feel themselves free, so long as part of their motherland is unfree. Like peace, freedom is indivisible. There is no such thing as being half free, as there is no such thing as being half alive.

(Prime Minister Kotelawala of Ceylon)

When the great powers of the West talk peace, their chances of agreement are weakened by the fact that each suspects the other's strength. We, by contrast, come to the conference table weak and relatively unarmed. We have no thermonuclear bombs in our pockets, no weapons of chemical or bacteriological warfare up our sleeves, no plans for armament factories or blueprints for ever more deadly methods of genocide in our brief cases.

We have, however, I venture to believe, something which the great and the mighty lack. That something is the strength of our weakness—the ability which our very defenselessness confers, to offer ourselves as mediators in the dispute between the giants of Communism and anti-Communism.

The time has gone by when the function of small countries in world affairs could be summed up by the words used by one of the war leaders at Yalta: 'The eagle should permit the small birds to sing and care not whereof they sing'.

Today, on the contrary, the salvation of the world depends not on great powers but on the lesser countries, many of whom are still voiceless in the councils of the nations. And I am sure that if Asia and Africa put forward an unambiguous and united demand for the reconstitution of the United Nations, by abolishing the Veto and converting the Security Council into a fully elected body responsible to the General Assembly, it will meet with powerful response from all the smaller nations of the world.

(Premier Chou En-Lai of Communist China)

The Chinese Delegation has come here to seek unity and not to quarrel. We Communists do not hide the fact that we believe in communism and that we consider the socialist system a good system. There is no need at this Conference to publicize one's ideology and the political system of one's country, although differences do exist among us.

The Chinese Delegation has come here to seek common ground, and not to create divergence. Is there any basis for seeking common ground among us? Yes, there is. The overwhelming majority of the Asian and African countries and peoples have suffered and are still suffering from the calamities of colonialism. This is acknowledged by all of us. If we seek common ground in doing away with the sufferings and calamities under colonialism, it will be very easy for us to have mutual understanding and respect, mutual sympathy and support, instead of mutual suspicion and fear, mutual exclusion and antagonism....

As a Chinese proverb says: 'Do not do unto others what you yourself do not desire.' We are against outside interference; how could we want to interfere in the internal affairs of others?...

The Chinese people have chosen and support their own government. There is freedom of religious belief in China. China has no intention whatsoever to subvert the governments of its neighbouring countries. On the contrary, it is China that is suffering from the subversive activities which are openly carried out by the United States of America without any disguise. If you do not believe in this you can come personally or send representatives to China to take a look. We allow people to have doubts who do not yet know the truth. There is a saying in

China: 'To hear a hundred times cannot be compared with seeing once.' We welcome the delegates of all the participating countries in this Conference to visit China at any time you like. We have no bamboo curtain, but there are people who are spreading a smokescreen between us.

Source: Noble Frankland (ed.), Documents on International Affairs, 1955 *(London: Royal Institute of International Affairs and Oxford University Press, 1958), pp. 400-412.*

DOCUMENT 3 EXCERPTS FROM THE FINAL COMMUNIQUE OF THE BANDUNG CONFERENCE (APRIL 24, 1955)

1. The Asian-African Conference recognised the urgency of promoting economic development in the Asian-African region. There was general desire for economic co-operation among the participating countries on the basis of mutual interest and respect for national sovereignty. The proposals with regard to economic co-operation within the participating countries do not preclude either the desirability or the need for co-operation with countries outside the region, including the investment of foreign capital. It was further recognised that the assistance being received by certain participating countries from outside the region, through international or under bilateral arrangements, had made a valuable contribution to the implementation of their development programmes.

....

1. The Asian-African Conference was convinced that among the most powerful means of promoting understanding among nations is the development of cultural co-operation. Asia and Africa have been the cradle of great religions and civilisations which have enriched other cultures and civilisations while themselves being enriched in the process. Thus the cultures of Asia and Africa are based on spiritual and universal foundations.

....

2. The Asian-African Conference took note of the fact that the existence of colonialism in many parts of Asia and Africa, in whatever form it may be, not only prevents cultural co-operation but also suppresses the national cultures of the people. Some colonial powers have denied to their dependent peoples basic rights in the sphere of education and culture which hampers the development of their personality and also prevents cultural intercourse with other Asian and African peoples.

....

The Conference condemned such a denial of fundamental rights in the sphere of education and culture in some parts of Asia and Africa by this and other forms of cultural suppression.

In particular, the Conference condemned racialism as a means of cultural suppression.

....

Human Rights and Self-Determination

1. The Asian-African Conference declared its full support of the fundamental principles of Human Rights as set forth in the Charter of the United Nations and took note of the Universal Declaration of Human Rights as a common standard of achievement for all peoples and all nations.

The Conference declared its full support of the principle of self-determination of peoples and nations as set forth in the Charter of the United Nations and took note of the United Nations resolutions on the rights of peoples and nations to self-determination, which is a pre-requisite of the full enjoyment of all fundamental Human Rights.

2. The Asian-African Conference deplored the policies and practices of racial segregation and discrimination which form the basis of government and human relations in large regions of Africa and in other parts of the world. Such conduct is not only a gross violation of human

rights but also a denial of the dignity of man. The Conference extended its warm sympathy and support for the courageous stand taken by the victims of racial discrimination.

....

1. The Asian-African Conference discussed the problems of dependent peoples and colonialism and the evils arising from the subjection of peoples to alien subjugation, domination and exploitation.

The Conference is agreed:

(a) in declaring that colonialism in all its manifestations is an evil which should speedily be brought to an end;

(b) in affirming that the subjection of peoples to alien subjugation, domination and exploitation constitutes a denial of fundamental human rights, is contrary to the Charter of the United Nations and is an impediment to the promotion of world peace and co-operation;

(c) in declaring its support of the cause of freedom and independence for all such peoples, and

(d) in calling upon the powers concerned to grant freedom and independence to such peoples.

....

2. The Asian-African Conference having considered the dangerous situation of international tension existing and the risks confronting the whole human race from the outbreak of global war in which the destructive power of all types of armaments, including nuclear and thermo-nuclear weapons, would be employed, invited the attention of all nations to the terrible consequences that would follow if such a war were to break out.

The Conference considered that disarmament and the prohibition of production, experimentation and use of nuclear and thermonuclear weapons of war are imperative to save mankind and civilisation from the fear and prospect of wholesale destruction. It considered that the nations of Asia and Africa assembled here have a duty towards humanity and civilisation to proclaim their support for disarmament and for the prohibition of these weapons and to appeal to nations principally concerned and to world opinion, to bring about such disarmament and prohibition.

Source: Noble Frankland (ed.), Documents on International Affairs, 1955 *(London: Royal Institute of International Affairs and Oxford University Press, 1958), pp. 429-438.*

Independence movements in some European colonies in Asia and Africa began even before the 20th century, but it took World War Two to fundamentally alter the international balance of power and allow for widespread "decolonization". The European powers were in shambles at the end of World War Two, and so their imperial outposts quickly became economic and political liabilities. Moreover, both of the two "superpowers" opposed the restoration of colonial rule in the new international order. The initial stages of decolonization in Asia and Africa were for the most part peaceful, but the interplay of Cold War tensions with ethnic and regional rivalries often made the process of independence chaotic and bloody. Such was the case in the former Belgian Congo, where a civil war shortly after independence drew international attention and superpower intervention.

DOCUMENT 4

SOVIET PREMIER NIKITA KHRUSHCHEV ON THE CONGO CRISIS (JULY 14-15, 1960)

15. Mr. Khrushchev's reply to the Congolese telegram of 14 July, 15 July 1960

The Soviet Government and the peoples of the Soviet Union are closely following the developments in the Republic of Congo which has become the victim of imperialist aggression. We realise the difficulty of your position and take into account the tremendous international significance of the heroic struggle of the Congolese people for the independence and integrity of the Republic of Congo.

The face of the colonialists is very familiar to the peoples: they are aware of the innumerable outrages the colonialists have committed in the Congo, as well as in other areas of Africa, of the extermination of millions of people, and of their attempts to isolate the Congo completely from the outside world. For decades they have been indulging in idle talk about a 'civilising mission' in the Congo but they strove to ensure that no Congolese person could receive a higher education or become an officer in the army. The conduct of the Belgian ruling circles cannot but call forth condemnation—they signed a treaty of friendship with the independent Republic of Congo and immediately trampled it underfoot before the eyes of the whole world, as if it were only a scrap of paper.

It is not difficult to see that those who have undertaken armed intervention against the Congo and those who have egged the Belgians on, want to deal a blow at all the African peoples and want to preserve medievalism and slavery over a large part of the African continent. The aggressors' hand raised against the independence of the Congo is at the same time threatening Nigeria, Madagascar, Mali, Togo and other African countries which have just gained their independence or are about to obtain it in the near future.

Your struggle is the struggle of millions upon millions of people in Africa, Asia and Latin America. Indo-China, Algeria, Suez, Guatemala, Lebanon and Jordan, Guinea and Cuba, and now the Congo—all these are links in the same chain of the imperialist postwar policy aimed at preventing the enslaved peoples from gaining their independence, from gaining national freedom and building a new life.

....

It is common knowledge that the old Congo was not only a Belgian colony. The bayonet was Belgian, but the masters were the big American, Belgian, British and West German monopolies. And when the Congolese people shook off the Belgian colonialist yoke, they also threw off the collective colonial yoke of imperialism in the Congo. That is why the present aggression against the Congo, carried out with the help of Belgian troops, is actually collective imperialist aggression by the powers whose big monopolies have entrenched themselves in the Congo and, above all, in her richest province—Katanga.

The Soviet Union has already raised its voice in resolute condemnation of the imperialist intervention against the Republic of Congo. It has gone on record for United Nations measures to end the aggression and completely restore the sovereign rights of the independent Republic of Congo.

In an atmosphere of growing resentment of the peoples, who are incensed by the imperialist aggression in the Congo, the United Nations Security Council has done a good deed by passing a resolution urging the Government of Belgium to withdraw Belgian troops from the territory of the Congo.

If aggression were to continue in spite of this decision, the Soviet Government declares that the necessity would arise for more effective measures both on the part of the United Nations and on the part of the peaceloving states which come out in solidarity with the cause of the Congo.

If the states that are directly involved in imperialist aggression against the Republic of Congo and those that are egging them on in this continue their criminal actions, the Soviet Union will not hesitate to take the most resolute measures to cut short the aggression.

....

The demand of the Soviet Union is simple—hands off the Republic of Congo!

Source: Richard Gott, John Major and Geoffrey Warner, (eds.), Documents on International Affairs, 1960 *(London: Royal Institute of International Affairs and Oxford University Press, 1964), pp. 279-280.*

DOCUMENT 5 U.S. SECRETARY OF STATE CHRISTIAN HERTER ON THE CONGO CRISIS (JULY 21, 1960)

18. Statement by the United States Secretary of State, Mr. Herter, 21 July 1960

I want to report briefly on the situation in the Congo as it affects our interests.

Our first concern was for the welfare and safety of the some 2,000 Americans living in this widespread area.

The breakdown of public order in the Congo shortly after independence and the appeal of that young country to the United Nations for help drew immediate response from that body. On July 13 the Security Council adopted a resolution authorizing the Secretary-General to take the necessary steps... to provide...military assistance in the Congo, until the Congolese Government can maintain order.

The United States not only voted in support of this resolution but put its logistic and communications resources at the disposal of the United Nations. At the request of the Secretary-General we have, I think, set a remarkable record in bringing aid and assistance to the Congo. Starting from scratch on July 14, the United States had as of today transported approximately 3,500 troops with 300 tons of equipment from three African countries and one European country. We have flown in 400 tons of desperately needed flour and airlifted from the United States and Europe communications and transport equipment essential to the proper functioning of the U.N. Command in the Congo. In this brief time a total of over 125 flights of transport planes provided by the United States have been made to the Congo. This support operation is continuing day and night. By the end of this week we shall have transported an additional 2,000 troops and approximately 100 tons of equipment to the U.N. Command in Leopoldville.

The United States effort, of course, is conducted entirely in response to a request of the United Nations. Our own troops are not involved in the United Nations action. You will recall that it was mutually understood that the major powers should not supply troops. The United States has abided by the letter and spirit of this understanding. However, we have been shocked by the attitude and statements of the Soviet Union regarding this matter. The representative of the U.S.S.R. voted in the United Nations Security Council for the same resolution as the United States which I quoted above. This action had hardly been completed, however, when Mr. Khrushchev was publicly assuring the leaders of the Congo that he was prepared to intervene militarily in the Congo if the United Nations action did not proceed to his satisfaction. I submit that such statements and threats, whether intended to be carried out or not, are recklessly irresponsible.

....

We must ask ourselves which policy the Soviet Union really intends to pursue. I find it hard to believe that the Soviet Union is prepared to set itself against the United Nations in the effort to restore order to the Congo which is progressing so rapidly and well.

Source: Richard Gott, John Major and Geoffrey Warner, (eds.), Documents on International Affairs, 1960 *(London: Royal Institute of International Affairs and Oxford University Press, 1964), pp. 283-284.*

DOCUMENT 6 THE MURDER OF CONGO'S LEFTIST LEADER PATRICE LUMUMBA (FEBRUARY 13, 1961)

Statement by the Minister of the Interior in Katanga on the murder of congo's leftist leader Patrice Lumumba, allegedly by a CIA-backed para-military squad.

I have called you here to announce the death of Lumumba and of his accomplices Okito and Mpolo. ...Massacred yesterday morning by the inhabitants of a small village situated quite a distance from the place where the vehicle had been discovered, so that we are still wondering how the three fugitives could have got there.

....

We flew to the spot this morning, the party consisting of a number of persons capable of identifying the three bodies, the Minister Kibwe, the Minister Kitenge and myself. We were accompanied by a doctor who was to make out a death certificate if the bodies did in fact prove to be those of Lumumba, Okito and Mpolo. They were identified beyond any possibility of doubt and their death was certified. The bodies were immediately buried in a place which we shall not reveal, if only to prevent any pilgrimages being made to it.

Nor shall we disclose the name of the village whose inhabitants put an end to the sorry exploits of Lumumba and his accomplices, for we do not want these Katangans, the name of whose tribe will not even be revealed, to be the object of possible reprisals on the part of Lumumba supporters.

Nor do we wish to be exposed to pressure to make us bring to trial for murder these Katangans who have perhaps acted somewhat precipitately, which is excusable in view of the fact that they believed the fugitives to be armed, but whom we cannot honestly blame for having rid Katanga, the Congo, Africa and the world of a problem which some persons had unduly magnified and which threatened to be a source of trouble to mankind.

...I shall tell you nothing more about the circumstances of the fugitives' death. I should be lying if I said that Lumumba's death grieves me. You know how I fell about him: he is an ordinary criminal who is responsible for thousands of deaths in Katanga and tens of thousands in Kasai, not to mention the persecutions and exterminations in Oriental province and Kivu.

....

I am of course aware that the United Nations will say that the whole thing was a plot and that we murdered them ourselves. Such an accusation is inevitable. If Lumumba had died in Katanga of sickness, old age or some other natural cause, we should still have been charged with murder, solely because the death occurred in Katanga. I am going to speak frankly and bluntly, as I usually do. We shall be accused of having murdered them. My reply is: prove it. To demonstrate our good faith, we have placed no obstacles in the way of the journalists' mission.

I also expect the friends of the communist Lumumba to raise the question of the death of the three fugitives in the United Nations Security Council. Even if we had executed them—which is categorically denied and in no way proved—I refuse in advance to recognize any right on the part of the United Nations to take a position on this question.

....

There are some who would deny us this right solely because we are black and belong to a young nation. The young nations of Africa, among others, would not understand such a flagrant disregard of the sovereignty of another African nation....

Source: D.C. Watt (ed.), Documents on International Affairs, 1961 *(London: Royal Institute of International Affairs, 1965), p. 734.*

As the pace of decolonization quickened the non-aligned movement's ranks swelled. However, the criteria for membership was often questionable. Many of the members engaged both the superpowers for economic and even military support, and few were actually "peace-loving" in the conduct of their foreign policies.

By the early 1960s the movement also become somewhat divided in its leadership and orientation. Faced with religious and ethnic divisions, tensions with Pakistan and border clashes against China, India began to drift away from strict neutralism. Its more pacifist leadership gradually lost support, especially after the death of Nehru in 1964. Similarly, domestic conflict in Indonesia undermined that country's leadership role, while others like Burma experimented with isolationism instead. Consequently the non-aligned movement came to be more and more associated with nationalistic states like Egypt and Yugoslavia. While the rhetoric remained the same, under the direction of leaders like Egypt's Gamal Abdul Nasser neutralism became a more fragmented and militant property in international relations.

DOCUMENT 7 GAMAL ABDAL NASSER TO KHRUSHCHEV (JUNE 9, 1961)

...The Arab nationalism in which we believe neither stands for narrow racialism nor for regional expansion which aims to acquire more land. It is the movement of a people who lived the same history and spoke the same language, and consequently acquired a unity of conscience and thinking. In trying to eliminate the traces of industrial discrimination which imperialism imposed, Arab nationalism is also trying to do away with all the traces and vestiges which imperialism left on its lands and among its people.

As to our belief in Arab nationalism, we do not believe that it contradicts our belief in the unity of world destiny and the imminent solidarity of peoples under the principle of peaceful coexistence. Perhaps we are more sensitive than anybody else with regard to national motives because of two things: first, our belief in the need that our future development must emanate from the potential power of our people and from its suppressed needs and demands over the long centuries of oppression and exploitation; and second, the fact that we are newly experiencing independence and we are very anxious to preserve it, sometimes to the extent of sensitivity.

For all these reasons, we refuse capitalism not only because we hate it, but also because we believe that it contradicts the nature, circumstances, hopes, needs, and requirements of our people. But this refusal does not mean that communism, whose success was proved under the conditions prevalent in other people's countries can be applied and can succeed in our country. Our people refuse to be limited to this choice and believe that the scope of world thinking is now wider than these closed circuits. Our people believe that without isolating themselves from the wealth of world thinking they can, by their skill and creative power, add new things to this wealth. In fact, in its experience with us, imperialism has always fallen into the error that capitalism and communism are the only alternatives for each other. This error always justified, in its eyes, the launching of war against our socialist co-operative ideas and the branding of these ideas as steps leading to communism. From this point, imperialism used to attack the policy of non-alignment which we pursued in the international field and which is, in fact, a true reflection of our national beliefs.

Source: D.C. Watt, (ed.), Documents on International Affairs, 1961 *(London: Royal Institute of International Affairs, 1965), pp. 602-604.*

DOCUMENT 8 THE CONFERENCE OF NON-ALIGNED COUNTRIES AT BELGRADE (SEPTEMBER 1961)

We call ourselves a conference of non-aligned countries. Now, the word non-aligned may be differently interpreted but basically it was used, and coined almost, with the meaning non-aligned with the great Power blocs of the world. Non-aligned has a negative meaning, but if you give it a positive connotation it means nations which object to this lining-up for war purposes—military blocs, military alliances and the like. Therefore we keep away from this and we want to throw our weight, such as it is, in favour of peace.

....

I therefore submit that we must look at things in the proper perspective today. First things must come first, and nothing is more important or has more priority than this world situation of war and peace. Everything else, however vital to us—and other things are vital to us—has secondary place. If, in this crisis, something we do, some action of ours or some words of ours, helps to some extent to resolve the problem, to remove the fear of war, then we have justified ourselves and strengthened ourselves in order to meet all the other problems that face us. On the other hand, if we cannot face this matter straight forwardly and clearly in our own minds then somehow we fail mankind in this crisis, we give no lead. Of course we stand for anti-colonialism, anti-imperialism, anti-racialism, and all that.

....

It has become a commonplace for people in every country to refer to the dangers of modern nuclear warfare. Although we talk about it, I am not so sure that even those who talk about it fully and emotionally realize what this means. We talk about the destruction of civilization, the destruction of humanity, the destruction of the human race, if nuclear war comes. ...This should be put foremost and topmost, and perhaps be isolated to show that it is the main thing, that other things may be very important but they are secondary. If this is done it will undoubtedly create a far greater impression than would a mere record of the various other problems that face us, although they are very important problems.

....

Many of the countries represented here have only recently become free or independent. They have tremendous problems and, above all, the problem of making good and to advance their own people, economically, socially, etc., because we must recognize that most of these countries are under-developed—nearly all. We must recognize that they are socially and economically backward countries, and it is not an easy matter to get rid of this inheritance of backwardness and under-development. It requires clear thinking. It requires action. It requires a tremendous amount of hard work, and all of us have to face that. I think that it is right and proper that other countries, the affluent countries, the rich countries, should help in this process. They should do it. They have to some extent done it. I think they should do more of it, but whatever they may do the ultimate burden will lie on the people of our own countries. If it did not, if by some miracle or somebody else's help we stood up, well we would fall down again. When you stand up, you do not stand long when you do not have the strength. The ultimate burden is on us. So it is no good expecting others to do all of our work.

....

We must not imagine that we can order about great countries or as small countries do as we like. Our capacity is limited, but we have a certain capacity, a certain strength, call it what you like, moral strength, or other strength. Let us use it properly, rightly, without force but with courtesy and with a friendly approach so that we may influence those who have the power of war and peace in their hands, and thus try if not to prevent war for all time at any rate to push it away so that in the meantime the world may learn the better use of co-operation. Then ultimately the world may put an end to war itself.

Source: D.C. Watt, (ed.), Documents on International Affairs, 1961 *(London: Royal Institute of International Affairs, 1965), pp. 613-614, 619, 621.*

By 1960, twenty-five new nations in Africa alone were represented at the United Nations. Decolonization occurred throughout the 1960s at a furious pace, and with frequently violent consequences. Ethnic and tribal rivalries combined with competition between the superpowers to produce civil and even regional conflict. However there were attempts to establish the basis for African unity. Kwame Nkrumah of Ghana was the charismatic leader of "Pan-Africanism". He believed once African states ended their infighting that economic and political development would follow. Once this was achieved, Africa's international position would be greatly enhanced. The Organization of African Unity (OAU) was an important step in this direction, but it also illustrated the dissatisfaction of some African states with the non-aligned movement.

DOCUMENT 9 RESOLUTIONS OF THE UNITED NATIONS GENERAL ASSEMBLY ON DECOLONIZATION IN AFRICA (DECEMBER 1960)

The General Assembly,

Mindful of the determination proclaimed by the peoples of the world in the Charter of the United Nations to reaffirm faith in fundamental human rights, in the dignity and worth of the human person, in the equal rights of men and women and of nations large and small and to promote social progress and better standards of life in larger freedom,

Conscious of the need for the creation of conditions of stability and well-being and peaceful and friendly relations based on respect for the principles of equal rights and self-determination of all peoples, and of universal respect for, and observance of, human rights and fundamental freedom for all without distinction as to race, sex, language or religion,

Recognizing the passionate yearning for freedom in all dependent peoples and the decisive role of such peoples in the attainment of their independence,

Aware of the increasing conflicts resulting from the denial of or impediments in the way of the freedom of such peoples, which constitute a serious threat to world peace,

Considering the important role of the United Nations in assisting the movement for independence in Trust and Non-Self-Governing Territories,

Recognizing that the peoples of the world ardently desire the end of colonialism in all its manifestations,

Convinced that the continued existence of colonialism prevents the development of international economic co-operation, impedes the social, cultural and economic development of dependent peoples and militaries against the United Nations ideal of universal peace,

Affirming that peoples may, for their own ends, freely dispose of their natural wealth and resources without prejudice to any obligations arising out of international economic co-operation, based upon the principle of mutual benefit, and international law,

Believing that the process of liberation is irresistible and that, in order to avoid serious crises, an end must be put to colonialism and all practices of segregation and discrimination associated therewith,

Welcoming the emergence in recent years of a large number of dependent territories into freedom and independence, and recognizing the increasingly powerful trends towards freedom in such territories which have not yet attained independence,

Convinced that all peoples have an inalienable right to complete freedom, the exercise of their sovereignty and the integrity of their national territory, *Solemnly proclaims* the necessity of bringing to a speedy and unconditional end colonialism in all its forms and manifestations;

And to this end

Declares that:

1. The subjection of peoples to alien subjugation, domination and exploitation constitutes a denial of fundamental human rights, is contrary to the Charter of the United Nations and is an impediment to the promotion of world peace and co-operation.

2. All peoples have the right to self-determination; by virtue of that right they freely determine their political status and freely pursue their economic, social and cultural development.

3. Inadequacy of political, economic, social or educational preparedness should never serve as a pretext for delaying independence.

4. All armed action or repressive measures of all kinds directed against dependent peoples shall cease in order to enable them to exercise peacefully and freely their right to complete independence, and the integrity of their national territory shall be respected.

5. Immediate steps shall be taken, in Trust and Non-Self-Governing Territories or all other territories which have not yet attained independence, to transfer all powers to the peoples of those territories, without any conditions or reservations, in accordance with their freely expressed will and desire, without any distinction as to race, creed or colour, in order to enable them to enjoy complete independence and freedom.

6. Any attempt aimed at the partial or total disruption of the national unity and the territorial integrity of a country is incompatible with the purposes and principles of the Charter of the United Nations.

7. All States shall observe faithfully and strictly the provisions of the Charter of the United Nations, the Universal Declaration of Human Rights and the present Declaration on the basis of equality, non-interference in the internal affairs of all States, and respect for the sovereign rights of all peoples and their territorial integrity.

Source: Ian Brownlie, Basic Documents on African Affairs *(London: Oxford University Press, 1971), pp. 366-368.*

DOCUMENT 10

CHARTER OF THE ORGANIZATION OF AFRICAN UNITY (OAU) (MAY 25, 1963)

Convinced that it is the inalienable right of all people to control their own destiny;

Conscious of the fact that freedom, equality, justice and dignity are essential objectives for the achievement of the legitimate aspirations of the African peoples;

Conscious of our responsibility to harness the natural and human resources of our continent for the total advancement of our peoples in spheres of human endeavour;

Inspired by a common determination to promote understanding among our peoples and cooperation among our States in response to the aspirations of our peoples for brotherhood and solidarity, in a larger unity transcending ethnic and national differences;

Convinced that, in order to translate this determination into a dynamic force in the cause of human progress, conditions for peace and security must be established and maintained;

Determined to safeguard and consolidate the hard-won independence as well as the sovereignty and territorial integrity of our States, and to resist neocolonialism in all its forms;

Dedicated to the general progress of Africa;

Persuaded that the Charter of the United Nations and the Universal Declaration of Human Rights, to the principles of which we reaffirm our adherence, provide a solid foundation for peaceful and positive cooperation among States;

Desirous that all African States should henceforth unite so that the welfare and well-being of their peoples can be assured;

Resolved to reinforce the links between our States by establishing and strengthening common institutions;

Have agreed to the present Charter.

ESTABLISHMENT

Article I. 1. The High Contracting Parties do by the present Charter establish an Organization to be known as the *'Organization of African Unity'.*

2. The Organization shall include the Continental African States, Madagascar and other Islands surrounding Africa.

PURPOSES

Article II. 1. The Organization shall have the following purposes:

(a) To promote the unity and solidarity of the African States;

(b) To coordinate and intensify their collaboration and efforts to achieve a better life for the peoples of Africa;

(c) To defend their sovereignty, their territorial integrity and independence;

(d) To eradicate all forms of colonialism from Africa; and

(e) To promote international cooperation, having due regard to the Charter of the United Nations and the Universal Declaration of Human Rights.

2. To these ends, the Member States shall coordinate and harmonize their general policies, especially in the following fields:

(a) Political and diplomatic cooperation;

(b) Economic cooperation, including transport and communications;

(c) Educational and cultural cooperation;

(d) Health, sanitation, and nutritional cooperation;

(e) Scientific and technical cooperation; and

(f) Cooperation for defence and security.

PRINCIPLES

Article III. The Member States, in pursuit of the purposes stated in Article II, solemnly affirm and declare their adherence to the following principles:

1. The sovereign equality of all Member States;

2. Non-interference in the internal affairs of States;

3. Respect for the sovereignty and territorial integrity of each State and for its inalienable right to independent existence;

4. Peaceful settlement of disputes by negotiation, mediation, conciliation or arbitration;

5. Unreserved condemnation, in all its forms, of political assassination as well as of subversive activities on the part of neighboring States or any other States;

6. Absolute dedication to the total emancipation of the African territories which are still dependent;

7. Affirmation of a policy of non-alignment with regard to all blocs.

Source: J.A.S. Grenville, The Major International Treaties 1914-1973 *(London: Meuthen and Co. Ltd., 1974), pp. 484-485.*

One of the most important issues in African decolonization was the persistence of racial discrimination among non-African states. But the problem also extended to the continent itself, as some countries remained dominated by a minority population of white colonists. The most striking example of this was South Africa, where the policy of apartheid maintained a strict division between the races in almost every sense. How to deal with South Africa was a major problem for independent black African states. Many needed the trade that the more developed South African economy provided, while others were too focused on their own domestic problems to worry about racial discrimination elsewhere. South Africa played a major role in the economic, political and military balance of power in the southern half of the continent throughout the Cold War, and it continues to do so today with the tremendous recent changes that have ended apartheid. The process of combating racial discrimination in Africa was long and bloody, and in many respects is still going on today.

DOCUMENT 11 OAU RESOLUTION ON RACIAL DISCRIMINATION IN AFRICA (May 1964)

Noting with grave concern the consistent refusal of the South African Government to give consideration to appeals made by every sector of world opinion and their non-compliance with the resolutions of the United Nations Security Council and the General Assembly;

Noting further that the attitude of certain states towards the Government of South Africa and their continued close relations with that Government only encourages it to persist in its policies of apartheid and its contempt for the United Nations;

Convinced of the desirability of stepping up as a matter of urgency the action of the African States in regard to the application of sanctions against the South African Government;

Expressing its deep concern for the trials conducted according to the arbitrary and inhuman laws of the Government of South Africa against the opponents of policies of apartheid and for the recent convictions and sentences passed on African nationalists, particularly Nelson Mandela and Walter Sisulu;

I. Calls for the release of Nelson Mandela, Walter Sisulu, Mangalisso Sobukue and all other Nationalists imprisoned or detained under the arbitrary laws of South Africa;

....

3. Appeals to all oil producing countries to cease, as a matter of urgency, their supply of oil and petroleum products to South Africa;

4. Calls on all African States to implement forthwith the decision taken in Addis Ababa in May 1963 to boycott South African goods and to cease the supply of mineral and other raw materials and the importation of South African goods;

5. Requests the co-operation of all countries and in particular that of the Major Trading Partners in the boycott of South Africa;

6. Establishes a body within the OAU General Secretariat, entrusted, among others, with the following functions:

(a) to plan co-ordination among the Member States and to ensure the strictest implementation of the resolutions of the Organization of African Unity;

(b) to harmonize co-operation with friendly States with a view to implementing an effective boycott of South Africa;

(c) to collect and disseminate information about States, foreign financial, economic and commercial institutions which trade with the Government of South Africa;

(d) to promote, in co-operation with other international bodies, the campaign for international economic sanctions against South Africa by all appropriate means, in particular countering the propaganda and pressures of the South African Government.

Source: Ian Brownlie, Basic Documents on African Affairs *(London: Oxford University Press, 1971), pp. 372-373.*

DOCUMENT 12 THE FREEDOM CHARTER OF THE AFRICAN NATIONAL CONGRESS (July 1969)

The ANC rejected the claims of the European settlers to domination, and fought against all attempts to subjugate them in the land of their birth. But in the face of the gravest injustices the ANC never once abandoned the principle that all those who had their home in the country of the Africans, were welcome, provided only that they accepted full and consistent equality and freedom for all. In this the ANC was not merely bowing to history and reality but believed that it was correct in principle to make this position clear. Over and over again in the face of manifest inhumanity the ANC absolutely refused to be provoked into abandoning its democratic principles.

The ruling white minority rejected the concepts of the ANC and to that extent the movement and the people fought and will fight them.

....

The Charter was not the statement of this or that section of the population. It was a declaration of all the people of South Africa. It was a simple, honest, unpretentious document reflecting the desires and ideas of millions of common people. Therein lay the power of its revolutionary message. And always it should be borne in mind that both in its wording and intent the Charter projected the view not of present-day South Africa but that of the country as it should and will be after the victory of the revolution.

....

In South Africa not only does the system at present enforce discrimination against individuals by reason of their colour or race but in addition some national groups are privileged, as such, over others. At the moment the Afrikaner national group is lording it over the rest of the population with the English group playing second-fiddle to them. For all the non-White groups—the Africans, Indians and the Coloureds the situation is one of humiliation and oppression. As far as languages are concerned only Afrikaans and English have official status in the bodies of state such as Parliament or Provincial Councils; in the courts, schools and in the administration. The culture of the African, Indian and Coloured people is barely tolerated. In fact everything is done to smash and obliterate the genuine cultural heritage of our people. If there is reference to culture by the oppressors it is for the purpose of using it as an instrument to maintain our people in backwardness and ignorance.

Day in and day out White politicians and publicists are regaling the world with their theories of national, colour and racial discrimination and contempt for our people. Enshrined in the laws of South Africa are a host of insulting provisions directed at the dignity and humanity of the oppressed people.

A Democratic government of the people shall ensure that all national groups have equal rights, as such, to achieve their destiny in a united South Africa.

There shall be equal status in the bodies of state, in the courts and in the schools for the African, Indian, Coloured and Whites as far as their national rights are concerned. All people shall have equal right to use their own languages, and to develop their own folk culture and customs; all national groups shall be protected by laws against insults to their race or national pride; the preaching and practice of national, racial or colour discrimination and contempt shall be a punishable crime; and all laws and practices based on *apartheid* or racial discrimination shall be set aside.

....

The courts of South Africa are manned by White officials, magistrates, judges. As a result the courts serve as instruments of oppression. The democratic state shall create courts representative of all the people.

South Africa has the highest proportion of prisoners of any state in the world. This is because there are so many petty infringements to which a penalty of imprisonment is attached. In a new South Africa, imprisonment shall only be for serious crimes against the people, and shall aim at re-education, not vengeance.

It has been a standing policy of White governments in South Africa to prevent Africans and other non-Whites from holding responsible positions in the police force. The present police force and army are instruments of coercion to protect White supremacy. Their whole aim is punitive and terroristic against the majority of the population.

....

On the wake of the victorious revolution a Democratic People's Republic shall be proclaimed in South Africa. This shall be a fully independent state which respects the rights and sovereignty of nations.

South Africa shall strive to maintain world peace and the settlement of international disputes by negotiation—not war.

Peace and friendship amongst all people shall be secured by upholding the equal rights, opportunities and status of all.

....

Democratic South Africa shall take its place as a member of the OAU and work to strengthen Pan-African unity in all fields. Our country will actively support national liberation movements of the peoples of the world against imperialism, colonialism and neo-colonialism.

....

The revolutionary struggle is in its infancy. It will be a long hard road. To accomplish the glorious task of the revolution maximum unity among all national groups and revolutionary forces must be created and maintained. All South African patriots whatever their race must take their place in the revolution under the banner of the African National Congress. Forward to revolution and the victory of the people's programme of liberation!

Source: Ian Brownlie, Basic Documents on African Affairs *(London: Oxford University Press, 1971), pp. 437-447.*

Despite the appeal of both non-alignment and regional solidarity, the developing world witnessed even more conflict in the 1970s and 1980s. Heightened competition between the superpowers for control of strategic resources and potential military bases fed the internal struggles of many countries brought on by decolonization. Communist victories and the U.S. withdrawal from Indochina appeared to be a definite success for the Soviet Union and China, but in Africa it was a different story. Although several African states proclaimed themselves Marxist and communist movements continued, by the late 1970s it was apparent that the Soviet Union had failed to gain a solid foothold on the continent. The need for economic development appeared to win out over ideological conviction, and in this regard the United States and western world were much more appealing to many Africans. However, this did not mean that the "proxy wars" were over. Nor did it mean that the suffering of African people was alleviated. International indifference, ethnic strife, economic underdevelopment and natural calamities all continue to plague the continent. On the whole Africa produces less food per capita today than it did twenty years ago, while its population has nearly tripled in the past half-century. The Cold War may be over, but the process of decolonization and the struggle for development are ongoing.

DOCUMENT 13 THE ANGOLA CRISIS

Excerpts from a speech on the Angola crisis and Soviet intentions, by William E. Schaufele Jr., Assistant Secretary of State for African Affairs (February 6, 1976)

We are told that we are overreacting—that the Africans will never be Communists and we should not worry about what the Soviets are doing. This argument misses the whole point of Moscow's strategy in less developed areas like Africa. When the Soviets speak about changing the "correlation of forces" in the world, they are talking about extending their influences in countries where it has not been strong before and, conversely, neutralizing Western influence in countries where it was previously dominant. It is true that Moscow claims to see this as a long, slow process growing out of internal social and other conflicts. It also believes, however, that Communist countries have a certain role to play as "midwives of progress" assisting leftist forces in each country.

....

Angola is an illustration of how the U.S.S.R. now feels it can behave in one of these conflict situations in Africa. The issue here is not merely one of principle: real democracy versus totalitarianism, something which used to concern American liberals. But it is also a basic question of how social change is to come about in the developing world. We and the Soviets can both agree that many changes are needed, and we also thought we had agreed to use mutual restraint and avoid trying to take unilateral advantage of each other in future conflict situations; but certainly the sending of a 12,000-man Cuban army to Angola to promote "progressive" social change is a curious form of restraint.

....

Some say that African nationalism will take care of the Russians and the Cubans and cite countries where excessive Soviet influence has been eliminated.

But there is no precedent in Africa for a government of a newly independent African state which owes its very existence to the Soviet Union. Certainly the fact that the Soviet Union was permitted to mount such a massive intervention from neighboring Congo (Brazzaville) would not indicate that its influence has seriously diminished in the 10 years it has had a privileged position there.

Certainly the fact that there are some 3,300 Soviet military and civilian advisers in certain African states would not indicate that this influence is diminishing. Certainly the fact that Soviet military assistance deliveries had been three times their delivery of economic assistance is a clear indication of what they really seek in Africa.

....

Only now are many Americans and Africans beginning to see the implications of the presence of 12,000 Cubans in Angola. When the Cuban Deputy Prime Minister announced during the OAU summit meeting that Cuba would continue to send its troops to Angola as long as Neto wanted them, the Daily Mail of Lusaka exploded at this arrogant insistence that Cuba "would continue to send troops to Angola to kill Africans whether the OAU liked it or not."

Source: Elaine P. Adam, (ed), American Foreign Relations 1976: A Documentary Record *(New York: Council on Foreign Relations and New York University Press, 1979), pp. 280-282.*

DOCUMENT 14 U.S. POLICY IN SOUTHERN AFRICA IN THE 1970S

Excerpts from speeches on U.S. policy in southern Africa by Secretary of State Henry Kissinger in Lusaka, Zambia (April 22, 1976) and Washington (May 13, 1976).

I have come to Africa because in so many ways the challenges of Africa are the challenges of the modern era. Morally and politically, the drama of national independence in Africa over the last generation has transformed international affairs. More than any other region of the world, Africa symbolizes that the previous era of world affairs, the colonial era, is a thing of the past. The great tasks you face—in national building, in keeping the peace and integrity of this continent, in economic development, in gaining an equitable role in world councils, in achieving racial justice—these reflect the challenges of building a humane and progressive world order.

I have come to Africa with an open mind and an open heart to demonstrate my country's desire to work with you on these great tasks. My journey is intended to give fresh impetus to our cooperation and to usher in a new era in American policy.

The United States was one of the prime movers of the process of decolonization. The American people welcomed the new nations into the world community and for two decades have given aid and encouragement to economic and social progress in Africa. And America's responsibilities as a global power give us a strong interest today in the independence, peace, and well-being of this vast continent comprising a fifth of the world's land surface. For without peace, racial justice, and growing prosperity in Africa, we cannot speak of a just international order.

There is nothing to be gained in a debate about whether in the past American has neglected Africa or been insufficiently committed to African goals. The United States has many responsibilities in the world. Given the burden it has carried in the postwar period, it could not do everything simultaneously. African nations, too, have their own priorities and concerns, which have not always accorded with our own. No good can come of mutual recrimination. Our differing perspectives converge in a common purpose to build a secure and just future for Africa. In active collaboration there is much we can do; in contention or apart we will miss great opportunities. President Ford and the American Government and people are prepared to work with you with energy and good will if met in the same spirit.

So it is time to put aside slogans and to seek practical solutions. It is time to find our common ground and act boldly for common ends.

Africa is a continent of hope, a modern frontier. The United States from the beginning has been a country of the frontier, built by men and women of hope. The American people know from their history and meaning of the struggle for independence, for racial equality, for economic progress, for human dignity.

I am not here to give American prescriptions for Africa's problems. Your program must be African. The basic decisions and goals must be African. But we are prepared to help.

Nor am I here to set African against African, either among your governments or among factions of liberation movements. African problems cannot be solved, and your destiny cannot be fulfilled, except by a united Africa.

America supports African unity. We urge all other countries to do the same.

Here in Africa the range of mankind's challenges and potential can be seen in all its complexity and enormous promise.

The massive power and grandeur of nature is before us in all its aspects—as the harsh master and as a bountiful servant of mankind.

Here we can feel the rich and living cultures which have changed and invigorated art, music, and thought around the world.

And here on this continent we are tested, all of us, to see whether our future will be determined for us or by us, whether humanity will be the victim or the architect of its destiny.

....

A sound relationship between America and Africa is crucial to an international structure of relations that promotes peace, widening prosperity, and human dignity. When I began my African trip, war had already begun in the south of the continent, risking possible great-power conflict. Africa's hopes for steady economic development were being distorted by increasingly radical forces, and the course of peaceful social change threatened to degenerate into widespread bloodshed.

....

Africa is of immense size, strategically located, with governments of substantial significance in numbers and growing influence in the councils of the world. The interdependence of America and our allies with Africa is increasingly obvious. Africa is a continent of vast resources.

....

Thus, an independent and prospering Africa is of considerable consequence to the security, political, and economic interests of all the great industrial democracies.

For her part, Africa recognizes full well the crucial importance of our markets and investments to her own prosperity. And politically, the emphasis which African leaders placed in conversations with me on the need and importance of American action and support is proof that our assets and our moral influence are recognized and valued on the continent.

We are, in addition, bound by a moral dimension—the cultural heritage of 23 million Americans and the moral sympathy of over 200 million Americans who understand the motivations of peoples who would establish their freedom and prosperity against great odds.

....

—Never before in history has so revolutionary a change occurred with such rapidity as Africa's transition from colonialism to independence. Many African states are but a decade or so old.

—Moreover, a continent of nearly 50 nations cannot easily, if at all, be encompassed by a single, coherent policy. Africa's drive for unity is a reality; yet Africa's great diversity makes clear-cut general formulations difficult to achieve and apply.

—If Africa is not to become a grave source of great-power conflict and of international tensions, Africa's problems must be for Africans to solve. They must not be permitted to become the subject of great-power rivalry and confrontation. Their ultimate resolution lies in the processes of Africa's own internal political and social evolution.

Source: Elaine P. Adams (ed.), American Foreign Relations 1976: A Documentary Record *(New York: Council on Foreign Relations and New York University Press, 1979), pp. 283-285, 294-296.*

DOCUMENT 15

EXCERPTS FROM A SPEECH BY PRESIDENT JIMMY CARTER IN LAGOS, NIGERIA (APRIL 1, 1968)

We share with you a commitment to majority rule and individual human rights. In order to meet the basic needs of the people, we share with you a commitment to economic growth and to human development. We share with you a commitment to an Africa that is at peace, free from colonialism, free from racism, free from military interference by outside nations, and free from the inevitable conflicts that can come when the integrity of national boundaries are not respected. We share these things with you as well.

....

Our concern for human rights extends throughout this continent and throughout the world. Whatever the ideology or the power or the race of a government that abuses the rights of its people, we oppose those abuses.

We in America welcome the real progress in human rights that is being made in many countries, in Africa as well as in other regions.

....

Each country must, of course, adapt the instruments of democracy to fit its own particular needs, a process now being completed by your constituent assembly. The basic elements are participation by individuals in the decisions that affect their lives, respect for civil liberties through the rule of law, and thus, protection of the dignity of all men and women.

Wherever these fundamental principles exist, a government can accommodate to necessary change without breaking, and its people can demand such change without being broken.

These principles are necessary for democracy, and they sustain development as well. For in a democracy, the people themselves can best ensure that their government will promote their economic rights, as well as their political and civil liberties.

....

Africans themselves can best find peaceful answers to African disputes through the Organization of African Unity and, when needed, with the help of the United Nations.

....

I know something about social change. In my own lifetime, I've seen the region of my birth, the southern part of the United States, changed from a place of poverty and despair and racial division to a land of bright promise and opportunity and increasing racial harmony.

I've seen the towering wall between the races taken down, piece by piece, until the whites and the blacks of my country could reach across it to each other.

I know that our own society is different from any other, and I know that we still have much to do in the United States. But nothing can shake my faith that in every part of the world, peaceful change can come and bless the lives of human beings. Nothing can make me doubt that this continent will win its struggle for freedom—freedom from racism and the denial of human rights, freedom from want and suffering, and freedom from the destruction of war and foreign intervention.

....

We know that Africans can always take the lead in shaping the destiny of your own people. And we know that this continent will enjoy the liberation that can come to those who put racial division and injustice behind them.

I believe that this day is coming for Africa. And on that day, blacks and whites alike will be able to say, in the words of a great man from my own State, Dr. Martin Luther King, Jr., "Free at last, free at last, great God Almighty, we are free at last."

Source: Elaine P. Adam (ed.), American Foreign Relations 1976: A Documentary Record *(New York: Council on Foreign Relations and New York University Press, 1979), pp. 308-314 .*

STUDY QUESTIONS FOR SECTION TEN: DECOLONIZATION AND NONALIGNMENT

1. What impact did decolonization have on international relations?

2. Explain the origins and meaning of the policy of non-alignment.

3. Who were the key figures in the nonaligned movement? What were their motives for supporting it?

4. What are wars of national liberation and why did the Soviet Union support them?

5. Is there any truth in the opinion held by many in the West that the non-aligned movement tilted towards the Soviet Union?

SECTION ELEVEN

LATIN AMERICA IN INTERNATIONAL RELATIONS, 1900-1990

DOCUMENTS

CHRONOLOGY

1890	first meeting of the Pan-American Union regional political forum
1898	Spanish-American War
1901	Platt Amendment; Hay-Pauncefort Treaty ending British claims in the region
1903	Roosevelt Corollary; U.S. troops stationed in Panama (to 1914)
1904	Panama Canal Treaty authorizes the U.S. to construct and defend the canal
1906	U.S. troops intervene in the Dominican Republic and Cuba (to 1909)
1907	U.S. troops intervene in Honduras
1910	U.S. troops intervene in Nicaragua; Mexican Revolution (1910-11)
1911	U.S. troops intervene in Honduras
1912	U.S. troops intervene in Nicaragua (to 1925)
1914	U.S. troops intervene in Haiti, the Dominican Republic and Mexico (to 1917)
1915	U.S. troops intervene in Haiti (to 1934)
1916	U.S. troops intervene in the Dominican Republic (to 1924)
1917	U.S. troops intervene in Cuba (to 1933)
1918	U.S. troops intervene in Mexico (to 1919)
1919-20	U.S. troops intervene in Honduras and Guatemala
1925	U.S. troops intervene in Honduras and Panama
1926	U.S. troops intervene in Nicaragua (to 1933)
1933	FDR's "Good Neighbour" policy; U.S. troops out of Cuba and Nicaragua
1934	abrogation of the Platt Amendment; U.S. troops out of Haiti

1947	Rio Treaty establishing a permanent regional defensive alliance
1948	the Organization of American States (OAS) formed (replaces Pan-American Union)
1954	CIA-backed right-wing coup in Guatemala, bringing military dictatorship to power
1958	anti-American demonstrators attack Vice-President Richard Nixon in Caracas
1958-59	Cuban Revolution and civil war, bringing Fidel Castro to power
1960	Castro nationalizes American financial holdings; U.S. embargo on Cuba
1961	break in Cuba-U.S. diplomatic relations; Kennedy's "Alliance for Progress" policy; Bay of Pigs invasion; assassination of Trujillo in the Dominican Republic
1962	Cuban Missile Crisis
1964	CIA-backed military coup in Brazil
1965	U.S. troops intervene in the Dominican Republic (remaining to 1966)
1967	Marxist guerilla leader Ernesto (Che) Guevara killed in Bolivia
1970	Salvador Allende elected in Chile; he nationalizes U.S. financial interests
1973	CIA-backed military coup and assassination of Allende
1977	Carter signs treaty with Panama ending American canal jurisdiction
1979	Marxist "Sandinista" revolution in Nicaragua; reformist coup in El Salvador
1981	Reagan orders CIA aid to "Contra" rebels in Nicaragua and military in El Salvador
1982	Falkland Islands War between Argentina and Great Britain
1983	U.S. troops intervene in Grenada coup to put down "pro-Castro" forces
1994	U.S. troops intervene in Haiti after several years of turmoil

Many states in Latin America and the Caribbean earned their independence in the early 19th century as Spanish and Portuguese authority collapsed. With common religious, linguistic and cultural bonds, prospects for the political integration of the region were good. Moreover, considerable resource wealth and fertile agricultural land gave the new republics the essential ingredients needed to maintain autonomous economic development. Instead, political divisions and a lack of economic coordination left many of the states backward, and produced an enormous power vacuum in the western hemisphere. Contrary to popular belief, the United States did not immediately fill this void. In fact, in the early 19th century the United States was itself only a young and struggling republic. British and French influence in the Caribbean and South America remained strong, and focused on its own political and economic consolidation, the U.S. was really in no position to test its strength elsewhere in the Americas. Despite such limitations, the expansionist impulse was very much alive among many Americans who viewed the re-establishment of European colonialism in the hemisphere as a threat to the U.S. In 1823, President James Monroe issued what amounted to a rather presumptuous warning to the European powers to stay out of the Americans' "backyard". Although the U.S. initially lacked the military power and political influence to back-up the rhetoric, the Monroe Doctrine was a crucial component of American foreign policy perception well into the 20th century.

DOCUMENT 1 EXTRACTS FROM PRESIDENT MONROE'S SEVENTH ANNUAL MESSAGE TO CONGRESS (DECEMBER 2, 1823)

In the discussions to which this interest has given rise and in the arrangements by which they may terminate the occasion has been judged proper for asserting, as a principle in which the rights and interests of the United States are involved, that the American continents, by the free and independent condition which they have assumed and maintain, are henceforth not to be considered as subjects for future colonization by any European powers....

It was stated at the commencement of the last session that a great effort was then making in Spain and Portugal to improve the condition of the people of those countries, and that it appeared to be conducted with extraordinary moderation. It need scarcely be remarked that the result has been so far very different from what was then anticipated. Of events in that quarter of the globe, with which we have so much intercourse and from which we derive our origin, we have always been anxious and interested spectators. The citizens of the United States cherish sentiments the most friendly in favor of the liberty and happiness of their fellow-men on that side of the Atlantic. In the wars of the European powers in matters relating to themselves we have never taken any part, nor does it comport with our policy so to do. It is only when our rights are invaded or seriously menaced that we resent injuries or make preparation for our defense. With the movements in this hemisphere we are of necessity more immediately connected, and by causes which must be obvious to all enlightened and impartial observers. The political system of the allied powers is essentially different in this respect from that of America. This difference proceeds from that which exists in their respective Governments; and to the defense of our own, which has been achieved by the loss of so much blood and treasure, and matured by the wisdom of their most enlightened citizens, and under which we have enjoyed unexampled felicity, this whole nation is devoted. We owe it, therefore, to candor and to the amicable relations existing between the United States and those powers to declare that we should consider any attempt on their part to extend their system to any portion of this hemisphere as dangerous to our peace and safety. With the existing colonies or dependencies of any European power we have not interfered and shall not interfere. But with the Governments who have declared their independence and maintained it, and whose independence we have, on great consideration and on just principles, acknowledged, we could not view any interposition for the purpose of oppressing them, or controlling in any other manner their destiny, by any European power in any other light than as the manifestation of an unfriendly disposition toward the United States.

....

Our policy in regard to Europe, which was adopted at an early stage of the wars which have so long agitated that quarter of the globe, nevertheless remains the same, which is, not to interfere in the internal concerns of any of its powers; to consider the government *de facto* as the legitimate government for us; to cultivate friendly relations with it, and to preserve those relations by a frank, firm, and manly policy, meeting in all instances the just claims of every power, submitting to injuries from none. But in regard to those continents circumstances are eminently and conspicuously different. It is impossible that the allied powers should extend their political system to any portion of either continent without endangering our peace and happiness; nor can anyone believe that our southern brethren, if left to themselves, would adopt it of their own accord. It is equally impossible, therefore, that we should behold such interposition in any form with indifference.

....

It is still the true policy of the United States to leave the parties to themselves, in the hope that other powers will pursue the same course....

Source: Henry Steele Commager, (ed.), Documents of American History (8th edition) *(New York: Appleton-Century-Crofts, 1968), pp. 235-237.*

After the American Civil War and the era of westward expansion, political stability and a national consensus developed in the U.S. This in turn facilitated tremendous economic growth and, as some historians contend, the inevitable pressure to seek out new resources and markets. By the end of the 19th century the United States was fast becoming one of the world's predominant economic and military powers, so much so that the ideals enshrined in the Monroe Doctrine were no longer simply bravado. Confronted with challenges elsewhere in its empire and the threat of German military expansion, Great Britain gradually acquiesced to the U.S. and began to withdraw from South America and the Caribbean. France too turned its attentions to other matters, but the remnants of Spanish influence in the region remained an affront to the U.S. Many Americans believed in a hemispheric solidarity between "sister republics", and Spanish colonialism, particularly in Cuba, represented the antithesis of "liberty" in the Americas. The U.S. fought and won a war with the declining Spanish empire in 1898, and as a result Americans found themselves the undisputed hegemon in the western hemisphere. The question was whether the U.S. would become simply another "imperialist" power.

DOCUMENT 2 THE PLATT AMENDMENT (TREATY WITH CUBA) (MAY 22, 1903)

ART. I. The Government of Cuba shall never enter into any treaty or other compact with any foreign power or powers which will impair or tend to impair the independence of Cuba, nor in any manner authorize or permit any foreign power or powers to obtain by colonization or for military or naval purposes, or otherwise, lodgement in or control over any portion of said island.

....

ART. III. The Government of Cuba consents that the United States may exercise the right to intervene for the preservation of Cuban independence, the maintenance of a government adequate for the protection of life, property, and individual liberty, and for discharging the obligations with respect to Cuba imposed by the treaty of Paris on the United States, now to be assumed and undertaken by the government of Cuba.

ART. IV. All Acts of the United States in Cuba during its military occupance thereof are ratified and validated, and all lawful rights acquired thereunder shall be maintained and protected.

....

ART. VII. To enable the United States to maintain the independence of Cuba, and to protect the people thereof, as well as for its own defense, the government of Cuba will sell or lease to the United States lands necessary for coaling or naval stations at certain specified points to be agreed upon with the President of the United States....

Source: Henry Steele Commager, (ed.), Documents of American History (8th edition) *(New York: Appleton-Century-Crofts, 1968), p. 29.*

DOCUMENT 3

THE ROOSEVELT COROLLARY TO THE MONROE DOCTRINE 1904-5

... It is not true that the United States feels any land hunger or entertains any projects as regards the other nations of the Western Hemisphere save such as are for their welfare. All that this country desires is to see the neighboring countries stable, orderly, and prosperous. Any country whose people conduct themselves well can count upon our hearty friendship. If a nation shows that it knows how to act with reasonable efficiency and decency in social and political matters, if it keeps order and pays its obligations, it need fear no interference from the United States. Chronic wrongdoing, or an impotence which results in a general loosening of the ties of civilized society, may in America, as elsewhere, ultimately require intervention by some civilized nation, and in the Western Hemisphere the adherence of the United States to the Monroe Doctrine may force the United States, however reluctantly, in flagrant cases of such wrongdoing or impotence, to the exercise of an international police power.

....

Our interests and those of our southern neighbors are in reality identical. They have great natural riches, and if within their borders the reign of law and justice obtains, prosperity is sure to come to them. While they thus obey the primary laws of civilized society they may rest assured that they will be treated by us in a spirit of cordial and helpful sympathy. We would interfere with them only in the last resort, and then only if it became evident that their inability or unwillingness to do justice at home and abroad had violated the rights of the United States or had invited foreign aggression to the detriment of the entire body of American nations. It is a mere truism to say that every nation, whether in America or anywhere else, which desires to maintain its freedom, its independence, must ultimately realize that the right of such independence can not be separated from the responsibility of making good use of it.

...It must be understood that under no circumstances will the United States use the Monroe Doctrine as a cloak for territorial aggression. We desire peace with all the world, but perhaps most of all with the other peoples of the American Continent. There are, of course, limits to the wrongs which any self-respecting nation can endure. It is always possible that wrong actions toward this Nation, or toward citizens of this Nation, in some State unable to keep order among its own people, unable to secure justice from outsiders, and unwilling to do justice to those outsiders who treat it well, may result in our having to take action to protect our rights; but such action will not be taken with a view to territorial aggression, and it will be taken at all only with extreme reluctance and when it has become evident that every other resource has been exhausted.

Source: Henry Steele Commager, (ed.), Documents of American History (8th edition) *(New York: Appleton-Century-Crofts, 1968), pp. 33-34.*

American military intervention in Latin America and the Caribbean was almost routine after the War with Spain right up until the 1930s. On most occasions the pretext was to protect American lives that were allegedly threatened by political turmoil in the various countries. More and more it became evident that the relationship between the "sister republics" was not so equal, and that the United States was determined to secure its own political and economic interests regardless of any nation's "independence". However, the Great Depression and fear of another war in Europe and Asia helped to change that attitude. President Franklin Roosevelt believed that the nearly constant intervention was costly and only served to worsen relations with other countries in the hemisphere. Moreover, FDR realized that disgruntled neighbours could make valuable allies for any potential enemy the U.S. might face if involved in a war. His "Good Neighbour" policy was designed to change the view that the Caribbean was just an "American lake".

DOCUMENT 4 EXTRACTS FROM FDR SPEECH AT WOODROW WILSON FOUNDATION DINNER (DECEMBER 28, 1933)

'Comprehension must be the soil in which shall grow all the fruits of friendship.' These words, used by President Wilson in the Mobile speech in 1913, can well serve as a statement of policy by the Government of the United States. That policy applies equally to a comprehension of our internal problems and our international relations....

In that speech in Mobile, President Wilson first enunciated the definite statement 'that the United States will never again seek one additional foot of territory by conquest'. The United States accepted that declaration of policy.

President Wilson went further, pointing out with special reference to our Latin American neighbours that material interests must never be made superior to human liberty.

Nevertheless, and largely as a result of the convulsion of the World War and its after effects, the complete fruition of that policy of unselfishness has not in every case been obtained. And in this we, all of us, have to share the responsibility.

I do not hesitate to say that, if I had been engaged in a political campaign as a citizen of some other American republic, I might have been strongly tempted to play upon the fears of my compatriots of that republic by charging the United States of North America with some form of imperialistic desire for selfish aggrandizement.

As a citizen of some other republic I might have found it difficult to believe fully in the altruism of the richest American republic. In particular, as a citizen of some other republic, I might have found it hard to approve of the occupation of the territory of other republics, even as a temporary measure.

It therefore has seemed clear to me as President that the time has come to supplement and to implement the declaration of President Wilson by the further declaration that the definite policy of the United States from now on is one opposed to armed intervention.

The maintenance of constitutional government in other nations is not a sacred obligation devolving upon the United States alone. The maintenance of law and the orderly processes of government in this hemisphere is the concern of each individual nation within its own borders first of all.

It is only if and when the failure of orderly processes affects the other nations of the continent that it becomes their concern; and the point to stress is that in such event it becomes the joint concern of a whole continent in which we are all neighbours.

....

I believe that I express the views of my countrymen when I state that the old policies, alliances, combinations and balances of power have proved themselves inadequate for the preservation of world peace.

Source: Stephen Heald, (ed.), Documents on International Affairs, 1936 *(London: Royal Institute of International Affairs and Oxford University Press, 1937), pp. 472-473.*

DOCUMENT 5 EXTRACTS FROM FDR SPEECH AT INTER-AMERICAN CONFERENCE (DECEMBER 1, 1936)

... Members of a family need no introduction or formalities when, in pursuance of excellent custom, they meet together for their common good....

In this Western Hemisphere the night of fear has been dispelled. Many of the intolerable burdens of economic depression have been lightened and, due in no small part to our common efforts, every nation of this hemisphere is to-day at peace with its neighbours.

This is no conference to form alliances, to divide the spoils of war, to partition countries, to deal with human beings as though they were the pawns in a game of chance. Our purpose, under happy auspices, is to assure the continuance of the blessing of peace.

Three years ago, recognizing that a crisis was being thrust upon the New World, with splendid unanimity our twenty-one Republics set an example to the whole world by proclaiming a new spirit, a new day in the affairs of this hemisphere.

....

Events elsewhere have served only to strengthen our horror of war and all that war means. The men, women, and children of the Americas know that warfare in this day and age means more than the mere clash of armies: they see the destruction of cities and of farms—they foresee that children and grandchildren, if they survive, will stagger for long years not only under the burden of poverty, but also amid the threat of broken society and the destruction of constitutional government.

I am profoundly convinced that the plain people everywhere in the civilized world to-day wish to live in peace one with another. And still leaders and governments resort to war. Truly, if the genius of mankind that has invented the weapons of death cannot discover the means of preserving peace, civilization as we know it lives in an evil day.

But we cannot now, especially in view of our common purpose, accept any defeatist attitude. We have learned by hard experience that peace is not to be had for the mere asking; that peace, like other great privileges, can be obtained only by hard and painstaking effort. We are here to dedicate ourselves and our countries to that work.

You who assemble to-day carry with you in your deliberations the hopes of millions of human beings in other less fortunate lands. Beyond the ocean we see continents rent asunder by old hatreds and new fanaticism. We hear the demand that injustice and inequality be corrected by resorting to the sword and not by resorting to reason and peaceful justice. We hear the cry that new markets can be achieved only through conquest. We read that the sanctity of treaties between nations is disregarded.

....

We know that nations guilty of these follies inevitably face the day either when their weapons of destruction must be used against their neighbours or when an unsound economy, like a house of cards, will fall apart.

In either case, even though the Americans become involved in no war, we must suffer too. The madness of a great war in other parts of the world would affect us and threaten our good in a hundred ways. And the economic collapse of any nation or nations must of necessity harm our own prosperity.

Can we, the Republics of the New World, help the Old World to avert the catastrophe which impends? Yes, I am confident that we can.

....

In the determination to live at peace among ourselves we in the Americas make it at the same time clear that we stand shoulder to shoulder in our final determination that others who, driven by war madness or land-hunger, might seek to commit acts of aggression against us, will find a hemisphere wholly prepared to consult together for our mutual safety and our mutual good.

....

I cannot refrain here from reiterating my gratification that in this, as in so many other achievements, the American Republics have given a salutary example to the world.

....

There are many other causes for war—among them, long festering feuds, unsettled frontiers, territorial rivalries. But these sources of danger which still exist in the Americas, I am thankful to say, are not only few in number, but already on the way to peaceful adjudication. While the settlement of such controversies may necessarily involve adjustments at home or in our relations with our neighbours which may appear to involve material sacrifice, let no man or woman forget that there is no profit in war. Sacrifices in the cause of peace are infinitely small compared with the holocaust of war.

Peace comes from the spirit, and must be grounded in faith. In seeking peace, perhaps we can best begin by proudly affirming the faith of the Americas; the faith in freedom and its fulfillment which has proved a mighty fortress beyond reach of successful attack in half the world.

That faith arises from a common hope and a common design given us by our fathers in differing form, but with a single aim—freedom and security of the individual, which has become the foundation of our peace.

If, then, by making war in our midst impossible, and if within ourselves and among ourselves we can give greater freedom and fulfillment to the individual lives of our citizens, the democratic form of representative government will have justified the high hopes of the liberating fathers. Democracy is still the hope of the world. If we in our generation can continue its successful applications in the Americas, it will spread and supersede other methods by which men are governed and which seem to most of us to run counter to our ideals of human liberty and human progress.

....

Our hemisphere has at last come of age. We are here assembled to show it united to the world. We took from our ancestors a great dream. We here offer it back as a great unified reality.

Finally, in expressing our faith of the Western World, let us affirm:

That we maintain and defend the democratic form of constitutional representative government.

That through such government we can more greatly provide a wider distribution of culture, of education, of thought, and of free expression.

That through it we can obtain a greater security of life for our citizens and a more equal opportunity for them to prosper.

That through it we can best foster commerce and the exchange of art and science between nations; that through it we can avoid the rivalry of armament, avert hatred, and encourage good will and true justice.

That through it we offer hope for peace and a more abundant life to the peoples of the whole world.

....

The faith of the Americans, therefore, lies in the spirit. The system, the sisterhood of the Americas is impregnable so long as her nations maintain that spirit.

In that faith and spirit we will have peace over the Western World. In that faith and spirit we will all watch and guard our hemisphere. In that faith and spirit may we also, with God's help, offer hope to our brethren overseas.

Source: John W. Wheeler-Bennett, (ed.), Documents on International Affairs, 1933 *(London: Royal Institute of International Affairs and Oxford University Press, 1934), pp. 563-567.*

In the first few years following World War Two, the United States was committed to assisting in the reconstruction of western Europe and Japan. While FDR moved away from the more overt demonstrations of American intervention in Latin America and the Caribbean, U.S. influence there remained strong, especially with respect to economics. The days of colonial rivalries were past, but the U.S. still perceived a threat to its role as the hemispheric overseer. Communism posed a new challenge to the world order, and although Russian tanks were far away from the Americas the U.S. was determined to maintain the region within its own sphere of influence. Along the lines of the Marshall Plan and North Atlantic Treaty Organization (NATO), Washington pushed hard to consolidate its political, economic and military interests with those of the other American states.

DOCUMENT 6 EXTRACTS FROM THE INTER-AMERICAN TREATY OF RECIPROCAL ASSISTANCE (RIO TREATY) (SEPTEMBER 2, 1947)

In the name of their Peoples, the Governments represented at the Inter-American Conference for the Maintenance of Continental Peace and Security, desirous of consolidating the strengthening their relations of friendship and good neighborliness, and

Considering: That Resolution VIII of the Inter-American Conference on Problems of War and Peace, which met in Mexico City, recommended that conclusion of a treaty to prevent and repel threats and acts of aggression against any of the countries of America;

That the High Contracting Parties reiterate their will to remain united in an inter-American system consistent with the purposes and principles of the United Nations, and reaffirm the existence of the agreement which they have concluded concerning those matters relating to the maintenance of international peace and security which are appropriate for regional action;

That the High Contracting Parties reaffirm their adherence to the principles of inter-American solidarity and cooperation, and especially to those set forth in the preamble and declarations of the Act of Chapultepec, all of which should be understood to be accepted as standards of their mutual relations and as the juridical basis of the Inter-American System;

That the American States propose, in order to improve the procedures for the pacific settlement of their controversies, to conclude the treaty concerning the "Inter-American Peace System" envisaged in Resolutions IX and XXXIX of the Inter-American Conference on Problems of War and Peace;

That the obligation of mutual assistance and common defense of the American Republics is essentially related to their democratic ideals and to their will to cooperate permanently in the fulfillment of the principles and purposes of a policy of peace;

That the American regional community affirms as a manifest truth that juridical organization is a necessary prerequisite of security and peace, and that peace is founded on justice and moral order and, consequently, on the international recognition and protection of human rights and freedoms, on the indispensable well-being of the people, and on the effectiveness of democracy for the international realization of justice and security,

Have resolved, in conformity with the objectives stated above, to conclude the following Treaty, in order to assure peace, through adequate means, to provide for effective reciprocal assistance to meet armed attacks against any American State, and in order to deal with threats of aggression against any of them:

Article 1

The High Contracting Parties formally condemn war and undertake in their international relations not to resort to the threat or the use of force in any manner inconsistent with the provisions of the Charter of the United Nations or of this Treaty.

Article 2

As a consequence of the principle set forth in the preceding Article, the High Contracting Parties undertake to submit every controversy which may arise between them to methods of peaceful settlement and to endeavor to settle any such controversy among themselves by means of the procedures in force in the Inter-American System before referring it to the General Assembly or the Security Council of the United Nations.

Article 3

1. The High Contracting Parties agree that an armed attack by any State against an American State shall be considered as an attack against all the American States and, consequently, each one of the said Contracting Parties undertakes to assist in meeting the attack in the exercise of the inherent right of individual or collective self-defense recognized by Article 51 of the Charter of the United Nations.

2. On request of the State or States directly attacked and until the decision of the Organ of Consultation of the Inter-American System, each one of the Contracting Parties may determine the immediate measures which it may individually take in fulfillment of the obligation contained in the preceding paragraph and in accordance with the principle of continental solidarity. The Organ of Consultation shall meet without delay for the purpose of examining those measures and agreeing upon the measures of a collective character that should be taken.

....

Article 6

If the inviolability or the integrity of the territory or the sovereignty or political independence of any American State should be affected by an aggression which is not an armed attack or by an extra-continental or intra-continental conflict, or by any other fact or situation that might endanger the peace of America, the Organ of Consultation shall meet immediately in order to agree on the measures which must be taken in case of aggression to assist the victim of the aggression or, in any case, the measures which should be taken for the common defense and for the maintenance of the peace and security of the Continent.

....

Article 9

In addition to other acts which the Organ of Consultation may characterize as aggression, the following shall be considered as such:

a) Unprovoked armed attack by a State against the territory, the people, or the land, sea or air forces of another State;

b) Invasion, by the armed forces of a State, of the territory of an American State, through the trespassing of boundaries demarcated in accordance with a treaty, judicial decision, or arbitral award, or, in the absence of frontiers thus demarcated, invasion affecting a region which is under the effective jurisdiction of another State.

Source: Arthur M. Schlesinger, Jr. (gen. ed.), The Dynamics of World Power: A Documentary History of United States Foreign Policy 1945-1973 *(volume 3) (New York: Chelsea House, 1973), pp. 30-33.*

DOCUMENT 7

EXTRACTS FROM THE CHARTER OF THE ORGANIZATION OF AMERICAN STATES (APRIL 30, 1948)

IN THE NAME OF THEIR PEOPLES, THE STATES REPRESENTED AT THE NINTH INTERNATIONAL CONFERENCE OF AMERICAN STATES,

Convinced that the historic mission of America is to offer to man a land of liberty, and a favorable environment for the development of his personality and the realization of his just aspirations;

Conscious that the mission has already inspired numerous agreements, whose essential value lies in the desire of the American peoples to live together in peace, and, though their mutual understanding and respect for the sovereignty of each one, to provide for the betterment of all, in independence, in equality and under law;

Confident that the true significance of American solidarity and good neighborliness can only mean the consolidation on this continent, within the framework of democratic institutions, of a system of individual liberty and social justice based on respect for the essential rights of man;

Persuaded that their welfare and their contribution to the progress and the civilization of the world will increasingly require intensive continental cooperation;

Resolved to persevere in the noble undertaking that humanity has conferred upon the United Nations, whose principles and purposes they solemnly reaffirm;

Convinced that juridical organization is a necessary condition for security and peace founded on moral order and on justice; and

In accordance with Resolution IX of the Inter-American Conference on Problems of War and Peace, held at Mexico City,

Have agreed upon the following CHARTER OF THE ORGANIZATION OF AMERICAN STATES

Part One

Chapter I: Nature and purposes

Article I. The American States establish by this Charter the international organization that they have developed to achieve an order of peace and justice, to promote their solidarity, to strengthen their collaboration, and to defend their sovereignty, their territorial integrity and their independence. Within the United Nations, the Organization of American States is a regional agency.

....

Article 4. The Organization of American States, in order to put into practice the principles on which it is founded and to fulfill its regional obligations under the Charter of the United Nations, proclaims the following essential purposes:

a) To strengthen the peace and security of the continent;

b) To prevent possible causes of difficulties and to ensure the pacific settlement of disputes that may arise among the Member States;

c) To provide for common action on the part of those States in the event of aggression;

d) To seek the solution of political, juridical and economic problems that may arise among them; and

e) to promote, by cooperative action, their economic, social and cultural development.

Chapter II: Principles

[Article 5. These affirm good faith, condemn aggression, aspire to social justice and economic cooperation.]

Chapter III: Fundamental rights and duties of States

Article 6. States are juridically equal, enjoy equal rights and equal capacity to exercise these rights, and have equal duties. The rights of each State depend not upon its power to ensure the exercise thereof, but upon the mere fact of its existence as a person under international law.

[*Articles 7-14.* Set out the rights and duties.]

Article 15. No State or group of States has the right to intervene, directly or indirectly, for any reason whatever, in the internal or external affairs of any other State. The foregoing principle prohibits not only armed force but also any other form of interference or attempted threat against the personality of the State or against its political, economic and cultural elements.

Article 16. No State may use or encourage the use of coercive measures of an economic or political character in order to force the sovereign will of another State and obtain from it advantages of any kind.

Article 17. The territory of a State is inviolable; it may not be the object, even temporarily, of military occupation or of other measures of force taken by another State, directly or indirectly, on any grounds whatever. No territorial acquisitions or special advantages obtained either by force or by other means of coercion shall be recognized.

Article 18. The American States bind themselves in their international relations not to have recourse to the use of force, except in the case of self-defense in accordance with existing treaties or in fulfillment thereof.

Article 19. Measures adopted for the maintenance of peace and security in accordance with existing treaties do not constitute a violation of the principles set forth in Articles 15 and 17.

Chapter IV: Pacific settlement of disputes

Article 20. All international disputes that may arise between American States shall be submitted to the peaceful procedures set forth in this Charter, before being referred to the Security Council of the United Nations.

Chapter V: Collective security

Article 24. Every act of aggression by a State against the territorial integrity or the inviolability of the territory or against the sovereignty or political independence of an American State shall be considered an act of aggression against the other American States.

Article 25. If the inviolability or the integrity of the territory or the sovereignty or political independence of any American State should be affected by an armed attack or by an act of aggression that is not an armed attack, or by an extra-continental conflict, or by a conflict between two or more American States, or by any other fact or situation that might endanger the peace of America, the American States, in furtherance of the principles of continental solidarity or collective self-defense, shall apply the measure and procedures established in the special treaties on the subject.

Source: J.A.S. Grenville, The Major International Treaties 1914-1973 *(London: Meuthen and Co. Ltd., 1974), pp. 328-330.*

Cold War tensions were increasing throughout the 1950s, and so too were pressures for economic and political reform within many of Latin American states. Although communism did make inroads into the region through revolutionary movements in various countries, much of the reformist impulse was more nationalistic in orientation. American economic domination was staggering. In some cases, U.S. corporations in Latin American countries wielded so much financial power that they seemed to virtually control Washington's policy towards those states. CIA-backed coups and the assassination of nationalist leaders became frighteningly familiar to the region. U.S. policy often favoured oppressive, dictatorial regimes that would be both vehemently anti-communist and sympathetic to American commercial interests. Yet the establishment of these so-called "banana republics" was not so easy. There was often violent opposition from many segments in society, and not just communists or nationalists. Moreover, Washington was inextricably linked with the dictators. Consequently, at the same time that the U.S. was seen by Latin Americans as the guarantor of freedom and liberty, it was also closely wedded to the indignation and exploitation they endured under these regimes. Vice-President Richard Nixon discovered first-hand the extent of anti-American sentiment on a trip through South America in 1958.

DOCUMENT 8 EXCERPTS FROM ACCOUNTS OF NIXON'S VISIT TO SAN MARCOS, PERU AND CARACAS, VENEZUELA (MAY 7, 1958)

When the motorcade arrived, there were more than two thousand students milling about, shouting out catcalls, carrying *"Fuera Nixon"* signs, and an occasional cry of *"Muera Nixon"* (Death to Nixon).

Nixon stopped the motorcade and got out of his car, ...he walked toward the students, smiling, asking the police not to push them back. With Walters shouting the translation, Nixon called out, "I would like to talk to you. What's the matter, you afraid of the truth?" One of the demonstrators shouted back, "Go home." "I'll be glad to go home," Nixon replied, "but don't you want the truth first?"

The crowd slowly gave way as Nixon moved toward the university gates. Students near enough to hear what he was saying were impressed—Walters heard one of them say, *"El gringo tiene cojones"* (The Yankee has balls)—but it was all show without substance, as there was not the slightest possibility the three men could force their way through the gates and into the university, especially not with Nixon ordering the police to stay out of it.

As Nixon continued to try to engage the students around him in conversation, those in the rear began throwing oranges, bottles, and an occasional small rock. Tad Szulc, who was back with the motorcade, watching, reported: "Pale with anger, but keeping a tight smile on his lips, Mr. Nixon stood his ground for four minutes. When one policeman tried to arrest a demonstrator, Nixon said, 'Let him go, I want to talk to him.'"

Then one of the rocks grazed Nixon's shoulder and landed on Sherwood's face, breaking a tooth. "Let's get out of here," Nixon said to Sherwood and Walters, "but move back slowly, keep facing them." When they reached their vehicle, a convertible, Nixon stood up in the backseat, Sherwood bracing him. Nixon threw his hands above his head and shouted, "Cowards, you are cowards! You are afraid of the truth! You are the worst kind of cowards!"

....

Nixon paid a price for seeking confrontation. As Hartmann wrote, "this crowd was really worked up. Spit, fruit and pebbles again rained on Nixon and his party, including the two dozen U.S. newsmen." Nixon fared worst of all. A tobacco-chewing agitator stood face-to-face with him at the door of the hotel and let fly a wad of tobacco spittle that caught Nixon full in the face. Nixon went through "a terrible test of temper control"; as he explained later, "One must experience the sensation to realize why spitting in a person's face is the most infuriating insult ever conceived by man." Nixon's instinct was to strike out at the agitator, but before he could recover from the shock of the spit, Sherwood threw the man aside. Nixon got in one blow, "planting a healthy kick on his shins. Nothing I did all day made me feel better."

Pat watched all this from a fourth-story window. "I've never been more proud of him," she said later. Hartmann shared her sentiments. "Throughout the ordeal," he wrote, "Nixon himself was completely self-possessed and bore himself with dignity and strength, a credit to his country."

....

There was a large crowd when Nixon arrived, gathered outside the gate and on the balcony of the airport terminal. People, mostly teen-agers, were shouting slogans and waving *"Feura Nixon"* signs. A group of dignitaries gathered at the foot of the ramp. At the airplane door, as Nixon waved at the crowd, Walters whispered into his ear, "They aren't friendly, Mr. Vice President." Nixon made a quick inspection of the military honor guard, then broke away to a nearby hangar, where some mechanics were standing around gaping. He shook hands, returned to the host committee, and said he had decided to skip the usual airport welcome speeches, because "no one could possibly hear what we said over the noise of this mob." He took Pat's arm and led the way toward the terminal building, over a red carpet specially laid out for the occasion. It was lined by soldiers and looked safe enough. But the soldiers simply stood, as did the police, as the mob began throwing little whistles, fruit, and other objects, along with vicious obscenities, at the Nixons.

....

As the Nixons approached the terminal door, directly under the observation balcony, which was packed with howling demonstrators, the army band struck up the Venezuelan national anthem. The Nixons came to attention. Then the unbelievable happened. A shower of spit began to rain down upon them. A torrent of the stuff, much of it brown, from the tobacco chewers. Pat's new red suit was covered with it. It was running down her face. Still Nixon stood, although he admitted that no one could hear the anthem anyway, due to the noise.

No one ever asked him directly how he could have stood there and let this happen to his wife. He did explain his own reasoning: "We preferred the indignity of spit to that of letting the mob see the Vice President of the United States duck and run away. And we also wanted to show them that we respected their national anthem even if they did not . . . Pat shared this trial at my side. In one sense, I was horrified that she should be subjected to it. In another sense, I was proud that she was with me."

....

The mob closed in again as the Secret Service pushed back. Spit flew. A teen-ager grabbed Pat's hand and screeched a question about Nixon torturing "little black boys" in Little Rock. "He was one of the very mean young boys," Pat later told Mazo. "I pretended that I didn't understand him. I just said, 'How are you? So nice to be here.' . . . They must have been told that we were horrible people."

....

The Foreign Minister attempted an explanation: "The Venezuelan people have been without freedom so long that they tend now to express themselves more vigorously perhaps than they should. In our new government we do not want to do anything which would be interpreted as a suppression of freedom."

Nixon shut him up. "If your new government doesn't have the guts and good sense to control a mob like the one at the airport, there soon will be no freedom for anyone in Venezuela. Don't you realize that that mob was Communist-led?"

....

A mob began to descend on them from the side streets, waving placards with Nazi swastikas alongside the doctored photo of Nixon that made him look like a fanged monster. But the ambush failed, because there was a way through the roadblock which the driver successfully negotiated.

....

As the motorcade stopped, yet another mob—about two hundred strong—emerged from the side streets. "Here they come," someone shouted. To Mazo it was "like a scene from the French Revolution." They were screaming, shouting, waving banners, placards, pipes, clubs, and bare fists. They swarmed around Nixon's car.

"Seven Venezuelan motorcycle police," Hartmann wrote, "formed in a V around the Nixon car, rested one foot to the pavement and just sat there as the mob spilled past. The military police who had flanked the motorcade at the airport had disappeared." But at least the motorcycle police kept the crowd from the front of Nixon's car. To the rear, in the car carrying Pat, the driver pulled up bumper to bumper, so that the rear was protected. But the side windows and doors were unprotected.

Four of the Secret Service men dashed forward from cars in the rear. They took positions guarding the door handles, pushing people away with their bare hands, "coolly," as Hartmann saw it, but heroically. Then, Hartmann reported, "the mob smashed against the glass [of Nixon's car] with rocks, pipes, jagged beer cans and their naked fists. They kicked and hammered at the doors and fenders.

....

The other reporters gathered around. "Let's go," Nixon said. "You can get your pictures later at the Embassy." No one thought to write a description of what he looked like—whether ashen-faced with fear and worry, or red-faced from anger, but he must have been a sight, his suit covered with spit and broken glass, standing beside a limousine whose side windows were all broken, covered with spit and dents.

At the embassy, as he hurried inside, the reporters caught up with him. In a short, impromptu response to a dozen questions hurled all at once, he was calm and unruffled. "These incidents are against Venezuela," he declared. "No patriotic Venezuelan would have torn down his country's flag as the mob did to the Venezuelan flag and also to ours. I don't feel it at all as a personal offense. If anything, the future relations of the United States and Venezuela will be better than ever." When some Venezuelans attempted to apologize, he said, "As far as I'm concerned, the incident is closed."

Nixon told Bill Key to cancel all his appearances, and to tell members of the ruling junta that they should come to the embassy to see him. Then he went to an upstairs room, threw away his stained clothes, and went to bed. "It was," Mazo wrote, "Nixon's first afternoon nap in twelve years of public life. He slept for forty minutes."

Source: Stephen E. Ambrose, Nixon: The Education of a Politician 1913-1962 *(New York: Simon and Schuster, 1987), pp. 467-78.*

DOCUMENT 9

EXCERPTS FROM NEWS CONFERENCE BY SECRETARY OF STATE JOHN FOSTER DULLES ON ANTI-AMERICAN DEMONSTRATIONS IN VENEZUELA (MAY 20, 1958)

In the first place I would not say that there is any general or preponderant anti-American sentiment among the people of Venezuela. You cannot judge a people on the basis of sporadic, organized outbursts of rowdyism. I am confident that what happened there is not a reflection of the general views of the Venezuelan people.

....

The miscalculation in the case of the visit to Caracas was primarily a miscalculation as to the adequacy and efficiency of the police force. It virtually melted away at the sight of trouble. That wasn't anticipated. I don't know whether it could have been anticipated or not. But if there had been an adequate handling of that situation by the police, such as occurs in most countries, there would not have been any reason whatever to have concluded that the trip was unwise to have undertaken.

....

On the basis of noninterference with the internal affairs of countries and in the case of South America—Latin America—if we tried to deal with those governments on the basis of our appraisal as to whether they were a good government or a bad government, whether they were a dictatorial or not a dictatorial government, we would find ourselves, I am afraid, deeply enmeshed in their internal affairs.

As you know, one of the cardinal doctrines for this hemisphere, which is affirmed and reaffirmed on every occasion by the American Republics, is the doctrine of noninterference in the internal affairs of other countries. Their economic and political interdependence with the United States is such that to a peculiar degree—a greater degree than probably any other area in the world—if we attempted to adjust our relations according to our appraisal of their government, we would become involved in their internal affairs.

I would like to point out there is no clearcut distinction. You can talk about dictators and nondictators, but it isn't quite as easy to classify on that basis. There are quasi-dictators and almost-dictators and "dictators of the proletariat" and all sorts of things in gradations. If you begin to grade and say, if it is a certain type of government, you give 100 percent support, and, if it is not quite as good by our standards, you give 90 percent, and, if it is less good, you give 70 percent support, that would get us involved in an intolerable situation.

It is obvious the American Government and the American nation and the American people like to see governments which rest upon the consent of the governed and where the governed are educated people able to carry the responsibilities of self-government. Wherever that exists, there almost automatically results a closer and more intimate friendly relationship than where that doesn't exist. But any formula whereby we try to apply a sort of slide rule to their governments would be, in fact, an interference in their internal affairs....

Source: Arthur M. Schlesinger, Jr. (gen. ed.), The Dynamics of World Power: A Documentary History of United States Foreign Policy 1945-1973 *(volume 3) (New York: Chelsea House, 1973), pp. 380-383.*

Despite frequent demonstrations of anti-Americanism, most Latin American states remained firmly supportive of and supported by Washington. However, Cuba was an exception. In 1958 a nationalist revolution toppled the long-time pro-American regime and brought Fidel Castro to power. The Eisenhower administration was initially uncertain as to how to handle Castro, but after he nationalized American financial holdings on the island and proclaimed his adherence to socialism, U.S. policy quickly counted him as an enemy. Castro became a spokesman for revolution in the Americas and criticized U.S. domination in the region. More importantly he sought friendly relations with the Soviet Union, which made Cuba a major foreign policy concern for Washington.

DOCUMENT 10

EXCERPTS FROM CASTRO'S SPEECH TO THE UNITED NATIONS GENERAL ASSEMBLY (SEPTEMBER 26, 1960)

Reference has been made to the universal desire for peace, which is the desire of all peoples and accordingly the desire of our people also. But this peace which the world wishes to preserve is a peace which we Cubans have been without for a long time. The perils which other peoples of the world may regard as more or less remote are problems and anxieties which are very close to us. It was not easy to come here to lay Cuba's problems before this Assembly. It was not easy for us to get here. I do not know whether we received special treatment. Can it be that we, the members of the Cuban delegation, represent the worst type of government in the world? Can it be that we, the representatives of the Cuban delegation, deserve the bad treatment which we have received? Why our delegation in particular? Cuba has sent many delegations to the United Nations. Cuba has been represented by many different persons, and yet, these exceptional measures were reserved for us: confinement to the island of Manhattan; instructions to all hotels not to rent us rooms, hostility and, on the pretext of security, isolation....

Personal humiliation, attempts at extortion, eviction from the hotel in which we were staying, and our removal to another hotel, after doing everything possible to avoid difficulties, refraining absolutely from leaving our lodgings, going nowhere except to this Assembly hall at the United Nations (on the few occasions when we have been present), and to a reception at the Soviet Embassy, in order to avoid problems and difficulties, even all this was not enough for us to be left in peace.

Over the years there had been considerable Cuban immigration into this country. During the last twenty years over 100,000 Cubans have come to this country from their own homeland, where they would have liked to remain always and where they wish to return as do all who are forced for social or economic reasons to leave their country. This Cuban population is employed; they respected and still respect the law and, very naturally, they felt deeply for their country and for the revolution. They never had any problems.

But one day there began to arrive in this country another kind of visitor; war criminals began to arrive; there began to arrive persons who, in some cases, had murdered hundreds of our compatriots. At once they were welcomed by the Press; they were welcomed by the authorities and naturally they reflected this welcome in their conduct and that is the reason for their many clashes with Cuban immigrants who had been working honestly in this country for years.

One of these incidents, provoked by persons who feel themselves strengthened by the systematic campaign against Cuba and the complicity of the authorities, resulted in the death of a little girl. This was a matter for regret, for all of us. But the guilty parties were not the Cubans who live here. Much less was the Cuban delegation guilty, and yet all of you have undoubtedly seen these headlines in the newspapers saying that pro-Castro groups had killed a ten-year-old girl; with the characteristic hypocrisy of all those who have anything to do with relations between Cuba and this country, a spokesman for the White House immediately made a statement drawing the whole world's attention to this act and to all intents and purposes laying the guilt at the door of the Cuban delegation. The United States representative to this Assembly added the crowning touch to the farce by sending a telegram to the Government of Venezuela and another telegram of condolences to the little girl's family, as though he felt obliged to give an explanation from the United Nations for something for which the Cuban delegation was virtually responsible.

But that was not all. When we were forced to leave one of the hotels in this city and come to United Nations Headquarters while other arrangements were being made, a modest hotel here, a Negro hotel in Harlem, offered us accommodation. The offer came during our conversation with the Secretary-General. Nevertheless, an official of the State Department did everything in his power to prevent us from being accommodated in this hotel.

At that moment, as if by magic, hotels began to spring up all over New York, hotels which had previously refused to house the Cuban delegation, offering to do so for nothing. Naturally, out of common courtesy, we agreed to go to the Harlem hotel. We thought that we had a right to hope that we would be left in peace. But we were not left in peace. As it had not been possible to prevent our stay in Harlem, a whispering campaign was started at once and the world was told that the Cuban delegation had taken up residence in a brothel.

No doubt to some gentlemen, a modest hotel in Harlem, where the Negroes of the United States live, could not be anything but a brothel. But besides this it was a matter of trying to cast a slur on the Cuban delegation, thus showing no respect even for the women members of our delegation or of its staff.

....

The problem of Cuba? Some representatives are perhaps well-informed; some of them not so well—it depends on your sources of information—but there is no doubt that for the world as a whole the Cuban problem is one that has arisen in the last two years; it is a new problem. Formerly the world had little reason to know that Cuba existed. To many people it was rather like an appendix to the United States. Even for many citizens of this country, Cuba was a colony of the United States. It was not so on the map. On the map we were shown in a different colour from the United States; in reality, we were a colony.

....

The new colonization of our country then began: the best agricultural land was acquired by the United States companies; concessions were granted for exploiting our natural resources and mines, concessions for the operation of public utilities, commercial concessions, concessions of every kind which, combined with the constitutional right, based on force, to intervene in our country transformed it from a Spanish into a United States colony.

....

Aware of our economy's dependence on the United States market, the United States Government began its series of warnings that it would deprive us of our sugar quota. Concurrently, other activities were taking place in the United States of America, the activities of the counterrevolutionaries.

One afternoon an aircraft coming from the north flew over one of our sugar mills and dropped a bomb. That was a strange, an unusual event, but of course we knew where that aircraft came from.

Another afternoon another aircraft flew over our sugarcane fields and dropped some small incendiary bombs. And what started in a haphazard fashion was then continued systematically.

One afternoon—when a large number of United States tourist agents were visiting Cuba in connexion with a campaign by the Revolutionary Government to encourage tourism as a source of national income—an aircraft of United States manufacture, of a type used in the Second World War, flew over our capital, dropping leaflets and some hand-grenades. Naturally, some anti-aircraft guns went into action. what with the grenades dropped by the aircraft and the anti-aircraft fire, because, as you know, some of the projectiles explode on contact with any hard object, the result was more than forty casualties. There were children and old people with their entrails ripped out. Was this the first time for us? No, children and old people, men and women had often been wiped out in our Cuban villages by bombs of United States manufacture supplied to the tyrant Batista.

....

Dozens of war victims; eighty families destroyed by an explosion; forty casualties caused by an aircraft that leisurely flew over our territory. The authorities of the United States Government denied that those aircraft had come from United States territory. What is more, they said the aircraft was standing quietly in a hangar. But when one of our periodicals published a photograph of the aircraft, it was only then that the United States authorities seized it, and immediately issued a statement to the effect that the matter was of no importance and that the casualties had been caused not by bombs but by anti-aircraft fire; and meanwhile those who had committed this foul deed, this crime, were going about the United States undisturbed, and not hindered in any way from continuing to commit such acts of aggression.

I take this opportunity of telling the representative of the United States that there are many mothers in Cuba still waiting for a telegram of condolences from him for their children murdered by United States bombs.

Source: Arthur M. Schlesinger, Jr. (gen. ed), The Dynamics of World Power: A Documentary History of United States Foreign Policy 1945-1973 *(volume 3) (New York: Chelsea House, 1973), pp. 463-467, 474-475.*

DOCUMENT 11 — EXCERPTS FROM JFK'S INAUGURAL SPEECH (JANUARY 21, 1961) AND SPEECH TO THE LATIN AMERICAN DIPLOMATIC CORPS IN WASHINGTON (MARCH 13, 1961)

John F. Kennedy inherited the Cuban dilemma when he came to power in January 1961. He also inherited the Eisenhower administration's plan to launch an attack on Cuba in the hopes of ousting Castro. In April 1961, Kennedy authorized the operation, conducted by CIA-trained, anti-Castro Cuban exiles. The "Bay of Pigs" invasion was a failure, and Kennedy was humiliated. Castro's fears of another invasion attempt in part led to the Soviets' decision to try and place nuclear missiles in Cuba. The Cuban missile crisis of October 1962 was one of the most dramatic events in history, as the world teetered on the brink of a nuclear holocaust. Contrasting the Bay of Pigs fiasco, the Kennedy administration was also responsible for initiating a gradual and favourable change in American policy towards Latin America. Learning from the anti-Americanism of the 1950s, he tried to change the perception that many young Latin Americans had of the U.S. by developing better economic and cultural ties.

January 21, 1961

Let the word go forth from this time and place, to friend and foe alike, that the torch has been passed to a new generation of Americans—born in this century, tempered by war, disciplined by a hard and bitter peace, proud of our ancient heritage—and unwilling to witness or permit the slow undoing of those human rights to which this nation has always been committed, and to which we are committed today at home and around the world.

Let every nation know, whether it wishes us well or ill, that we shall pay any price, bear any burden, meet any hardship, support any friend, oppose any foe, to assure the survival and the success of liberty.

....

To those new states whom we welcome to the ranks of the free, we pledge our word that one form of colonial control shall not have passed away merely to be replaced by a far more iron tyranny. We shall not always expect to find them supporting our view. But we shall always hope to find them strongly supporting their own freedom—and to remember that in the past, those who foolishly sought power by riding the back of the tiger ended up inside.

To those peoples in the huts and villages of half the globe struggling to break the bonds of mass misery, we pledge our best efforts to help them help themselves, for whatever period is required—not because the Communists may be doing it, not because we seek their votes, but because it is right. If a free society cannot help the many who are poor, it cannot save the few who are rich.

....

Let all our neighbors know that we shall join with them to oppose aggression or subversion anywhere in the Americas. And let every other power know that this hemisphere intends to remain the master of its own house.

....

March 13, 1961

We meet together as firm and ancient friends, united by history and experience and by our determination to advance the values of American civilization. For this New World of ours is not a mere accident of geography. Our continents are bound together by a common history, the endless exploration of new frontiers. Our nations are the product of a common struggle, the revolt from colonial rule. And our people share a common heritage, the quest for the dignity and the freedom of man.

....

Our hemisphere's mission is not yet completed. For our unfulfilled task is to demonstrate to the entire world that man's unsatisfied aspiration for economic progress and social justice can best be achieved by free men working within a framework of democratic institutions. If we can do this in our own hemisphere, and for our own people, we may yet realize the prophecy of the great Mexican patriot, Benito Juárez, that "democracy is the destiny of future humanity."

....

Throughout Latin America, a continent rich in resources and in the spiritual and cultural achievements of its people, millions of men and women suffer the daily degradations of poverty and hunger. They lack decent shelter or protection from disease. Their children are deprived of the education or the jobs which are the gateway to a better life. Each day the problems grow more urgent. Population growth is outpacing economic growth—low living standards are further endangered—and discontent, the discontent of a people who know that abundance and the tools of progress are at last within their reach, is growing. In the words of José Figueres, "once dormant peoples are struggling upward toward the sun, toward a better life."

If we are to meet a problem so staggering in its dimensions, our approach must itself be equally bold—an approach consistent with the majestic concept of Operation Pan America. Therefore I have called on all people of the hemisphere to join in a new Alliance for Progress—*Alianza para el Progreso*—a vast cooperative effort, unparalleled in magnitude and nobility of purpose, to satisfy the basic needs of the American people for homes, work and land, health and schools—*techo, trabajo y tierra, salud y escuela*.

First, I propose that the American republics begin on a vast new Ten Year Plan for the Americas, a plan to transform the 1960s into a historic decade of democratic progress.

These ten years will be the years of maximum progress, maximum effort, the years when the greatest obstacles must be overcome, the years when the need for assistance will be the greatest.

If we are successful, if our effort is bold enough and determined enough, then the close of this decade will mark the beginning of a new era in the American experience. The living standards of every American family will be on the rise, basic education will be available to all, hunger will be a forgotten experience, the need for massive outside help will have passed, most nations will have entered a period of self-sustaining growth, and though there will be still much to do, every American republic will be the master of its own revolution and its own hope and progress.

Let me stress that only the most determined efforts of the American nations themselves can bring success to this effort. They, and they alone, can mobilize their resources, enlist the energies of their people, and modify their social patterns so that all, and not just a privileged few, share in the fruits of growth. If this effort is made, then outside assistance will give vital impetus to progress; without it, no amount of help will advance the welfare of the people.

Thus if the countries of Latin America are ready to do their part, and I am sure they are, then I believe the United States, for its part, should help provide resources of a scope and magnitude sufficient to make this bold development plan a success—just as we helped to provide, against equal odds nearly, the resources adequate to help rebuild the economies of Western Europe. For only an effort of towering dimensions can insure fulfillment of our plan for a decade of progress.

....

To achieve this goal political freedom must accompany material progress. Our Alliance for Progress is an alliance of free governments, and it must work to eliminate tyranny from a hemisphere in which it has no rightful place.

Source: Theodore C. Sorensen, (ed.), Let The Word Go Forth: The Speeches, Statements and Writings of John F. Kennedy *(New York: Delacorte Press, 1988), pp. 12-13 / 351-352 / 356.*

During most of the 1960s United States foreign policy was focused on the wrenching trauma of the war in Indochina. President Lyndon Johnson seemed to return to the Monroe Doctrine when he ordered U.S. troops into the Dominican Republic during political upheaval there in 1965. OAS members eventually gave their reluctant support for the American operation, but they began to wonder if the goals of social and economic progress outlined by John Kennedy were shared by his successor. When Richard Nixon took over the Presidency in 1968 any such doubts were confirmed. Nixon's policy focused on the suppression of communist and even nationalist activity through massive support to pro-American military dictatorships. He was determined to enforce hemispheric solidarity and isolate Castro's Cuba, no matter what that meant for the independence of Latin American states. Chile was the case in point for the Nixon administration in the early 1970s when Salvador Allende became the first democratically elected Marxist president in the western hemisphere. His social and economic reforms quickly earned the wrath of American corporations there, and soon Washington was heavily involved in Chilean politics.

DOCUMENT 12 COMMENTS ON THE ALLENDE GOVERNMENT IN CHILE BY ASSISTANT SECRETARY OF STATE MEYER BEFORE THE HOUSE SUBCOMMITTEE ON INTER-AMERICAN AFFAIRS (OCTOBER 15, 1971)

The Controller General [Hector Humeres Magnan] of Chile announced his findings on October 11 that no compensation would be paid for the U.S. copper mining investments expropriated on July 16 except for modest amounts in the cases of two smaller properties.

The United States Government is deeply disappointed and disturbed at this serious departure from accepted standards of international law. Under established principles of international law, the expropriation must be accompanied by reasonable provision for payment of just compensation. The United States had made clear to the Government of Chile its hope that a solution could be found on a reasonable and pragmatic basis consistent with international law.

It appears that the major factor in the Controller General's decision with respect to the larger producers was the determination on September 28 of alleged "excess profits." The unprecedented retroactive application of the excess profits concept, which was not obligatory under the expropriation legislation adopted by the Chilean Congress, is particularly disquieting. The U.S. companies which are affected by this determination of the Chilean Government earned their profits in Chile in accordance with Chilean law and under specific contractual agreements made directly with the Government of Chile. The excess profits deductions punish the companies today for acts that were legal and approved by the Government of Chile at the time. No claim is being made that these excess profits deductions are based on violations of Chilean law. This retroactive determination has serious implications for the rule of law.

Should Chile fail to meet its international obligations, it could jeopardize flows of private funds and erode the base of support for foreign assistance, with possible adverse effects on other developing countries. The course of action which the Chilean Government appears to have chosen, therefore, could have an adverse effect on the international development process.

The United States hopes that the Government of Chile, in accordance with its obligations under international law, will give further careful consideration to this matter.

....

The statement contains no threat.

....

We have no reason or desire to seek or welcome a confrontation with the Government of Chile. The entire thrust of our policy in the past year has been to try our level best to minimize the chances of a confrontation. Nor do we question Chile's right to self-determination. We cannot be expected, however, to be indifferent or to remain silent when established international norms applicable to our nationals are in jeopardy.

....

I wish to make it clear that any differences we may have with Chile are neither political nor ideological in their origin. President Nixon has stated clearly that the United States is prepared to have the kind of relationship with the Chilean Government that it is prepared to have with us. We deal with governments as they are. Our relations depend not on their internal structures or social systems, but on actions which affect us and the inter-American system. In pursuit of this policy we have maintained a correct and positive attitude toward the present Government of Chile since its inception.

We would like to believe that the Chilean Government shares our desire for normal relations, but we cannot ignore the fact that there are some important elements among the political forces within the present Chilean Government which have appeared to welcome a confrontation with the United States for ideological as well as for internal political reasons.

Source: Richard P. Stebbins and Elaine P. Adam (eds.), American Foreign Relations 1971: A Documentary Record *(New York: Council on Foreign Relations and New York University Press, 1976), pp. 483-485.*

DOCUMENT 13

COMMENTS ON THE COUP IN CHILE BY ASSISTANT SECRETARY OF STATE FOR INTER-AMERICAN AFFAIRS KUBISCH BEFORE THE HOUSE SUBCOMMITTEE (SEPTEMBER 20, 1973)

...Perhaps I should take this opportunity at the outset to comment on false charges from some quarters that the U.S. Government had advance knowledge of or participated in some way in the overthrow and death of President Allende.

Gentlemen, I wish to state as flatly and as categorically as I possibly can that we did not have advance knowledge of the coup that took place on September 11. In the light of what I consider to be some rather imprecise reporting on the matter, I want to distinguish between our receiving reports about the *possibility* of a coup in Chile and our having advance *knowledge* that a coup would take place.

The facts are that we had received many reports over a long period of time about the possibility of a coup in Chile. Such reports and speculations are rife in Chile itself. Indeed, President Allende himself had commented publicly about them, and there was even a report in a Santiago daily newspaper on September 11 that a coup by the Chilean armed forces was scheduled for that very day.

All of the earlier reports that had speculated about or predicted coup attempts turned out to be false except the last one, which was received in our offices Tuesday morning, September 11, after the coup had already begun.

However, there was no contact whatsoever by the organizers and leaders of the coup directly with us, and we did not have definite knowledge of it in advance.

In a similar vein, either explicitly or implicitly, the U.S. Government has been charged with involvement or complicity in the coup. This is absolutely false. As official spokesmen of the U.S. Government have stated repeatedly, we were not involved in the coup in any way.

....

Much concern has naturally been shown for the human tragedy that has resulted from recent events in Chile. The American people and their government have traditionally demonstrated such concern for the suffering of others throughout the world. The United States has given active support in numerous ways to alleviating suffering and furthering the respect of human rights. With regard to Chile, we have already expressed regret at the loss of human lives and at the death of President Allende.

We have also been concerned with reports of violations of human rights in Chile. However, to my knowledge, many of these reports are unsubstantiated and not necessarily indicative of the policies to be followed by the new Government of Chile once the situation there has fully stabilized.

....

We are not responsible for the difficulties in which Chile found itself, and it is not for us to judge what would have been best or will now be best for the Chilean people.

Source: Richard P. Stebbins and Elaine P. Adam (eds.), American Foreign Relations 1971: A Documentary Record *(New York: Council on Foreign Relations and New York University Press, 1976), pp. 413-415.*

Throughout the 1970s Latin America's international position and relationship with the U.S. changed. Sustained economic growth in most countries helped to expand and diversify trade, which in turn brought in foreign investment from Europe and Japan. American economic domination of the region was no longer undisputed. This gave many of the countries a new self-confidence, which often translated into political assertiveness in their dealings with Washington. This shift was also facilitated by detente between the U.S. and Soviet Union. A warming trend in the Cold War made American policy in the region less rigid and more inclined to tolerate deviation from Washington's agenda. With President Jimmy Carter there was a renewed emphasis on political and social reform within the Americas, and an end to much of the military assistance Nixon gave to right-wing dictatorships. Focusing on human rights issues, Carter even seemed to condone coups against pro-American regimes that had a record of oppression. Such was the case in 1979 when revolutions flared in both El Salvador and Nicaragua. However, Carter lost the 1980 presidential election to Ronald Reagan, who quickly returned to a more "traditional" Latin American policy. Although the revolutions in both countries were broadly based and generally well-received by other Latin American states, Reagan was convinced that the new governments in place were communist. He authorized CIA support for counter-revolutionaries fighting the government in Nicaragua, while funding the military and police that dominated a more centrist regime in El Salvador. Many in the international community were appalled by such meddling, which brought with it death squads and numerous human rights abuses.

DOCUMENT 14

FINDINGS OF THE INTERNATIONAL COURT OF JUSTICE ON AMERICAN INTERVENTION IN NICARAGUA (MAY AND OCTOBER 1984)

The government of Nicaragua accuses the United States of repeated violations of its sovereign rights. The most serious accusation concerns the international crime of aggression, of which the United States is guilty by virtue of multiple illegal interventions with the goal of depriving Nicaragua of its right to self-determination.

The crime of aggression has been perpetrated by various types of acts, all of which violate the rights of Nicaragua and which, moreover, even imply certain violations of the laws of war or incite war.

This illegal conduct is aggravated by the persistent refusal of the government of the United States to abide by the various procedures for the peaceful settlement of differences, as required by the rights of peoples (cf. Algiers Declaration), notwithstanding the constant efforts of the Nicaraguan government to negotiate a peaceful solution.

Specifically, Nicaragua contends that the United States has organized, trained, and armed counterrevolutionary forces established in Honduran territory, whose main objective is to overthrow the legitimate Sandinista government. Nicaragua contends that this entire policy violates rules forbidding the recourse to force and intervention in the internal affairs of other nations, set forth most notably in Article 2 (4) of the Charter of the United Nations, in Articles 18 and 20 of the Charter of the Organization of American States, and Article I of the Havana Convention of February 20, 1928 on the rights and duties of states in the event of civil war.

These various violations, orchestrated by the Central Intelligence Agency (CIA) on behalf of the U.S. government, have caused suffering and death for the Nicaraguan people and led to numerous illegal incursions into their territory, with the aim of terrorizing the civilian population, and in a time of great economic shortages have abusively deprived them of food resources.

In particular, Nicaragua accuses the government of the United States of having violated in the most serious manner its most basic rights as a sovereign nation by mining its ports, which caused considerable damage to its port installations as well as to several ships operating under foreign flags. These mining operations, which are acts of war, constitute an aggression on the part of a country which is officially at peace with Nicaragua and which still maintains diplomatic relations with it.

Nicaragua also accuses the United States of threatening a major invasion of its territory, a threat made credible by U.S. engagement in numerous air, sea, and land maneuvers on the basis of planned and disclosed strategic options. Such threats and plans constitute an aggression that makes a mockery of the sovereign rights of Nicaragua. The menace of this threatened invasion compels the Nicaraguan government to devote most of its already scarce resources to defense against these illegal activities, resources desperately required to meet the needs of its people.

Nicaragua contends that these illegal practices constitute criminal behavior, and entail personal accountability on the part of the Chief Executive of the United States and other policymakers in the sense of this term as defined by the Nuremberg Tribunal.

The Defense of the United States

In substance, the United States contends that it is acting in legitimate self-defense, according to the rights of peoples, and accuses Nicaragua of massive arms shipments to the Salvadoran rebels. This export of the Sandinista revolution constitutes, according to the United States, intervention in the internal affairs of El Salvador.

In this context, the United States claims that the mining of the ports of Nicaragua and the support given to the counterrevolutionary forces constitute an expression of the right of legitimate collective defense. Toward this end, the U.S. government relies on a broad and self-serving interpretation of Article 51 of the Charter of the United Nations, which confers the right of self-defense upon all states.

The United States accuses Nicaragua of supporting the rebel forces of El Salvador; and contends that such assistance constitutes an aggression according to the terms of Article 39 of the Charter and of the resolution on the definition of aggression adopted by the General Assembly of the United Nations in 1974.

The United States claims that its actions are a reasonable and appropriate effort to stop the flow of arms to El Salvador, with no intention of overthrowing the Sandinista government. It contends that it is no longer responsible for the conduct of the "contras" in their internal opposition to the Sandinista government.

The United States declares, finally, that Nicaragua has not fulfilled OAS norms regarding human rights and democracy, and that such deficiencies are sufficient to justify the external pressures exerted on Nicaragua to encourage respect for these norms.

THE FACTS

After having appraised the evidence presented, the Tribunal has arrived at the following conclusions:

—The government of the United States has not proven its principal accusation, that of the support given by Nicaragua to the rebel forces of El Salvador;

—The obvious objective of the rebel forces active along the border and in the interior of Nicaraguan territory is to destabilize, and if possible to overthrow, the government in Managua;

—By principal reliance on the CIA, an organ of the U.S. government, rebel forces are essentially equipped, directed, and controlled by the United States;

—The government of the United States has blocked efforts by Nicaragua to find a peaceful resolution of its disputes with foreign governments and has not shown good faith in trying to find a negotiated solution;

—The military and paramilitary operations have caused great suffering and great damage to the Nicaraguan people;

The United States has undertaken numerous military maneuvers which threaten Nicaraguan security, for purposes of provocation and intimidation, and has made plans for a large-scale invasion directed at Nicaragua.

....

The United States policies constitute the most serious violation of the rules of international law that forbid intervention in the internal affairs of others and protect the basic rights of each people and each country to set up a regime of their choice through the dynamics of national self-determination. These legal conclusions reflect also the norms of the Charter of the United Nations, especially as specified in resolutions 2131 (XX), 2625 (XXV), 2734 (XXV), and 36/103 of the General Assembly of the United Nations. Those resolutions have been adopted with the approval of the United States and their validity cannot now be contested.

In this case, the evidence presented leaves no reason to doubt the democratic achievement of the Nicaraguan revolution. The Tribunal rejects the allegations made by the United States government concerning Nicaragua's failure to live up to its democratic promises, and denies the right of any government to judge the democratic character of other governments.

Under these conditions, there is no humanitarian justification for the intervention in Nicaragua. The problems existing in Nicaragua do not justify intervention, especially as the worst of these problems have been instigated by the United States itself.

. . .

Finally, there exists the gross disproportion between the massive amount of power unleashed by the United States in its intervention to destroy the legal authority of Nicaragua, and the legitimate defense that it claims to be pursuing. The United States policy, moreover, has no foundation in terms of the force that would have been necessary to guard against alleged aggression by Nicaragua, assuming it had been established. That is, in any event, U.S. force is so excessive as by itself to condemn it as an abuse of the doctrine of legitimate defense.

On these various grounds, the Tribunal considers that the validity of the accusation of aggression made by Nicaragua against the United States is convincingly established beyond any reasonable doubt.

....

In carrying out its aggression, the United States uses an army comprised mainly of former officers and soldiers of the Somoza dictatorship, fugitives pardoned by a revolution which in its hour of triumph condemned no one. This army, whose goal is to annihilate Nicaragua, has its principal bases in Honduras and Miami; it is common knowledge that it is recruited, financed, armed, and directed by the government of the United States. North American military advisers participate directly in its actions. Although the principal target of aggression is Nicaragua, the war also affects the bordering countries, which are gradually being transformed into large military bases and thus function as part of an imperial, geopolitical strategy that sees Central America as an integral part of the United States.

. . .

Nicaragua is under attack not because it *is* democratic but rather to ensure that *it does not become so*. Nicaragua is under attack not because it *could become* a military dictatorship but to make sure that it *does*. Nicaragua is under attack not because it *could become* the satellite of a great power but rather to ensure that it *will*.

Source: Marlene Dixon, (ed.), On Trial: Reagan's War Against Nicaragua *(San Francisco: Synthesis Publications, 1985), pp. 225-228 / 230 / 232-233.*

On May 10, 1984, the International Court of Justice at The Hague issued a historic order favorable to Nicaragua's complaint against the United States for laying mines in its ports and other actions. The Court also rejected on a temporary basis the U.S. position that the World Court had no authority in the case (on the technical grounds that Nicaragua had never officially recorded its 1929 decision recognizing the Court).

A few hours before the original filing of Nicaragua's complaint, President Reagan had said the U.S. would not submit to World Court jurisdiction on Central American disputes for two years.

On November 26, 1984, the Court ruled permanently that it did have authority in the case and it rejected Reagan's declaration. A full hearing on the case was expected to take place in May 1985

Here are excerpts from the Interim Order of Protection of May 10, 1984, which reflects worldwide opinion that Nicaragua's charges are justified. The Court's decision also embodies the concept of a community of nations in which relationships must be subject to forms of global order. In the first excerpt, the Court reviews the charges brought by Nicaragua; the second contains the main part of the ruling itself.

ORDER

Present: President Elias; *Vice President* Sette-Camara; *Judges* Lachs, Morozov, Nagendra Singh, Ruda, Mosler, Oda, Ago, El-Khani, Schwebel, Sir Robert Jennings, de Lacharriére, Mbaye, Bedjaoui; *Registrar* Torres Bernardez.

The International Court of Justice,

Composed as above,

After deliberation,

Having regard to Articles 41 and 48 of the Statute of the Court,

Having regard to Articles 73 and 74 of the Rules of Court,

Having regard to the Application by the Republic of Nicaragua filed in the Registry of the Court on 9 April 1984, instituting proceedings against the United States of America in respect of a dispute concerning responsibility for military and paramilitary activities in and against Nicaragua;

Makes the following Order:

1. Whereas in the above-mentioned Application the Republic of Nicaragua, invoking the declarations of acceptance of the jurisdiction of the Court deposited by both States under Article 36 of the Statute of the Court, recounts a series of events over the period from March 1981 up to the present day, as a result of which Nicaragua claims to have suffered grievous consequences, and claims that

"the United States of America is using military force against Nicaragua and intervening in Nicaragua's internal affairs, in violation of Nicaragua's sovereignty, territorial integrity and political independence and of the most fundamental and universally-accepted principles of international law";

and whereas, on the basis of the facts alleged in the Application, it requests the court adjudge and declare:

"(a) That the United States, in recruiting, training, arming, equipping, financing, supplying and otherwise encouraging, supporting, aiding, and directing military and paramilitary actions in and against Nicaragua, has violated and is violating its express charter and treaty obligations to Nicaragua and, in particular, its charter and treaty obligations under:

—Article 2 (4) of the United Nations Charter;

—Articles 18 and 20 of the Charter of the Organization of American States;

—Article 8 of the Convention on Rights and Duties of States;

—Article I, Third, of the Convention concerning the Duties and Rights of States in the Event of Civil Strife.

(b) That the United States, in breach of its obligation under general and customary international law, has violated and is violating the sovereignty of Nicaragua by:

—armed attacks against Nicaragua by air, land and sea;

—incursions into Nicaragua territorial waters;

—aerial trespass into Nicaraguan airspace;

—efforts by direct and indirect means to coerce and intimidate the Government of Nicaragua.

(c) That the United States, in breach of its obligation under general and customary international law, has used and is using force and the threat of force against Nicaragua.

(d) That the United States, in breach of its obligation under general and customary international law, has intervened and is intervening in the internal affairs of Nicaragua.

(e) That the United States, in breach of its obligation under general and customary international law, has infringed and is infringing the freedom of the high seas and interrupting peaceful maritime commerce.

(f) That the United States, in breach of its obligation under general and customary international law, has killed, wounded, and kidnapped and is killing, wounding, and kidnapping citizens of Nicaragua.

(g) That, in view of its breaches of the foregoing legal obligations, the United States is under a particular duty to cease and desist immediately:

From all use of force—whether direct or indirect, overt or covert—against Nicaragua, and from all threats of force against Nicaragua;

from all violations of the sovereignty, territorial integrity, or political independence of Nicaragua, including all intervention, direct or indirect, in the internal affairs of Nicaragua;

from all support of any kind—including the provision of training, arms, ammunition, finances, supplies, assistance, direction or any other form of support—to any nation, group, organization, movement, or individual engaged or planning to engage in military or paramilitary actions in or against Nicaragua;

from all efforts to restrict, block, or endanger access to or from Nicaraguan ports;

and from all killings, woundings, and kidnappings of Nicaraguan citizens.

(h) That the United States has an obligation to pay Nicaragua, in its own right and as *parens patriae* for the citizens of Nicaragua, reparations for damages to person, property, and the Nicaraguan economy caused by the foregoing violations of international law in a sum to be determined by the Court. Nicaragua reserves the right to introduce to the Court a precise evaluation of the damages caused by the United States;

2. Having regard to the request dated 9 April 1984 and filed in the Registry the same day, whereby the Republic of Nicaragua, relying on Article 41 of the Statute of the Court and Articles 73, 74, 75, and 78 of the Rules of Court, urgently requests the Court to indicate the following provisional measures to be in effect while the Court is seised of the case introduced by the abovementioned Application:

"—That the United States should immediately cease and desist from providing, directly or indirectly, any support—including training, arms, ammunition, supplies, assistance, finances, direction, or any other form of support—to any nation, group, organization, movement, or individual engaged or planning to engage in military or paramilitary activities in or against Nicaragua;

—That the United States should immediately cease and desist from any military or paramilitary activity by its own officials, agents or forces in or against Nicaragua and from any other use or threat of force in its relations with Nicaragua;

THE COURT

A. Unanimously,

Rejects the request made by the United States of America that the proceedings on the Application filed by the Republic of Nicaragua on 9 April 1984, and on the request filed the same day by the Republic of Nicaragua for the indication of provisional measures, be terminated by the removal of the case from the list;

B. *Indicates*, pending its final decision in the proceedings instituted on 9 April 1984 by the Republic of Nicaragua against the United States of America, the following provisional measures:

1. Unanimously,

The United States of America should immediately cease and refrain from any action restricting, blocking, or endangering access to or from Nicaraguan ports, and, in particular, the laying of mines;

2. By fourteen votes to one,

The right to sovereignty and to political independence possessed by the Republic of Nicaragua, like any other State of the region or of the world, should be fully respected and should not in any way be jeopardized by any military and paramilitary activities which are prohibited by the principles of international law, in particular the principle that States should refrain in their international relations from the threat or use of force against the territorial integrity or the political independence of any State, and the principle concerning the duty not to intervene in matters within the domestic jurisdiction of a State, principles embodied in the United Nations Charter and the Charter of the Organization of American States.

IN FAVOR: *President* Elias; *Vice-President* Sette-Camara; *Judges* Lachs, Morozov, Nagendra Singh, Ruda, Mosler, Oda, Ago, El-Khani, Sir Robert Jennings, de Lacharriere, Mbaye, Bedjaoui.

AGAINST: *Judge* Schwebel.

Source: Marlene Dixon, (ed.), On Trial: Reagan's War Against Nicaragua *(San Francisco: Synthesis Publications, 1985), pp. 255-258.*

Document 15

Personal account of Digna Barrera before the International Court of Justice

My name is Digna Barrera, 29 years old, mother of two children and from the heroic city of Esteí, in Nicaragua. To begin my story, I can tell you that I was kidnapped in the El Zapote community of the Department of Nueva Segovia of Region One, when my husband and I were going to a little farm that the Agrarian Reform gave us.

At about 4 p.m., we arrived at the house of Amadeo Fajardo, my uncle, and were offered a meal. After we ate dinner, at about 7 p.m., I went out of the kitchen to the corral, to get a cigarette from my husband who was talking with my uncle. Only my uncle was there, so I asked him where my husband was, and he answered that he was over there, under the tree talking with some *"compas"* (*compañeros*).

Very confidently, I went towards them. Two men answered my greetings very aggressively, and told me that the boss had ordered me to go with them. The man in charge was tall and dark, and wearing a black cap. He ordered me to give up all that I had, and they took my jewelry. I was asked to give up my guns, but I answered that I didn't have any, that we had just come to our farm nearby. At that moment, I saw my husband coming with his hands tied. He had been brutally beaten, and they told me: "We came from the Ministry of the Interior in Managua to arrest the two of you because you are contra supporters." I answered, "You are crazy, we are not contras, we are Sandinistas." A man who was traveling with us told them, "I came with this couple and I have three sons who are in the army in Managua." And they answered: "Then you'll come with us, too, that might help them." They took him and tied his hands. There were five of them altogether.

Two of the kidnappers stood with my husband and me under the tree, while the other three talked in secret with my uncle. After that, we all started walking, while the last man erased the footprints with a tree branch. After walking a while, we arrived at a place where about 50 men were waiting. There I was brutally raped many times, in my rectum and my vagina. I was forced down on my knees and raped at the same time that my husband was cruelly beaten. They kept asking us what the plans of the contras were, but we knew that they were the contras and they confirmed that to us, saying they were from the Nicaraguan Democratic Front (Frente Democrático Nicaragüense, FDN).

....

They kept raping me in front of my husband, I was in great pain and wanted to scream, but they covered my mouth very tightly with a handkerchief.

....

Then they let me go. But before that, they asked Juan Valladares, who had also been kidnapped, if he was with the revolution. Juan answered: "Yes, I love the revolution because under Somoza I never had any land. The revolution gave me land to work and live." They made him lie face up on the ground, and with a spoon they tore out his eyes. After that they shot him. He said only: "Oh, my mother!" Those were his last words.

....

When I got back to my uncle's house, he wasn't there but a peasant told me that he wanted me to go to the house of Rosario Vellorín. I went and found him. He asked me if my husband Agustín had been killed, and I said yes.

....

We owe all this to Ronald Reagan.

Source: Marlene Dixon, (ed.), On Trial: Reagan's War Against Nicaragua *(San Francisco: Synthesis Publications, 1985), pp. 90-92.*

DOCUMENT 16

LETTER TO THE PEOPLE OF THE UNITED STATES FROM AN INTERNATIONAL GROUP OF PROMINENT WRITERS INCLUDING GABRIEL GARCIA MARQUEZ AND GRAHAM GREENE

The present United States administration has gone to war against the people and government of Nicaragua.

It is an undeclared war, unauthorized by Congress and, therefore, unconstitutional. It is a covert war. The American people have not authorized the use of public funds for a war waged in the name of supposed intelligence operations.

It is an irrational war. It renounces diplomatic negotiations without giving them a serious try.

It is a reactionary war. The United States created and then supported the corrupt Somoza dictatorship during more than 40 years. Now it cannot tolerate an independent government in Nicaragua. It has armed the former guardsmen of the Somoza regime against the people of Nicaragua.

It is an inhuman war. It is destroying the modest but profound achievements of the Nicaraguan revolution. It is destroying the crops and schools of Nicaragua. It is killing the children and the peasants of Nicaragua.

It is a dangerous war. It wrenches the problems of Nicaragua and Central America out of their peculiar cultural and historical contexts and thrusts them onto the stage of east-west conflict. This distortion can internationalize the war and destroy opportunities for diplomacy, democracy and social advancements in the region.

It is a treacherous war. It is the fourth time in this century that the United States has invented pretexts to invade Nicaragua. This time, it is doing so by mercenary means, pitting brothers against brothers and countries against countries in the region. It is an immoral war. Once again, a superpower declares itself menaced by the independence of a small nation and attempts its submission by intimidation or its destruction by force.

We fear that the United States government is attempting to implement policy by "accomplished fact"—in Nicaragua, leaving no room for debate or opposition.

We are also confident that the people of the United States, their public opinion and their democratic institutions will speak out against this undeclared, covert, irrational, inhuman, dangerous and immoral adventure undertaken by the government of Ronald Reagan.

Source: Peter Rossett and John Vandermeer, The Nicaragua Reader: Documents of a Revolution Under Fire *(New York: Grove Press, 1983), pp. 241-242.*

The Reagan administration was not moved by any such appeals, nor was it bound to accept the judgement of the International Court of Justice. In fact, during the 1980s Reagan expanded an interventionist policy with respect to countries in the western hemisphere. The tiny Caribbean island of Grenada had a revolution in 1979 that brought to power Maurice Bishop, who openly pursued friendly ties with the Sandinistas in Nicaragua, Castro and even the Soviet Union.

DOCUMENT 17 LETTER FROM BISHOP TO DANIEL ORTEGA (HEAD OF THE NICARAGUAN GOVERNMENT) (JULY 17, 1981)

[*My dear Daniel*]

Warmest fraternal and Revolutionary greetings!

On the occasion of the second Anniversary of the glorious Nicaraguan Revolution Our Party, Government an People extend our total and complete solidarity with the FSLN, your Government of National Reconstruction and the fighting children of Sandino.

. . . I am certain, from reports we have been receiving, that our two situations are under similar pressures. It is clear that U.S. Imperialism has decided to make an all-out onslaught on our two Revolutions. The propaganda war, the economic aggression, the Political and Industrial destablisation and the threat of mercenary invasion all lead to the unmistakable conclusion that imperialism has decided to attempt to overthrow our popular Revolutions this year. That is their decision; but we have made our own decision that our Revolutions will continue and undoubtedly we will win out. As our People say in Grenada—A UNITED, CONSCIOUS, ORGANISED AND VIGILANT PEOPLE CAN NEVER BE DEFEATED.

....

LONG LIVE THE NICARAGUAN REVOLUTION:

LONG LIVE THE FSLN!

LONG LIVE THE UNBREAKABLE BONDS OF FRIENDSHIP BETWEEN THE PEOPLE OF GRENADA AND NICARAGUA!

FORWARD EVER, BACKWARD NEVER!

A Warm Embrace,
[Maurice]

Source: Paul Seabury and Walter A. MacDougall (eds.), The Grenada Papers *(San Francisco: ICS Press, 1984), pp. 31-32.*

DOCUMENT 18 EXTRACTS OF A MEMO FROM THE EMBASSY OF GRENADA IN MOSCOW ON RELATIONS WITH THE SOVIET UNION (JULY 11, 1983)

. . .There is a general acceptance among Soviet authorities that we are at the national democratic, anti-imperialist stage of socialist orientation. The USSR assigns a special place to these types of countries in its foreign policy. This is, of course, also the case with other socialist countries. In terms of their priorities, the countries of socialist orientation come right after the socialist community.

....

The Soviets have been burnt quite often in the past by giving support to Governments which have either squandered that support, or turned around and become agents of imperialism, or lost power. One is reminded of Egypt, Somolia, Ghana and Peru. They are therefore very careful, and for us sometimes maddingly slow, in making up their minds about who to support. They have decided to support us for two main reasons. 1. Cuba has strongly championed our cause. 2. They are genuinely impressed with our management of the economy and state affairs in general. They are impressed with our commitment to planning, the absence of corruption, the ethic of hard work among the leadership, the ability of the leadership to spread this ethic among the population, the willingness to sacrifice. They are also impressed with the policy on the communication media, the close links with the masses, the practice of popular democracy and the implementation of the policy of democratic centralism as a guiding principle and not a dogma. Also of importance is the stability of our leadership.

....

By itself, Grenada's distance from the USSR, and its small size, would mean that we would figure in a very minute way in the USSR's global relationships. Our revolution has to be viewed as a world-wide process with its original roots in the Great October Revolution. For Grenada to assume a position of increasingly greater importance, we have to be seen as influencing at least regional events. We have to establish ourselves as the authority on events in at least the English-speaking Caribbean, and be the sponsor of revolutionary activity and progressive developments in this region at least.

....

Recommendations

1. Continue high profile, well prepared participation in important events of the socialist community, eg Karl Marx Conference and World Peace Council.

2. Implement agreements between Grenada and other members of the socialist community promptly and faithfully.

3. Encourage officials to visit at least two countries in Eastern Europe during official missions to this part of the world.

....

Recommendations

1. Continue our international support for the Soviet line.

2. Strengthen our political efforts in the UN and OAS and their agencies.

3. Seek a more critical role in the non-aligned movement.

4. Examine the desirability, ways and means of developing closer relations with the "middle" and "off centre" countries.

Source: Paul Seabury and Walter A. MacDougall (eds.), The Grenada Papers *(San Francisco: ICS Press, 1984), pp. 199-201, 207, 210, 216.*

After economic and political pressure through neighbouring states by Washington, Bishop tried to distance himself from his revolutionary rhetoric. This however led to his overthrow and execution by some of his more radical followers in October 1983. On the pretext of protecting American medical students working there, the Reagan administration sent in the marines and toppled the new government. Cuban construction crews which had been there to help construct a new runway were quickly expelled, and a much more "favourable" regime was installed on the island. The invasion of Grenada was clearly a warning to Castro and Nicaragua, but by the end of the 1980s a new and different challenge presented itself to American foreign policy. The fight against drugs in the U.S. brought several Latin American countries to the attention of American law enforcement agencies. Government officials in several long-time American ally states were linked to international drug cartels, presenting a major dilemma for Washington. The most glaring case of corruption was in Panama, where strongman General Manuel Noriega was himself implicated in narcotics trafficking. Based on this, in 1989 President George Bush sent in the marines once again to force Noriega's extradition to the U.S. to face charges. However, many people questioned both the motive and legality of 'Operation Just Cause'. Given the history of American relations with other states in the western hemisphere, such doubts continue to question U.S. policy in the region today.

DOCUMENT 19 EXCERPTS FROM A 1977 FUND-RAISING LETTER WRITTEN BY RONALD REAGAN ABOUT PRESIDENT CARTER'S POLICY OF REVOKING U.S. CLAIMS ON THE PANAMA CANAL

. . .Unless you and I act now, one of the most vital shipping and defense waterways will be in the complete control of the anti-American, pro-Marxist dictator, General Torrijos.

You and I just can't let that happen. Too much is at stake. That's why I felt it was important that I alert you personally to what's been going on behind your back.

....

Here's why I am so worried:

1) Once the treaty is ratified, the U.S. can't build a new sea-level canal in or out of Panama without the express written permission of the Panamanian government. In the process of giving up our Canal, Mr. Carter has also surrendered our rights to build a new one if needed.

2) Once ratified, there's no guarantee our Naval Fleet will have the right of priority passage in time of war. Our Navy depends on safe, secure, unrestricted passage through the Canal. But if we lose this short-cut from the Atlantic to the Pacific, we'll lose the flexibility and quick response we need to protect our country and our holdings.

3) Once ratified, there is no guarantee the U.S. can intervene to protect and defend the neutrality of the Canal. Despite the way Mr. Carter "interprets" the treaty, Panamanian's [sic] chief negotiator, Mr. Betancourt [sic], says, flat out, "The U.S. does NOT have the right to intervene to defend the Canal."

4) Once ratified, we must close down 10 of our military bases, Americans in the Zone will be under Panamanian rule, and we must pay Torrijos millions more each year for the Canal.

...Believe me, I am counting on you to give me all the help you possibly can to defeat those who time and time again vote to weaken our national security.

....

Believe me, without your support, the Canal is as good as gone. Then we'll have to write off the Canal like we were forced to write off Vietnam, Cambodia and Laos.

....

It's time you and I counter the slick propaganda campaign that says our ownership of the Canal is "imperialistic." Nothing could be further from the truth.

We haven't made a nickel on the Canal. We've run it for the benefit of the entire world. And we've poured over $200 million a year into the Panamanian economy.

This debate concerns our national security. And that shouldn't be sacrificed to score a few political points with a regime in Panama that so blatantly violates the human rights of its own people.

With so much at stake, I urge you to send me your contribution so we can defeat those who vote time and time again against a strong U.S. foreign policy....

With deep concern,
Ronald Reagan

Source: Independent Commission of Inquiry on the U.S. Invasion of Panama, The U.S. Invasion of Panama: The Truth Behind Operation 'Just Cause' *(Boston: South End Press, 1991), pp. 128-130.*

DOCUMENT 20

EXCERPTS FROM NORIEGA'S WRITTEN STATEMENT ON CHARGES AGAINST HIM FOR THE FEDERAL DISTRICT COURT IN MIAMI (APRIL 2, 1990)

The reasons for the invasion of the Republic of Panama by the government of the United States include:

I. The Panamanian isthmus is of strategic importance to the United States! For that reason we see the interest in, and the phobia against Panama rather than Peru or Paraguay or Argentina or Venezuela or Guatemala; because none of them are either the passageway or the focus of geopolitical strategy, they don't have an interoceanic canal, and they are not the geographical center of intercontinental routes.

II. Because of the military bases, the United States has an interest in continuing to maintain troops at the crossroads of the American continent that can be deployed to control South, North and Central America and the Caribbean. The only ideal country in all of the Americas is Panama, with the Atlantic and Pacific regions correlated with the transit distances for air and maritime traffic. In addition, the vegetation and ecology of Panama provide a proving ground with terrain equivalent to that of Colombia and Venezuela and the jungles of Peru and Brazil.

III. The treaties signed by President Carter and Torrijos were to put an end to the armed presence and the military control of a Southern Command in the year 1999. The new United States administration and its "establishment" now consider that it was an error to have signed these treaties and are looking for a way to invalidate them. And for this reason they violate and continue violating their clauses.

IV. The administrator of the Canal is now supposed to be a Panamanian, reversing the majority from North Americans to Panamanians. It was necessary that this should be someone dependable and manageable for the North American government officials in order to continue using their CIA with its economic resources as the source for other hidden and secret funding not reported to the U.S. Treasury, for covert actions and illegal aggression such as the Iran-Gate operations against Nicaragua.

The consequences of the invasion include:

I. The physical destruction of the country by aerial bombardment and the devastation and destruction of buildings, material goods, etc.

II. Civilian and military deaths, including North Americans, whose death toll has been kept secret and the information denied to the North American people. There are families still searching for their missing relatives who disappeared into common graves or whose bodies were incinerated by flamethrowers. The death and destruction caused by this invasion are kept at reasonable levels and scientifically controlled. Like the devastation at Hiroshima and Nagasaki, one must look at the videotapes taken during that night to be able to appreciate the magnitude of savagery and inhumanity.

Source: Independent Commission of Inquiry on the U.S. Invasion of Panama, The U.S. Invasion of Panama: The Truth Behind Operation 'Just Cause' *(Boston: South End Press, 1991), pp. 121-122.*

DOCUMENT 21 RESOLUTION OF THE OAS ON THE INVASION OF PANAMA (DECEMBER 22, 1989)

THE PERMANENT COUNCIL OF THE ORGANIZATION OF AMERICAN STATES HAVING SEEN:

The serious events in the Republic of Panama, especially the armed clashes resulting from the military intervention by the United States and the deplorable loss of lives and property;

The obligation of States not to intervene, directly or indirectly, for any reason whatever, in the internal or external affairs of any other State, and

The obligation to respect the inviolability of the territory of a State, which may not be the object, even temporarily, of military occupation or of other measures of force taken by another State, directly or indirectly, on any grounds whatever,

....

That any just and lasting solution to the Panamanian problem must be based upon full respect for the right of its people to self-determination without outside interference;

That it is necessary to guarantee full respect for the sovereignty of Panama;

That it is also necessary to reestablish conditions that will guarantee the full exercise of the human rights and fundamental freedoms of the Panamanian people;

That the Panamanian people have the inalienable right to self-determination without internal dictates or external interference,

RESOLVES:

1. To deeply regret the military intervention in Panama.

2. To urge the immediate cessation of hostilities and bloodshed and to request the launching of negotiations between the various political sectors of the country that will lead to a concerted solution to the Panamanian institutional crisis.

3. To express its deepest concern over the serious incidents and the loss of lives taking place in the Republic of Panama.

4. To call for the withdrawal of the foreign troops used for the military intervention and to reaffirm that solving the crisis Panama is undergoing at this time necessarily requires full respect for the right of the Panamanian people to self-determination without outside interference and faithful adherence to the letter and spirit of the Torrijos-Carter treaties.

Source: Independent Commission of Inquiry on the U.S. Invasion of Panama, The U.S. Invasion of Panama: The Truth Behind Operation 'Just Cause' *(Boston: South End Press, 1991), 124-125.*

STUDY QUESTIONS FOR SECTION ELEVEN: LATIN AMERICA IN INTERNATIONAL RELATIONS

1. Assess American foreign policy towards Latin America before the 1930s.

2. How and why did American policy change during the administration of Franklin Roosevelt?

3. How did the Cold War affect American policy in the region in the late 1940s and the 1950s?

4. Did American policy towards Latin America change significantly during the Kennedy administration?

5. How did the breakdown of relations between the United States and Cuba affect Latin America?

6. What were the main developments in American policies towards Latin America in the 1970s and 1980s? What factors influenced those policies?

SECTION TWELVE

THE MIDDLE EAST IN INTERNATIONAL RELATIONS

DOCUMENTS

CHRONOLOGY

1914	World War I starts
1916	Arab revolt
1917	Sykes-Picot Agreement Balfour declaration
1918	World War I ends
1920	establishment of French mandates for Lebanon and Syria, and British Mandates for Iraq and Palestine
1922	end of the Ottoman Empire
1924	Ibn Saud ruler of Saudi Arabia
1939	World War II starts
1941	British occupy Syria and Lebanon British and Soviets occupy Iran
1942	Battle of El Alamein: German and Italian Retreat
1945	World War II ends Arab League founded
1946	Syria, Lebanon, Jordan independent
1947	British decide to pull out of Palestine; fighting starts between Jews and Arabs
1948	State of Israel proclaimed in Palestine
1952	Overthrow of King Farouk of Egypt; rise of Gamal Abdal Nasser
1956	Suez crisis
1957	Eisenhower Doctrine
1958	US troops into Lebanon Iraq revolution
1960	OPEC (Organization of Petroleum Exporting Countries) founded
1964	PLO (Palestine Liberation Organization) founded
1967	Six Days War
1969	War of Attrition Ghaddafi into power in Libya Nasser dies; Anwar Sadat into power in Egypt
1971	British responsibility for the Persian Gulf ends Jordan suppresses Palestinians
1972	Treaty of Friendship between Iraq and Soviet Union Black September kidnaps Israeli athletes at Munich Olympics

1973	October/Yom Kippur War
	OPEC uses oil weapon
1975	Lebanese civil war starts
1976	Syria invades Lebanon
1978	Camp David agreements
1979	treaty between Egypt and Israel
	Saddam Hussein into power in Iraq
	Shah deposed in Iran; Ayatollah Khomeini into power
	Soviet Union invades Afghanistan
1980	Iraq invades Iran; Iran-Iraq war starts
1982	Israel invades Lebanon
1985	Israel pulls back in Lebanon
1987	Intifada starts in West Bank and Gaza
1988	Iran-Iraq war ends
1990	Iraq invades Kuwait
1991	Gulf War
	Middle East peace conference in Madrid
1993	Oslo agreements between Israel and the PLO

DOCUMENT 1 THE ARAB REVOLT

By the end of the nineteenth century, in a number of centres such as Cairo, Damascus and Beirut, there was the revival of Arab culture and learning, as well as a growth in Arab nationalism. This took the form of antagonism to Ottoman Turkish rule. During World War I, both sides tried to use the Middle East against the other. The Germans attempted to stir up Muslim feeling against the British and the French; the British and French encouraged an Arab revolt against the Ottoman Turks, who were allied to Germany. The hereditary guardians of Mecca, the Hashemite family, were prepared to lead such a revolt, on certain conditions. The British, through their representative in Egypt, Sir Henry McMahon, indicated that they were willing to recognize Arab independence with the exception of parts of modern day Syria and Lebanon. McMahon sent the following letter to Hussein of Mecca:

October 24, 1915.

I have received your letter of the 29th Shawal, 1333, with much pleasure and your expression of friendliness and sincerity have given me the greatest satisfaction.

I regret that you should have received from my last letter the impression that I regarded the question of limits and boundaries with coldness and hesitation; such was not the case, but it appeared to me that the time had not yet come when that question could be discussed in a conclusive manner.

I have realised, however, from your last letter that you regard this question as one of vital and urgent importance. I have, therefore, lost no time in informing the Government of Great Britain of the contents of your letter, and it is with great pleasure that I communicate to you on their behalf the following statement, which I am confident you will receive with satisfaction.

The two districts of Mersina and Alexandretta and portions of Syria lying to the west of the districts of Damascus, Homs, Hama and Aleppo cannot be said to be purely Arab, and should be excluded from the limits demanded.

With the above modification, and without prejudice to our existing treaties with Arab chiefs, we accept those limits.

As for those regions lying within those frontiers wherein Great Britain is free to act without detriment to the interests of her ally, France, I am empowered in the name of the Government of Great Britain to give the following assurances and make the following reply to your letter:

(1) Subject to the above modifications, Great Britain is prepared to recognise and support the independence of the Arabs in all the regions within the limits demanded by the Sherif of Mecca.

(2) Great Britain will guarantee the Holy Places against all external aggression and will recognise their inviolability.

(3) When the situation admits, Great Britain will give to the Arabs her advice and will assist them to establish what may appear to be the most suitable forms of government in those various territories.

(4) On the other hand, it is understood that the Arabs have decided to seek the advice and guidance of Great Britain only, and that such European advisers and officials as may be required for the formation of a sound form of administration will be British.

(5) With regard to the *vilayets* of Bagdad and Basra, the Arabs will recognise that the established position and interests of Great Britain necessitate special administrative arrangements in order to secure these territories from foreign aggression to promote the welfare of the local populations and to safeguard our mutual economic interests.

I am convinced that this declaration will assure you beyond all possible doubt of the sympathy of Great Britain towards the aspirations of her friends the Arabs and will result in a firm and lasting alliance, the immediate results of which will be the expulsion of the Turks from the Arab counties and the freeing of the Arab peoples from the Turkish yoke, which for so many years has pressed heavily upon them.

I have confined myself in this letter to the more vital and important questions, and if there are any other matters dealt with in your letters which I have omitted to mention, we may discuss them at some convenient date in the future.

It was with very great relief and satisfaction that I heard of the safe arrival of the Holy Carpet and the accompanying offerings which, thanks to the clearness of your directions and the excellence of your arrangements, were landed without trouble or mishap in spite of the dangers and difficulties occasioned by the present sad war. May God soon bring a lasting peace and freedom of all peoples.

I am sending this letter by the hand of your trusted and excellent messenger, Sheikh Mohammed ibn Arif ibn Uraifan, and he will inform you of the various matters of interest, but of less vital importance, which I have not mentioned in this letter.

(Compliments).

(Signed): A. HENRY MCMAHON.

Source: Walter Laquer, ed., The Israeli-Arab Reader *(London: Bantam Books, 1968), pp. 16-17.*

DOCUMENT 2

THE SYKES-PICOT AGREEMENT

At the same time as they were encouraging the Arabs to revolt, Britain and France were determined to protect their interests and positions in the Middle East. Both depended on the Suez Canal to communicate with their possessions in Asia and both were using oil from the Middle East. Sir Mark Sykes, a British official, and Georges Picot, a French one, were delegated by their governments in 1915 to discuss the post-war division of the Middle East. They drew up the following agreement which was accepted by both governments.

THE INTER-ALLIED (SYKES-PICOT)
AGREEMENT OF 1916

It is accordingly understood between the French and British Governments—

1. That France and Great Britain are prepared to recognize and protect an independent Arab State or a Confederation of Arab States in the areas (A) and (B) marked on the annexed map, under the suzerainty of an Arab chief. That in area (A) France, and in area (B) Great Britain, shall have priority of right of enterprise and local loans. That in area (A) France, and in area (B) Great Britain, shall alone supply advisers or foreign functionaries at the request of the Arab State or Confederation of Arab States.

2. That in the blue area France, and in the red area Great Britain, shall be allowed to establish such direct or indirect administration or control as they desire and as they may think fit to arrange with the Arab State or Confederation of Arab States.

3. That in the brown area there shall be established an international administration, the form of which is to be decided upon after consultation with Russia, and subsequently in consultation with the other Allies, and the representatives of the Shereef of Mecca.

4. That Great Britain be accorded (1) the ports of Haifa and Acre, (2) guarantee of a given supply of water from the Tigris and Euphrates in area (A) for area (B). His Majesty's Government, on their part, undertake that they will at no time enter into negotiations for the cession of Cyprus to any third Power without the previous consent of the French Government.

5. That Alexandretta shall be a free port as regards the trade of the British Empire, and that there shall be no discrimination in port charges

or facilities as regards British shipping and British goods; that there shall be freedom of transit for British goods through Alexandretta and by railway through the blue area, whether those goods are intended for or originate in the red area, or (B) area, or area (A); and there shall be no discrimination, direct or indirect against British goods on any railway or against British goods or ships at any port serving the areas mentioned.

That Haifa shall be a free port as regards the trade of France, her dominions and protectorates, and there shall be no discrimination in port charges or facilities as regards French shipping and French goods. There shall be freedom of transit for French goods through Haifa and by the British railway through the brown area, whether those goods are intended for or originate in the blue area, area (A), or area (B), and there shall be no discrimination, direct or indirect, against French goods on any railway, or against French goods or ships at any port serving the areas mentioned.

6. That in area (A) the Baghdad Railway shall not be extended southwards beyond Mosul, and in area (B) northwards beyond Samarra, until a railway connecting Baghdad with Aleppo via the Euphrates Valley has been completed, and then only with the concurrence of the two Governments.

7. That Great Britain has the right to build, administer, and be sole owner of a railway connecting Haifa with area (B), and shall have a perpetual right to transport troops along such a line at all times.

It is to be understood by both Governments that this railway is to facilitate the connexion of Baghdad with Haifa by rail, and it is further understood that, if the engineering difficulties and expense entailed by keeping this connecting line in the brown area only make the project unfeasible, that the French Government shall be prepared to consider that the line in question may also traverse the polygon Banias-Keis Marib-Salkhab Tell Otsda-Mesmie before reaching area (B).

8. For a period of twenty years the existing Turkish customs tariff shall remain in force throughout the whole of the blue and red areas, as well as in areas (A) and (B), and no increase in the rates of duty or conversion from *ad valorem* to specific rates shall be made except by agreement between the two Powers.

There shall be no interior customs barriers between any of the above-mentioned areas. The customs duties leviable on goods destined for the interior shall be collected at the port of entry and handed over to the administration of the area of destination.

9. It shall be agreed that the French Government will at no time enter into any negotiations for the cession of their rights and will not cede such rights in the blue area to any third Power, except the Arab State or Confederation of Arab States without the previous agreement of His Majesty's Government, who, on their part, will give a similar undertaking to the French Government regarding the red area.

10. The British and French Governments, as the protectors of the Arab State, shall agree that they will not themselves acquire and will not consent to a third Power acquiring territorial possessions in the Arabian peninsula, nor consent to a third Power installing a naval base either on the east coast, or on the islands, of the Red Sea. This, however, shall not prevent such adjustment of the Aden frontier as may be necessary in consequence of recent Turkish aggression.

11. The negotiations with the Arabs as to the boundaries of the Arab State or Confederation of Arab States shall be continued through the same channel as heretofore on behalf of the two Powers.

12. It is agreed that measures to control the importation of arms into the Arab territories will be considered by the two Governments.

Source: Roger Adelson, Mark Sykes: Portrait of an Amateur *(London: Jonathan Cape, 1975) Appendix, pp. 302-4.*

DOCUMENT 3 ZIONISM

A further factor which was to complicate the subsequent history of the Middle East after World War 1 was Zionism. By the end of the 19th century, some European Jews had become convinced that the only long-term solution to "the Jewish question" was to establish a Jewish state. Since Jews had historical and religious ties to the Middle East, to the area in particular known as Palestine, this was an obvious choice for such a state. The local inhabitants, the Palestinian Arabs, seemed indifferent to the prospect and the nominal rulers, the Ottoman Turks, even welcomed outside investment and settlement. The movement to establish a homeland—which took the name Zionism from a Hebrew word for Jerusalem—had achieved considerable influence in Europe, although not in North America, by 1914. Theodore Herzl, usually recognized as the founder of modern Zionism, published *The Jewish State* in 1896, from which the following is taken:

...The Jewish question still exists. It would be foolish to deny it. It is a remnant of the Middle Ages, which civilized nations do not even yet seem able to shake off, try as they will. They certainly showed a generous desire to do so when they emancipated us. The Jewish question exists wherever Jews live in perceptible numbers. Where it does not exist, it is carried by Jews in the course of their migrations. We naturally move to those places where we are not persecuted, and there our presence produces persecution. This is the case in every country, and will remain so, even in those highly civilized—for instance, France—until the Jewish question finds a solution on a political basis. The unfortunate Jews are now carrying the seeds of Anti-Semitism into England; they have already introduced it into America.

I believe that I understand Anti-Semitism, which is really a highly complex movement. I consider it from a Jewish standpoint, yet without fear or hatred. I believe that I can see what elements there are in it of vulgar sport, of common trade jealousy, of inherited prejudice, of religious intolerance, and also of pretended self-defence. I think the Jewish question is no more a social than a religious one, notwithstanding that it sometimes takes these and other forms. It is a national question, which can only be solved by making it a political world-question to be discussed and settled by the civilized nations of the world in council.

We are a people—one people.

We have honestly endeavored everywhere to merge ourselves in the social life of surrounding communities and to preserve the faith of our fathers. We are not permitted to do so. In vain are we loyal patriots, our loyalty in some places running to extremes; in vain do we make the same sacrifices of life and property as our fellow-citizens; in vain do we strive to increase the fame of our native land in science and art, or her wealth by trade and commerce. In countries where we have lived for centuries we are still cried down as strangers, and often by those whose ancestors were not yet domiciled in the land where Jews had already had experience of suffering. The majority may decide which are the strangers; for this, as indeed every point which arises in the relations between nations, is a question of might. I do not here surrender any portion of our prescriptive right, when I make this statement merely in my own name as an individual. In the world as it now is and for an indefinite period will probably remain, might precedes right. It is useless, therefore, for us to be loyal patriots, as were the Huguenots who were forced to emigrate. If we could only be left in peace....

But I think we shall not be left in peace.

DOCUMENT 4 THE BALFOUR DECLARATION

By the time of World War I, a number of important British politicians were sympathetic to Zionism. In addition, by 1917, the British Government hoped to use it in the war effort. Support for Zionism, it was argued, might win over the significant Jewish community in the United States and thus put pressure on the American government to enter the war; it might weaken the support of Germany's Jews for their own government; and it might make it easier for the British government to raise money from Jewish bankers. After considerable debate, the British foreign secretary sent a cautiously-worded letter to Lord Rothschild, a leading British Zionist.

Foreign Office
November 2nd, 1917.

Dear Lord Rothschild,

I have much pleasure in conveying to you, on behalf of His Majesty's Government, the following declaration of sympathy with Jewish Zionist aspirations which has been submitted to, and approved by, the Cabinet.

"His Majesty's Government view with favour the establishment in Palestine of a national home for the Jewish people, and will use their best endeavours to facilitate the achievement of this object, it being clearly understood that nothing shall be done which may prejudice the civil and religious rights of existing non-Jewish communities in Palestine, or the rights and political status enjoyed by Jews in any other country."

I should be grateful if you would bring this declaration to the knowledge of the Zionist Federation.

Yours sincerely,
ARTHUR JAMES BALFOUR.

Source: Walter Laquer, ed., The Israeli-Arab Reader *(London: Bantam Books, 1968), p. 18.*

DOCUMENT 5 THE PEEL COMMISSION, 1937

Palestine was ruled by the British in the interwar years, under a mandate from the League of Nations. Jewish immigration came slowly at first but after Adolf Hitler and the Nazis came to power in Germany in 1933, it increased dramatically. The growing Jewish presence in Palestine led to tension with the Palestinian Arabs. There were serious disturbances from the end of the 1920s. The British, who found themselves under attack from both Arabs and Jews, made repeated but unsuccessful efforts to find a compromise. In 1937, the Palestine Royal Commission (the Peel Commission) reported:

. . . To foster Jewish immigration in the hope that it might ultimately lead to the creation of a Jewish majority and the establishment of a Jewish State with the consent or at least the acquiescence of the Arabs was one thing. It was quite another to contemplate, however remotely, the forcible conversion of Palestine into a Jewish State against the will of the Arabs. For that would clearly violate the spirit and intention of the Mandate System. It would mean that national self-determination had been withheld when the Arabs were a majority in Palestine and only conceded when the Jews were a majority. It would mean that the Arabs had been denied the opportunity of standing by themselves: that they had, in fact, after an interval of conflict, been bartered about from Turkish sovereignty to Jewish sovereignty. It is true that in the light of history Jewish rule over Palestine could not be regarded as foreign rule in the same sense as Turkish; but the international recognition of the right of the Jews to return to their old homeland did not involve the recognition of the right of the Jews to govern the Arabs in it against their will. The case stated by Lord Milner against an Arab control of Palestine applies equally to a Jewish control....

An irrepressible conflict has arisen between two national communities within the narrow bounds of one small country. About 1,000,000 Arabs are in strife, open or latent, with some 400,000 Jews. There is no common ground between them. The Arab community is predominantly Asiatic in character, the Jewish community predominantly European. They differ in religion and in language. Their cultural and social life, their ways of thought and conduct, are as incompatible as their national aspirations. These last are the greatest bar to peace. Arabs and Jews might possibly learn to live and work together in Palestine if they would make a genuine effort to reconcile and combine their national ideals and so build up in time a joint or dual nationality. But this they cannot do. The War and its sequel have inspired all Arabs with the hope of reviving in a free and united Arab world the traditions of the Arab golden age. The Jews similarly are inspired by their historic past. They mean to show what the Jewish nation can achieve when restored to the land of its birth. National assimilation between Arabs and Jews is thus ruled out. In the Arab picture the Jews could only occupy the place they occupied in Arab Egypt or Arab Spain. The Arabs would be as much outside the Jewish picture as the Canaanites in the old land of Israel. The National Home, as we have said before, cannot be half-national. In these circumstances to maintain that Palestinian citizenship has any moral meaning is a mischievous pretense. Neither Arab nor Jew has any sense of service to a single State....

Source: Walter Laquer, ed., The Israeli-Arab Reader *(London: Bantam Books, 1968), pp. 57-8.*

DOCUMENT 6 THE PROCLAMATION OF THE STATE OF ISRAEL

By the end of World War II, Britain had lost all interest in remaining in Palestine, where the situation was as far from being resolved as ever. In a controversial move, the British Government announced that it intended to pull out by 1948 and that it was handing over responsibility for Palestine to the newly-formed United Nations. The UN decided on partition of Palestine into an Arab and a Jewish state, with Jerusalem as an international city. Neither side was satisfied and fighting broke out almost immediately. Arabs elsewhere in the Middle East took up the cause of the Palestinian Arabs and a number of Arab contingents made their way to Palestine. The Jews were able to resist successfully and to seize more territory than they had been allotted by the UN. On May 14, 1948 the state of Israel proclaimed its independence.

Eretz Israel [the Land of Israel] was the birthplace of the Jewish people. Here their spiritual, religious and political identity was shaped. Here they first attained to statehood, created cultural values of national and universal significance and gave to the world the eternal Book of Books.

After being forcibly exiled from the land, the people kept faith with it throughout their Dispersion and never ceased to pray and hope for their return to it and for the restoration in it of their political freedom.

Impelled by this historic and traditional attachment, Jews strove in every successive generation to re-establish themselves in their ancient homeland. In recent decades, they returned in their masses. Pioneers...and defenders, they made deserts bloom, revived the Hebrew language, built villages and towns, and created a thriving community, controlling its own economy and culture, loving peace but knowing how to defend itself, bringing the blessings of progress to all the country's inhabitants, and aspiring towards independent nationhood.

In the year 5657 (1897), at the summons of the spiritual father of the Jewish state, Theodore Herzl, the First Zionist Congress convened and proclaimed the right of the Jewish people to national rebirth in its own country.

This right was recognised in the Balfour Declaration of the 2nd November, 1917, and re-affirmed in the Mandate of the League of Nations which, in particular, gave international sanction to the historic connection between the Jewish people and Eretz-Israel and to the right of the Jewish people to rebuild its National Home.

The catastrophe which recently befell the Jewish people—the massacre of millions of Jews in Europe—was another clear demonstration of the urgency of solving the problem of its homelessness by re-establishing in Eretz-Israel the Jewish State, which would open the gates of the homeland wide to every Jew and confer upon the Jewish people the status of a fully-privileged member of the family of nations.

Survivors of the Nazi holocaust in Europe, as well as Jews from other parts of the world, continued to migrate to Eretz-Israel, undaunted by difficulties, restrictions and dangers, and never ceased to assert their right to a life of dignity, freedom and honest toil in their national homeland.

In the Second World War, the Jewish community of this country contributed its full share to the struggle of the freedom and peace-loving nations against the forces of Nazi wickedness and, by the blood of its soldiers and its war effort, gained the right to be reckoned among the peoples who founded the United Nations.

On the 29th November, 1947, the United Nations General Assembly passed a resolution calling for the establishment of a Jewish State in Eretz-Israel; the General Assembly required the inhabitants of Eretz-Israel to take such steps as were necessary on their part for the implementation of that resolution. This recognition by the United Nations of the right of the Jewish people to establish their State is irrevocable.

This right is the natural right of the Jewish people to be masters of their own fate, like all other nations, in their own sovereign State.

ACCORDINGLY WE, MEMBERS OF THE PEOPLE'S COUNCIL, REPRESENTATIVE OF THE JEWISH COMMUNITY OF ERETZ-ISRAEL AND OF THE ZIONIST MOVEMENT, ARE HERE ASSEMBLED ON THE DAY OF THE TERMINATION OF THE BRITISH MANDATE OVER ERETZ-ISRAEL AND, BY VIRTUE OF OUR NATURAL AND HISTORIC RIGHT AND ON THE STRENGTH OF THE RESOLUTION OF THE UNITED NATIONS GENERAL ASSEMBLY, HEREBY DECLARE THE ESTABLISHMENT OF A JEWISH STATE IN ERETZ-ISRAEL, TO BE KNOWN AS THE STATE OF ISRAEL.

....

THE STATE OF ISRAEL will be open for Jewish immigration and for the Ingathering of the Exiles; it will foster the development of the country for the benefit of all its inhabitants; it will be based on freedom, justice and peace as envisaged by the prophets of Israel; it will ensure complete equality of social and political rights to all its inhabitants irrespective of religion, race or sex; it will guarantee freedom of religion, conscience, language, education and culture; it will safeguard the Holy Places of all religions; and it will be faithful to the principles of the Charter of the United Nations.

....

WE APPEAL—in the very midst of the onslaught launched against us now for months—to the Arab inhabitants of the State of Israel to preserve peace and participate in the upbuilding of the State on the basis of full and equal citizenship...

WE EXTEND our hand to all neighbouring states and their peoples in an offer of peace and good neighbourliness, and appeal to them to establish bonds of co-operation and mutual help with the sovereign Jewish people settled in its own land.

Source: I Laws of the State of Israel 3-5 (1948) [cited in John Norton Moore, ed., The Arab Israeli Conflict: Readings and Documents, *abridged edition (Princeton, New Jersey: Princeton University Press, 1977), pp. 935-7].*

DOCUMENT 7 THE SOVIET UNION AND THE MIDDLE EAST IN THE 1950S

In the years immediately after World War II, the Soviet Union took relatively little interest in the Middle East [or Near East, as the Soviets preferred to call it]. By the 1950s, however, it was beginning to realize that it could win influence by backing Arab nationalism against Israel and its Western supporters. In 1956, the Soviet Union supported Egypt and its leader, Nasser, during the Suez crisis. Nikita Khrushchev, Soviet leader after Stalin's death in 1953, explains Soviet thinking.

Our use of international influence to halt England, France, and Israel's aggression against Egypt in 1956 was a historic turning point. Before that time, the Soviet Union—and Imperial Russia before it—had always treated the Near East as belonging to England and France. King Farouk had once asked Stalin to give him arms so that he could force Great Britain to evacuate its troops from Egypt, but Stalin refused. Stalin said in my presence that the Near East was part of Britain's sphere of influence and that therefore we couldn't go sticking our noses into Egypt's affairs. Not that Stalin wouldn't have liked to move into the Near East—he would have liked to very much—but he realistically recognized that the balance of power wasn't in our favor and that Britain wouldn't have stood for our interference.

Things changed during the intervening years. Our economy, our armed forces, and the weight of our influence in international affairs all increased mightily, and by 1956 we were able to step in and assist President Nasser and the Arab peoples. It wasn't that we wanted to replace England as an exploiter of Egypt and other Arab countries. We weren't motivated by self-centred, mercantile interests. Quite the contrary, we wanted only to help these peoples cast off the yoke of their servile dependence on their colonial masters. Ours has been a noble mission in the Near East. We have incorporated into our diplomacy the tenets of Lenin's own foreign policy, and we have already begun to reap the fruits of our investment in the future of Arab nations.

Source: Strobe Talbott, ed., Khrushchev Remembers *(Boston and Toronto: Little, Brown and Company, 1970), p. 431.*

DOCUMENT 8 THE UNITED ARAB REPUBLIC MANIFESTO (1963)

The search for Arab unity has been a constant theme in the recent history of the Middle East. A number of movements, notably the Ba'ath Party and the Movement of Arab Nationalists, have been dedicated to bringing Arabs into some form of political grouping. In the 1950s, Gamal Abdal

Nasser, the ruler of Egypt, became a leading spokesman of pan-Arab nationalism. In 1958, he attempted to create a United Arab Republic between Egypt and Syria, and when that failed, to create another one in 1963 with Egypt, Iraq and Syria.

In the name of the Merciful Compassionate God,

In the name of the Almighty God,

The three delegations representing the United Arab Republic, Syria and Iraq met in Cairo and in response to the will of the Arab people in the three regions and the great Arab fatherland, brotherly talks began between the three delegations on Saturday, April 6, and ended on Wednesday, April 17, 1963.

The delegations in all their discussions were inspired by the faith that Arab unity was an inevitable aim deriving its principles from the oneness of language bearing culture and thought, common history-making sentiment and conscience, common national struggle deciding and defining destiny, common spiritual values stemming from Divine messages and common social and economic understanding based on liberty and socialism.

The delegations were guided by the will of the masses of the Arab peoples, demanding unity, struggling to attain it and sacrificing in its defence, and realising that the hard core of the union is to be formed by the unification of the parts of the homeland which have acquired their freedom and independence and in which nationalist, progressive governments have emerged with the determination to destroy the alliance of feudalism, capital, reaction and imperialism, and to liberate the working forces of the people in order to join them in alliance and to express their genuine will.

The revolution of July 23 was a historical turning point at which the Arab people in Egypt, discovering their identity and regaining their free will, set out on their quest for freedom, Arabism and union. The revolution of the 14th of Ramadan (February 8) illuminated the true Arab face of Iraq, and the path leading it to the horizons of unity, envisaged by the zealous elements of the July 14 revolution. The revolution of March 8 put Syria back into the line of the union destroyed by the setback of reactionary secession, having destroyed all the obstacles which the reactionaries and imperialism had determinedly put up in the path of union.

The three Revolutions thus met which affirmed again that unity is a revolutionary action deriving its conceptions from the people's faith, its power from their will, and its objectives from their aspirations for freedom and socialism.

Unity is a revolution—a revolution because it is popular, a revolution because it is progressive, and a revolution because it is a powerful tide in the current of civilisation.

Unity is especially a revolution because it is profoundly connected with the Palestine cause and with the national duty to liberate that country. It was the disaster of Palestine that revealed the conspiracy of the reactionary classes and exposed the treacheries of the hired regional parties and their denial of the people's objectives and aspirations. It was the disaster of Palestine that showed the weakness and backwardness of the economic and social systems that prevailed in the country, released the revolutionary energies of our people and awakened the spirit of revolt against imperialism, injustice, poverty and underdevelopment. It was the disaster of Palestine that clearly indicated the path of salvation, the path of unity, freedom and socialism. This was kept in mind by the delegations during their talks. If unity is a sacred objective, it is also the instrument of the popular struggle and its means to achieve its major objectives of freedom and security in liberating all the parts of the Arab homeland and in establishing a society of sufficiency and justice, a society of socialism, in continuing the revolutionary tide without deviation or relapse and its extension to embrace the greater Arab homeland, and in contributing to the progress of human civilisation and consolidation of world peace.

Source: Walter Laquer, ed., The Israeli-Arab Reader *(London: Bantam Books, 1968), pp. 131-133.*

DOCUMENT 9 UN SECURITY COUNCIL RESOLUTION 242

At the end of the 1967 war between Israel and its Arab neighbours, Israel remained in occupation of the Gaza strip, the Golan Heights, and the West Bank (including West Jerusalem).

Security Council Resolution 242 on the Arab-Israeli Crisis

November 22, 1967

The Security Council,

Expressing its continuing concern with the grave situation in the Middle East,

Emphasizing the inadmissibility of the acquisition of territory by war and the need to work for a just and lasting peace in which every State in the area can live in security,

Emphasizing further that all Member States in their acceptance of the Charter of the United Nations have undertaken a commitment to act in accordance with Article 2 of the Charter,

1. Affirms that the fulfilment of Charter principles requires the establishment of a just and lasting peace in the Middle East which should include the application of both the following principles:

(i) Withdrawal of Israeli armed forces from territories occupied in the recent conflict;

(ii) Termination of all claims or states of belligerency and respect for and acknowledgement of the sovereignty, territorial integrity and political independence of every State in the area and their right to live in peace within secure and recognized boundaries free from threats or acts of force;

2. Affirms further the necessity

(a) For guaranteeing freedom of navigation through international waterways in the area;

(b) For achieving a just settlement of the refugee problem;

(c) For guaranteeing the territorial inviolability and political independence of every State in the area through measures including the establishment of demilitarized zones,

3. Requests the Secretary-General to designate a Special Representative to proceed to the Middle East to establish and maintain contacts with the States concerned in order to promote agreement and assist efforts to achieve a peaceful and accepted settlement in accordance with the provisions and principles in this resolution;

4. Requests the Secretary-General to report to the Security Council on the progress of the efforts of that Special Representative as soon as possible.

Source: UN Security Council, Official Records, *22nd Year, 1968, pp. 8-9 [cited in Arthur M. Schlesinger, Jr.,* The Dynamics of World Power: A Documentary History of United States Foreign Policy 1945-73 *(New York: Chelsea House Books, 1973), pp. 425-6].*

DOCUMENT 10 THE ARAB SUMMIT CONFERENCE, SEPTEMBER 1, 1967

Neither side was ready to make peace after the 1967 War. The Arab states, whether radical or conservative, were not prepared to talk to Israel, as they made clear at the summit they held shortly after the war. Representatives, in many cases their countries' leaders, from Egypt, Saudi Arabia, Sudan, Jordan, Lebanon, Kuwait, Yemen, Iraq, Syria, Morocco, Libya, Tunisia, and Algeria, issued a statement.

First, the Conference affirmed Arab solidarity and the unification of Arab joint action in a cordial atmosphere of coordination and conciliation.

....

Second, the Conference affirmed the necessity of concerted joint efforts in the elimination of all traces of aggression on the basis that the recovery of all occupied Arab territory is the joint responsibility of all Arab countries.

Third, the Arab Heads of State agreed on unifying their efforts in joint political and diplomatic action at the international level to ensure the withdrawal of Israeli forces from the occupied Arab territory. This is within the framework of the basic Arab commitment, which entails non-recognition of Israel, no conciliation nor negotiation with her and the upholding of the rights of the Palestinian people to their land.

Fourth, the Ministers of Finance, Economy and Oil recommended the possibility of using oil as a weapon in the struggle.

Source: Arab News and Views, *no. 13 (September 1967) [cited in John Norton Moore, ed.,* The Arab Israeli Conflict: Readings and Documents, *abridged edition (Princeton, New Jersey: Princeton University Press, 1977), p. 1082].*

DOCUMENT 11 THE PALESTINE LIBERATION ORGANIZATION

The Palestine Liberation Organization was founded in 1964 under the guidance of Arab states, in particular Egypt, which hoped to use it in their conflict with Israel. The Palestinians, however, had their own views on the role of the PLO, and, by the late 1960s, it was taking an increasingly independent role. In July 1968, a PLO congress meeting in drew up the Palestinian National Charter.

Article 1: Palestine is the homeland of the Arab Palestinian people; it is an indivisible part of the Arab homeland, and the Palestinian people are an integral part of the Arab nation.

Article 2: Palestine, with the boundaries it had during the British mandate, is an invisible territorial unit.

Article 3: The Palestinian Arab people possess the legal right to their homeland and have the right to determine their destiny after achieving the liberation of their country in accordance with their wishes and entirely of their own accord and will.

Article 4. The Palestinian identity is a genuine, essential and inherent characteristic; it is transmitted from parents to children. The Zionist occupation and the dispersal of the Palestinian Arab people, through the disasters which befell them, do not make them lose their Palestinian identity and their membership of the Palestinian community, nor do they negate them.

Article 5: The Palestinians are those Arab nationals who, until 1947, normally resided in Palestine regardless of whether they were evicted from it or have stayed there. Anyone born after that date, of a Palestinian father—whether inside Palestine or outside it—is also a Palestinian.

Article 6: The Jews who had normally resided in Palestine until the beginning of the Zionist invasion will be considered Palestinian.

....

Article 8: The phase in their history, through which the Palestinian people are now living, is that of national struggle for the liberation of Palestine. Thus conflicts among the Palestinian national forces are secondary, and should be ended for the sake of the basic conflict that exists between the forces of Zionism and of imperialism on the one hand, and the Palestinian Arab people on the other.....

Article 9: Armed struggle is the only way to liberate Palestine.

....

Article 12: The Palestinian people believe in Arab unity. In order to contribute their share towards the attainment of that objective, however, they must, at the present stage of their struggle, safeguard their Palestinian identity and develop their consciousness of that identity, and oppose any plan that may dissolve or impair it.

....

Article 21: The Arab Palestinian people, expressing themselves by the armed Palestinian revolution, reject all solutions which are substitutes for the total liberation of Palestine and reject all proposals aiming at the liquidation of the Palestinian problem, or its internationalization.

Article 22: Zionism is a political movement organically associated with international imperialism and antagonistic to all action for liberation and to progressive movements in the world. It is racist and fanatic in its nature, aggressive, expansionist and colonial in its aims, and fascist in its methods. Israel is the instrument of the Zionist movement, and a geographical base for world imperialism placed strategically in the midst of the Arab homeland to combat the hopes of the Arab nation for liberation, unity and progress.

Source: Decisions of the National Congress of the Palestine Liberation Organization held in Cairo from 1-17 July 1968 [cited in John Norton Moore, ed., The Arab Israeli Conflict: Readings and Documents, *abridged edition (Princeton, New Jersey: Princeton University Press, 1977), pp. 1086-1090].*

DOCUMENT 12 UNITED NATIONS SECURITY COUNCIL RESOLUTION 338

Towards the end of the Yom Kippur/October War of 1973, the Security Council passed the following resolution:

The Security Council

1. Calls upon all parties to the present fighting to cease all firing and terminate all military activity immediately...

2. Calls upon the parties concerned to start immediately after the cease-fire the implementation of Security Council resolution 242 (1967) in all of its parts.

Source: cited in John Norton Moore, ed., The Arab Israeli Conflict: Readings and Documents, *abridged edition (Princeton, New Jersey: Princeton University Press, 1977), p. 1189.*

DOCUMENT 13 PRESIDENT ANWAR SADAT'S SPEECH TO THE ISRAELI PARLIAMENT, 1977

After the 1973 War, Egypt, under the leadership of Anwar Sadat, decided that the time had come to reach an understanding with Israel. In a very dramatic gesture, Sadat travelled to Israel in 1977, the first Arab leader to do so officially, and spoke to the Israeli parliament:

...I come to you today on solid ground to shape a new life and to establish peace. We all love this land, the land of God, we all, Moslems, Christians and Jews, all worship God.

....

But to be absolutely frank with you, I took this decision after long thought, knowing that it constitutes a great risk, for God Almighty has made it my fate to assume responsibility on behalf of the Egyptian people, to share in the responsibility of the Arab nation, the main duty of which, dictated by responsibility, is to exploit all and every means in a bid to save my Egyptian Arab people and the pan-Arab nation from the horrors of new suffering and destructive wars...

....

How can we achieve a durable peace based on justice? In my opinion, and I declare it to the whole world, from this forum, the answer is neither difficult nor is it impossible despite long years of feuds, blood, faction, strife, hatreds and deep-rooted animosity.

The answer is not difficult, nor is it impossible, if we sincerely and faithfully follow a straight line.

You want to live with us, part of the world.

In all sincerity I tell you we welcome you among us with full security and safety. This in itself is a tremendous turning point, one of the landmarks of decisive historical change. We used to reject you. We had our reasons and our fears, yes.

We refused to meet with you anywhere, yes.

....

Yet today I tell you, and I declare it to the whole world, that we accept to live with you in permanent peace based on justice. We do not want to encircle you or be encircled ourselves by destructive missiles ready for launching, nor by the shells of grudges and hatreds.

Source: Walter Laqueur and Barry Rubin, eds, The Israel-Arab Reader, *4th edition (New York and Oxford: Facts on File Publications, 1985), pp. 592-6*

DOCUMENT 14 THE ARAB REJECTION OF EGYPT'S OVERTURES TO ISRAEL

The PLO quickly condemned Sadat's 'treasonous' visit to Israel and on December 5, 1977 an Arab League Summit Conference took the following decision:

1. To condemn President Sadat's visit to the Zionist entity since it constitutes a great betrayal of the sacrifices and struggle of our Arab people in Egypt and their armed forces and of the struggle, sacrifices and principles of the Arab nation.

....

2. To work for the frustration of the results of President Sadat's visit to the Zionist entity and his talks with the leaders of the Zionist enemy and the subsequent measures including the proposed Cairo meeting. The conference warns that anyone who tries to pursue a similar line or to have any dealings with the said results shall be held responsible for his deed nationally and on the pan-Arab level.

3. To freeze political and diplomatic relations with the Egyptian Government, to suspend dealings with it on the Arab and international levels and to apply the regulations, provisions and decisions of the Arab boycott against Egyptian individuals, companies and firms which deal with the Zionist enemy.

Source: Walter Laqueur and Barry Rubin, eds, The Israel-Arab Reader, *4th edition (New York and Oxford: Facts on File Publications, 1985), pp. 603-4.*

DOCUMENT 15 THE CAMP DAVID FRAMEWORKS FOR PEACE (SEPTEMBER 1978)

President Carter invited President Sadat of Egypt and Prime Minister Begin of Israel to the presidential retreat of Camp David. Here intensive negotiations produced the basis for further negotiations which resulted, the following March, in a peace treaty between Egypt and Israel.

Preamble.

The search for peace in the Middle East must be guided by the following:

—The agreed basis for a peaceful settlement of the conflict between Israel and its neighbors is United Nations Security Council Resolution 242, in all its parts.

—After four wars in thirty years, despite intensive human efforts, the Middle East, which is the cradle of civilization and the birthplace of three great religions, does not yet enjoy the blessings of peace. The people of the Middle East yearn for peace so that the vast human and natural resources of the region can be turned to the pursuits of peace and so that this area can become a model for coexistence and cooperation among nations.

—The historic initiative of President Sadat in visiting Jerusalem and the reception accorded to him by the Parliament, government and people of Israel, and the reciprocal visit of Prime Minister Begin to Ismailia, the peace proposals made by both leaders, as well as the warm reception of these missions by the people of both countries, have created an unprecedented opportunity for peace which must not be lost if this generation and future generations are to be spared the tragedies of war.

....

Framework

Taking these factors into account, the parties are determined to reach a just, comprehensive, and durable settlement of the Middle East conflict through the conclusion of peace treaties based on Security Council Resolutions 242 and 338 in all their parts. ...

Source: Walter Laquer and Barry Rubin, eds, The Israel-Arab Reader, *4th edition (New York and Oxford: Facts on File Publications, 1985), pp. 609-10.*

DOCUMENT 16 THE SOVIET RESPONSE TO CAMP DAVID

In September 1979, Foreign Minister Andrei Gromyko spoke to the UN General Assembly:

A just settlement and the establishment of durable peace in the Middle East requires that Israel should end its occupation of all the Arab lands it seized in 1967, that the legitimate rights of the Arab people of Palestine including the right to create their own state be safeguarded and that the right of all states in the Middle East, including Israel, to independent existence under conditions of peace be effectively guaranteed.

The separate deal between Egypt and Israel resolves nothing. It is a means designed to lull the vigilance of peoples. It is a way of piling up on a still greater scale explosive material capable of producing a new conflagration in the Middle East. Moreover, added to the tense political atmosphere in this and the adjacent areas is the heavy smell of oil.

Source: Walter Laquer and Barry Rubin, eds, The Israel-Arab Reader, *4th edition (New York and Oxford: Facts on File Publications, 1985), p. 618.*

STUDY QUESTIONS FOR SECTION TWELVE: THE MIDDLE EAST IN INTERNATIONAL RELATIONS

1. Why have outside powers attempted to gain influence in the Middle East in the twentieth century?

2. What were the strengths and weaknesses of the peace settlements in the Middle East at the end of World War I?

3. Why did the establishment of the Jewish homeland in Palestine meet with opposition from many Arabs?

4. What was the significance of the Suez crisis of 1956?

5. When did the Cold War have its greatest impact on the Middle East?

SECTION THIRTEEN

BIBLIOGRAPHY

Sources

The Concise Columbia Encyclopedia (1983)
Encyclopedia Britannica
Humanities Index (monthly and annual)
Keesing's Contemporary Archives/Keesing's Record of World Events
Middleton, Hayden and Heater, Derek, *Atlas of Modern World* (1989)
New York Times Index
PAIS (Public Affairs Information Service (annual, CD-ROM & print)
The Penguin Atlas of World History. Volume two: *From the French Revolution to the Present* (Toronto, 1978)
Reader's Guide (annual)
Social Sciences Index (monthly and annual)

International Relations 1900-1995

Albrecht-Carrié, René, *A Diplomatic History of Europe since the Congress of Vienna* (London, 1965)
Bartlett, C.J., *The Global Conflict: The International Rivalry of the Great Powers, 1880-1970* (London, 1984)
Bull, Hedley and Watson, Adam, eds, *The Expansion of International Society* (Oxford, 1984)
Craig, Gordon, *Germany, 1866-1945* (New York, 1978)
Craig, Gordon and George, A.L., *Force and Statecraft: Diplomatic Problems of Our Time* (New York, 1983)
Gilpin, Robert, *The Political Economy of International Relations* (Princeton, 1987)
Grimwade, Nigel, *International Trade* (London, 1989)
Hobsbawm, Eric, *The Age of Extremes* (New York, 1995)
Kennedy, Paul, *The Rise and Fall of the Great Powers* (New York, 1987)
Keylor, W.R., *The Twentieth Century World: an international History* (New York, 1996)
Kindleberger, Charles P., *International Money: a collection of essays* (London, 1981)
Kissinger, Henry, *Diplomacy* (New York and London, 1995)
Mandelbaum, Michael, *The Fate of Nations: the search for national security in the nineteenth and twentieth centuries* (London and New York, 1988)
Morris, James, *Heaven's Command* (London, 1973)
__________, *Pax Britannica* (London, 1968)
__________, *Farewell the Trumpets* (London, 1978)
Odell, Peter, *Oil and World Power* (Harmondsworth, England, 1983)
Smil, Vaclav, *Energy in World History* (Boulder, Colorado, 1994)
Spero, Joan Edelman, *The Politics of International Economic Relations* (New York, several editions)
Turner, Louis, *Oil companies in the international system* (London, 1978)
Ulam, Adam, *Expansion and Coexistence: the History of Soviet Foreign Policy 1917-1973* (New York, 1974)
Walter, Andrew, *World Power and World Money: Hegemony and International Monetary Order* (1991)
Williamson, J. and Milner, C., *The World Economy* (London, 1991)
Yergin, Daniel, *The Prize: the epic quest for oil, money & power* (New York, 1991)

International Relations, 1900-1945

1900-1914

Evans, R.W.J. and Pogge von Strandmann, H., eds., *The Coming of the First World War* (London, 1988)
Geiss, Immanuel, *July 1914. The Outbreak of the First World War. Selected Documents* (London, 1967)
Gollwitzer, Heinz, *Europe in an Age of Imperialism* (London, 1969)
Herwig, Holger, *The Outbreak of World War I* (Toronto, 1991)
Hobsbawm, Eric, *The Age of Empire, 1875-1914* (London, 1987)
Joll, James, ed., *The Origins of the First World War* (London, 1984)
Kennan, George, *The Fateful Alliance: France, Russia, and the Coming of the First World War* (New York, 1984)
Kennedy, Paul, *The Rise and Fall of British Naval Mastery* (London, 1976)
__________, *The Rise of the Anglo-German Antagonism, 1860-1914* (London, 1980)
Koch, H.W., ed., *The Origins of the First World War* (London, 1982)
Massie, Robert K., *Dreadnought: Britain, Germany, and the Coming of the Great War* (New York, 1991)
Steiner, Zara, *Britain and the Origins of the First World War* (London, 1977)
Stone, Norman, *Europe Transformed. 1878-1919* (London, 1983)

1914-1919

Cooper, John M., *Causes and Consequences of World War I* (New York, 1972)
Nicolson, H., *Peacemaking 1919* (London, 1964)

Sharp, Alan, *The Versailles Settlement: Peacemaking in Paris, 1919* (London, 1991)
Stevenson, David, *The First World War and International Politics* (Oxford, 1988)
Stone, Norman, *The Eastern Front, 1914-1917* (London, 1975)
Wilson, Keith, ed., *Decisions for War* (London, 1995)
Zeman, Z.A.B., *A Diplomatic History of the First World War* (London, 1971)

1919-1939

Derek H. Aldcroft, *From Versailles to Wall Street* (London, 1977, 1987)
Bell, P.M.H., *The Origins of the Second World War in Europe* (London, 1986)
Carr, E.H., *The Twenty Years Crisis* (London, 1939)
Craig, Gordon and Gilbert, Felix, eds., *The Diplomats, 1919-1939*, 2 vols. (London, 1953)
Eubank, Keith, *World War II: Roots and Causes* (Toronto, 1992)
Hiden, John, *Germany and Europe 1919-1939* 2nd edition, 1993)
Iriye, Akira. *After Imperialism: The Search for a New Order in the Far East, 1921-1931* (New York, 1978)
Iriye, A., ed., *The Chinese and the Japanese* (Princeton, 1980)
___________, *The Origins of the Second World War in the Pacific* (London and New York, 1987)
Kennan, George, *Russia and the West under Lenin and Stalin* (Boston, 1971)
Kennedy, Paul, *The Rise and Fall of the Great Powers* (New York, 1987)
Kindleberger, Charles P., *The World in Depression, 1929-1939* (Berkeley, California, 1973)
King, F.P., *The New Internationalism: Allied Policy and the European Peace, 1939-1945* (Newton Abbott, England, 1973)
Kitchen, Martin, *Europe between the Wars: a Political History* (London and New York, 1988)
Marks, Sally, *The Illusion of Peace: International Relations in Europe 1918-1933*
Martel, Gordon, ed., *The Origins of the Second World War Reconsidered* (London,1986)
Millward, Alan, *War, Economy and Society, 1939-1945* (Berkeley, California, 1979)
Rubin, Barry, *The Great Powers in the Middle East, 1941-1947* (London, 1980)
Sontag, Raymond, *A Broken World, 1919-1939* (New York, 1971)
Thorne, Christopher, *The Approach of War, 1938-39* (London, 1967)
Watt,D.C., *Too Serious a Business: European Armed Forces and the Approach of the Second World War* (London, 1975)
Weinberg, Gerhard, *The Foreign Policy of Hitler's Germany* (Chicago, 1970, 1980), 2 vols.
Williams, Ann, *Britain and France in the Middle East and North Africa* (London, 1968)
Wiskemann, Elizabeth, *Europe of the Dictators, 1919-1945* (New York, 1966)
___________, *The Rome-Berlin Axis: a Study of the relations between Hitler and Mussolini* (London, 1966)
Wolfers, Arnold, *Britain and France between Two Wars* (New York, 1966)

1939-1945

Iriye, Akira, *Power and Culture: the Japanese-American War* (Cambridge, Mass., 1981)
Mastny, Vojtech, *Russials Road to the Cold War: Diplomacy, Warfare, and the Politics of Communism, 1941-1945* (New York, 1979)
Thorne, Christopher, *Allies of a Kind: the United States, Britain and the War Against Japan, 1941-45* (London and New York, 1978)
Weinberg, Gerhard, *A World At Arms: a Global History of World War II* (New York, 1994)
Wright, Gordon, *The Ordeal of Total War, 1939-1945* (New York, 1968)

International Relations, 1945-1995

1945-1990

Ansprenger, Franz, *The Dissolution of Colonial Empires* (London, 1989)
Brezinski, Z., *The Grand Failure: the Birth and Death of Communism in the Twentieth Century* (New York, 1989)
Bundy, McGeorge, *Danger and Survival: Choices about the Bomb in the First Fifty Years* (New York, 1990)
Calvocoressi, Peter, *World Politics since 1945* (London, 1987)
Crockatt, Richard, *The Fifty Years War: the United States and the Soviet Union in World Politics, 1941-1991* (London and New York, 1995)
Donelan, Michael D., *International disputes: case histories 1945-1970* (London, 1971)
Dunbabin, John P., *The Cold War: the Great Powers and their Allies* (London, 1994)
___________, *The Post-Imperial Age: the Great Powers and the Wider World* (London, 1994)
Fontaine, Andre, *A History of the Cold War*, 2 vols. (New York, 1968)
Freedman, Lawrence, *The Evolution of Nuclear Strategy* (London, 1982)
Gaddis, John Lewis *The Long Peace: Inquiries into the History of the Cold War* (New York, 1987)
___________, *Strategies of Containment: a Critical Appraisal of Postwar American National Security Policy* (New York, 1982)
___________, *The United States and the Origins of the Cold War, 1941-1947* (New York, 1972)
Grosser, Alfred, *The Western Alliance: European-American Relations since 1945* (New York, 1980)
Halle, Louis, *The Cold War as History* (New York, 1967)
Halliday, Fred, *Cold War, Third World* (London, 1989)

Hyland, William G., *The Cold War: fifty years of conflict* (New York, 1991)

__________, *Mortal Rivals: Understanding the Hidden Pattern of Soviet-American Relations* (New York, 1987)

Iriye, Akira, *The Cold War in Asia: a Historical Introduction* (New Jersey, 1974)

Kaplan, Lawrence, *NATO and the United States* (Boston, 1988)

Kapstein, Ethan, *The Insecure Alliance: Energy Crises and Western Politics since 1944* (New York, 1990)

Keohane, Robert O., *After Hegemony: co-operation and discord in the world political economy* (Princeton, 1984)

Kimche, David, *The Afro-Asian Movement* (New York, 1973)

LaFeber, Walter, *America in the Cold War: twenty years of revolution and response, 1947-1967* (New York, 1969)

Lundestad, Geir, *East, West, North, South: Major Developments in International Politics 1945-1990* (Oslo, 1991)

Mortimer, Robert A., *The Third-World coalition in international politics* (Boulder, Colorado, 1984)

Scammell, W., *The International Economy since 1945* (New York, 1984)

Tsoukalis, Loukas, ed., *Europe, America and the World Economy* (Oxford, 1986)

Ulam, Adam, *The Rivals: America and Russia since World War II* (New York, 1971)

Vadney, T.E., *The World since 1945* (London, 1987)

Walker, Martin, *The Cold War* (London and New York, 1993)

1945-1950

Barker, Elisabeth, *The British between the superpowers, 1945-50* (Toronto, 1983)

Buchan, Alastair, *End of the postwar era: a new balance of world power* (London, 1974)

Cook, Don, *Forging the Alliance: NATO, 1945-1950* (New York, 1989)

Deighton, Anne, *The Impossible Peace: Britain, the Division of Germany and the Origins of the Cold War* (Oxford, 1990)

Dockrill, Michael, *The Cold War 1945-1963* (Atlantic Highlands, N.J., 1988)

Feis, H.G., *From trust to terror: the onset of the Cold War, 1945-50* (New York, 1970)

Gaddis, John Lewis, *The United States and the Origins of the Cold War* (New York, 1972)

Kolko, Gabriel and Kolko, Joyce, *The Limits of Power: the World and United States Foreign Policy, 1945-54* (New York, 1972)

LaFeber, Walter, ed, *The Origins of the Cold War* (New York, 1971)

Maier, Charles, ed., *The Cold War in Europe* (New York, 1990)

Paterson, Thomas G., *On every front: the making of the Cold War* (New York, 1979)

Rees, David, *The Age of Containment* (London, 1967)

Seton-Watson, Hugh, *Neither war nor peace: the struggle for power in the post-war world* (London, 1960)

Thomas, Hugh, *Armed Truce: the beginnings of the cold war, 1945-46* (London and New York, 1986)

Yergin, Daniel, *Shattered Peace: Origins of the Cold War and the National Security State* (Boston, 1977)

1950-1970

Ambrose, Stephen, *Eisenhower: the President* (New York, 1984)

Beschloss, Michael, *The Crisis Years: Kennedy and Khrushchev 1960-1963* (New York, 1991)

Blight, James and Welch, David, *On the Brink: Americans and Soviets Reexamine the Cuban Missile Crisis* (New York, 1989)

Lowe, Peter, *The Origins of the Korean War* (London and New York, 1986)

Rees, David, *The Age of Containment: the Cold War 1945-1965* (London and New York, 1967)

Rees, David, *Korea: the limited war*

Reeves, Richard, *President Kennedy: profile of power*

1970-1989

Bell, Coral, *The Diplomacy of Detente* (New York, 1977)

Bowker, Mike and Williams, Phil, *Superpower Detente: A Reappraisal* (London, 1988)

Bromke, Adam, *East-west relations in the 1980s* (Ottawa, 1988)

Calleo, David P., *Beyond American Hegemony* (New York, 1987)

Chomsky, Noam, *Superpowers in Collision: the Cold War Now* (Harmondsworth, England, 1984)

Garthoff, Raymond, *Detente and Confrontation: American-Soviet Relations Nixon to Reagan* (Washington, 1985)

Halliday, Fred, *The making of the second Cold War* (London, 1988)

Hyland, William G., ed., *The Reagan Foreign Policy* (New York, 1987)

Isaacson, Walter, *Kissinger* (New York, 1992)

The 1990s

Carrère d'Encausse, Hélène, *The End of the Soviet Empire: the Triumph of Nations* (New York, 1993)

Cohen, Lenard J., *Broken Bonds: the Disintegration of Yugoslavia* (Boulder, Colorado, 1993)

Dunlop, J.B., *The Rise of Russia and the Fall of the Soviet Union* (Princeton, 1993)

Dawisha, Karen and Parrott, Bruce, *Russia and the New States of Eurasia* (New York: Cambridge University Press, 1994)

Glenny, Misha, *The Fall of Yugoslavia* (London and New York, 1992)

__________, *The Rebirth of History: Eastern Europe in the Age of Democracy* (1993)

Remnick, David, *Lenin's Tomb: The Last Days of the Soviet Empire* (New York, 1993)
Stokes, Gale, *The Walls Came Tumbling Down: the Collapse of Communism in Eastern Europe* (New York, 1993)
Suny, Ronald Grigor, *The Revenge of the Past: Nationalism, Revolution, and the Collapse of the Soviet Union* (Stanford, 1994)
Smith, Hedrick, *The New Russians* (New York, 1990)

International Relations by geographical area

Africa

Calvocoressi, Peter, *Independent Africa and the World* (London and New York, 1985)
Duignan, Peter and Gann, L.H., eds., *The United States and Africa* (New York, 1990)
Manning, Patrick, *Francophone Sub-Saharan Africa 1880-1985* (New York, 1990)
McKay, Vernon, *African Diplomacy: studies in the determinants of foreign Policy* (New York, 1966)

Asia

Cambridge History of Japan, vol. 2 (Cambridge, 1989)
Chang, Gordon H., *Friends and Enemies: the United States, China, and the Soviet Union, 1948-1972* (Stanford, 1990)
Davidson, Phillip, *Vietnam at War: the history 1946-1975* (New York, 1988)
Gungwu, Wang, *China and the World since 1949* (London, 1977)
Harding, Harry, ed., *China's Foreign Relations in the 1980s* (New Haven, Conn., 1984)
Herring, George C., *America's Longest War: the United States and Vietnam 1950-1975* (New York, 1986)
Iriye, Akira, *The Cold War in Asia: a historical introduction* (New York, 1974)
Karnow, Stanley, *Vietnam* (New York, 1984)
Lewy, G., *America in Vietnam* (New York, 1978)
Mancall, Mark, *China at the Center: 300 years of foreign policy* (New York, 1984)
Schaller, Michael, *The United States and China* (New York, 1979)
Shawcross, William, *Sideshow: Kissinger, Nixon, and the Destruction of Cambodia* (New York, 1979)
Zagoria, Donald S., *The Sino-Soviet Conflict, 1956-61* (Princeton, 1962)

Europe

DePorte, A.W., *Europe between the Super-Powers: The Enduring Balance* 2nd ed. (New Haven, 1986)
Garton-Ash, Timothy, *In Europe's Name: Germany and the Divided Continent* (New York, 1993)
Hallstein, Walter, *Europe in the Making* (New York, 1972)
Hanrieder, Wolfram, ed., *The United States and Western Europe* (Cambridge, Mass., 1974)
__________, ed., *West German Foreign Policy, 1949-1979* (Boulder, Colorado, 1980)
Kovrig, Bennett, *Of Walls and Bridges: the United States & Eastern Europe* (New York, 1991)
Laquer, Walter, *A Continent Astray: Europe 1970-1978*
Pinder, John, *European Community: the Building of a Union* (New York, 1991)
Reynolds, David, *Britannia Overruled: British Policy and World Power in the Twentieth Century* (London and New York, 1991)
Rothschild, Joseph, *Return to Diversity: a Political history of East Central Europe since World War II*, 2nd edition (New York, 1992)
Urwin, Derek, *The Community of Europe: A history of European integration since 1945* (London, 1991)
Wallace, William, *The Transformation of Western Europe* (New York, 1990)
Young, John W., *Cold War Europe* (London, 1991)
Zeman, Z.A.B., *The Making and Breaking of Communist Europe* (Cambridge, Mass., 1991)

The Soviet Union

Carrère d'Encausse, Hélène, *The End of the Soviet Empire: the Triumph of Nations* (New York, 1993)
Gromyko, Andrei, *Memoirs* (New York, 1989)
Heller, Mikhail and Nekrich, Aleksandr, *Utopia in Power: A History of the Soviet Union from 1917 to the Present* (New York, 1986)
Kennan, George, *Russia and the West under Lenin and Stalin* (Boston, 1971)
Malia, Martin, *The Soviet Tragedy: A History of Socialism in Russia, 1917-1991* (New York, 1994)
Veljko Micunovic, *Moscow Dairy*, (New York, 1980)
Remnick, David, *Lenin's Tomb: The Last Days of the Soviet Empire* (New York, 1993)
Suny, Ronald Grigor, *The Revenge of the Past: Nationalism, Revolution, and the Collapse of the Soviet Union* (Stanford, 1994)
Smith, Hedrick, *The New Russians* (New York, 1990)
Ulam, Adam, *Expansion and Coexistence: the history of Soviet Foreign Policy, 1917-1967* (New York, 1968)

Latin America

Baily, Samuel L., *The United States and the Development of South America, 1945-1975* (New York, 1976)
Davis, Harold Eugene et al, *Latin American Diplomatic History: an introduction* (Baton Rouge, 1977)
Gil, Frederico, *Latin American-United States Relations* (New York, 1971)
Parkinson, F., *Latin America, the Cold War and the World Powers, 1945-73* (Beverley Hills, 1974)

Middle East

Brown, Carl L., *International Politics in the Middle East* (Princeton, 1984)
Dawisha, Adeed and Dawisha, Karen, eds., *The Soviet Union* and the *Middle East* (New York and London, 1982)

Friedman, Thomas, *From Beirut to Jerusalem* (New York, 1989)
Glass, Charles, *Tribes with Flags* (London, 1990)
Halliday, Fred, *Threat from the East? Soviet Policy from Afghanistan and Iran to the Horn of Africa* (London, 1982)
Kelly, J.B., *Arabia, the Gulf and the West* (New York, 1980)
Laquer, Walter, *Confrontation: the Middle East in World Politics* (London, 1974)
Laquer, Walter, and Rubin, Barry, eds., *The Arab-Israeli Reader* (London, 1984)
Miller, Judith and Mylroie, Laurie, *Saddam Hussein and the Crisis in the Gulf* (New York, 1990)
Polk, W.R., *The United States and the Arab World* 3rd edition (Cambridge, Mass., 1975)
Shlaim, Avi, *War and Peace in the Middle East: a critique of American Policy* (New York, 1994)
Taylor, Alan R., *The Superpowers and the Middle East* (Syracuse, 1991)
Yapp, M.E., *The Making of the Modern Near East 1792-1923* (London and New York, 1987)
____________, *The Near East since the First World* War (London and New York, 1991)

North America

Canada

Granatstein, J.L., *Canadian foreign policy since 1945* (Toronto, 1969)
Granatstein, J.L. and Bothwell, Robert, *Pirouette: Pierre Trudeau and Canadian Foreign Policy* (Toronto, 1990)
Granatstein, J.L. and Hillmer, Norman, *Empire to Umpire: Canada and the World to the 1990s* (Toronto, 1994)
MacMillan, Margaret and Sorenson, David, eds., *Canada and NATO: Uneasy Past, Uncertain Future* (Waterloo, 1990)
Nossal, Kim, *The Politics of Canadian Foreign Policy*, 2nd ed. (Toronto, 1989)
Smith, Denis, *Diplomacy of Fear* (Toronto, 1988)
Stacey, Charles, *Canada and the Age of Conflict*, 2 vols. (Toronto, 1979)
Stairs, Denis, *Diplomacy of Constraint* (Toronto, 1974)

United States

Ambrose, Stephen, *Rise to Globalism: American Foreign Policy since 1938* (Toronto, 1988)
Brands, H.W., *The Devil We Knew: Americans and the Cold War* (New York, 1993)
Brands, H.W., *Problems in American Foreign Policy*, 2 vols. (New York, 1996)
Cambridge History of American Foreign Relations. Volumes 3 & 4 (New York, 1993)
Cohen, Warren, *Empire Without Tears: America's Foreign Relations, 1921-1933* (New York, 1984)
Costigliola, Frank, *Awkward Dominion: American Political, Economic and Cultural Relations with Europe, 1919-1933* (New York, 1984)
Dallek, Robert, *The American Style of Foreign Policy, Cultural Politics and Foreign Affairs* (New York, 1983)
Dallek, R., *Franklin D. Roosevelt and American Foreign Policy* (New York, 1979)
DeConde, Alexander, *A History of American Foreign Policy*, 2 vols. (New York, 1971)
Divine, Robert A., *Eisenhower and the Cold* War (New York, 1981)
Duignan, Peter and Gann, L.H., eds., *The United States and Africa* (New York, 1990)
Fairbank, John K., *The United States and China*, 4th edition (Cambridge, Mass., 1976)
Ferrell, Robert, *Woodrow Wilson and World War One* (New York, 1985)
Gaddis, John Lewis, *Strategies of Containment: a Critical Appraisal of Postwar American National Security Policy* (New York, 1982)
Graebner, Norman, *America as a World Power: A Realist Appraisal from Wilson to Reagan* (Wilmington, Delaware, 1984)
Isaacson, Walter, *Kissinger* (New York, 1992)
Kennan, George F., *Realities of American Foreign Policy* (Princeton, 1954)
Knock, Thomas, *To End All Wars: Woodrow Wilson and the Quest for a New World Order* (New York, 1992)
Link, Arthur S., *Woodrow Wilson: Revolution, War and Peace* (Princeton, 1979)
Paterson, Thomas, Clifford, J. Garry, and Hagan, Kenneth, *American Foreign Policy: a History* (New York, 1977)
Polk, W.R., *The United States and the Arab World* (Cambridge, Mass., 1975)
Rosenberg, Emily, *Spreading the American Dream: American Economic and Cultural Expansion 1896-1945.*
Schaller, Michael, *The United States and China* (New York, 1979)
Smith, Tony, *America's Mission: The United States and the Worldwide Struggle for Democracy in the Twentieth Century* (Princeton, 1994)

Section Fourteen

Films

All the following are available on video. While they may not be historically accurate, they can help to give students a sense of the past.

Europe before 1914

Mayerling (French: suicide of heir to the Austrian throne in 1889)

The Shooting Party (British: the English aristocracy in the last days before the War)

Colonel Redl (German: Austria-Hungary before the War)

1900 (Italian [Bertolucci]: the rise of socialism and fascism in Italy)

World War I

All Quiet on the Western Front (2 versions: German and American)

Battleship Potemkin Russian [Eisenstein]: mutiny of sailors during Russian revolution)

Black and White in Colour (French: the war in Africa)

Dr. Zhivago (British: the Russian Revolution)

Gallipoli (Australian: the Australian forces on the Gallipoli expedition)

La Grande Illusion (French [Jean Renoir]: French prisoners of war)

Lawrence of Arabia (British: the Arab revolt)

The Lighthorsemen (Australian: the war in the desert)

October (Russian [Eisenstein]: the storming of the Winter Palace)

Reds (American: the Russian Revolution)

The Red and the White (Hungarian: the fighting between reds and whites after the Russian Revolution)

Asia before 1941

55 Days at Peking (American: the Boxer Rebellion)

Gandhi (Britain: the story of the Indian national leader and the British)

The Inn of the Sixth Happiness (American: Ingrid Bergman saving orphans in China during the Japanese invasion)

The Last Emperor (Italian: China from the fall of the dynasty to Communist takeover)

The Sand Pebbles (American: American sailor in China in 1925)

Europe between the Wars

Burnt by the Sun (Russian: the effect of Stalin's purges on one family)

The Garden of the Finzi-Continis (Italian: Italian Jews and fascism)

Ship of Fools (American: passengers on German luxury liner sailing from Mexico to Germany just before Nazi takeover)

The Inner Circle (Russian-American: life in Stalin's court)

World War II

Ashes and Diamonds (Polish: resistance fighter at end of WW2)

Au Revoir, Les Enfants (French [Malle]: fate of Jewish children in occupied France)

Das Boot (German: U-boats)

The Bridge at Remagen (American: the German attempt to hang on to one of the last bridges leading into Germany from the West)

Bridge over the River Kwai (British: British and American prisoners of war)

A Bridge Too Far (British: Allied attempt to capture bridgehead on Rhine)

Casablanca (American: intrigue and drama in occupied Morocco)

Closely Watched Trains (Czechoslovak: Czechoslovakia under Nazi occupation)

Empire of the Sun (American [Spielberg]: the fate of an English boy during the Japanese occupation of China)

Europa, Europa (German and Russian: Jewish teenager during War)

Forbidden Games (French: French child in War)

From Here to Eternity (American: the United States on the verge of World War II)

Hope and Glory (British: child's life during Blitz)

The Immortal Battalion (aka The Way Ahead) (British: creation of a combat team)

Kanal (Polish: Polish resistance)

The Longest Day (American: D-Day)

The Marriage of Maria Braun (German: the fate of a German woman married to an army officer)

Midway (American: the battle in the Pacific)

Notorious (American [Hitchcock]: Ingrid Bergman as the daughter of a Nazi in Brazil)

Open City (Italian [Rossellini]: occupation and resistance in Italy during WW2)

Radio Days (American [Woody Allen]: the United States during the War)
Red Sorghum (Chinese: Chinese resistance to the Japanese)
Sands of Iwo Jima (American: the war against Japan)
Schindler's List (American [Spielberg]: the Holocaust)
Stalingrad (Russian: the decisive German defeat)
Tora! Tora! Tora! (Japanese & American: the attack on Pearl Harbour)
Von Ryan's Express (American: escape from a German prisoner-of-war camp
Wake Island (American: US marines trying to hold out against Japanese attack)
The Wannsee Conference (German: the Nazis taking the decision for the "Final Solution"

The Cold War

Dr. Strangelove or How I Learned to Stop Worrying and Love the Bomb (American: black comedy about the Bomb)
The Front (American: the blacklist of suspected Communists in Hollywood in the 1950s)
The Manchurian Candidate (American: Communist plots in United States)
Missiles of October (American: Cuban missile crisis)
No Way Out (American: government intrigue in Washington)
On the Beach (American: the world after nuclear war)

Europe since 1945

Day of the Jackal (American: attempt by hardliners opposed to Algerian independence to assassinate General De Gaulle)
Eleni (American: the civil war in Greece between the communists and the non-communists
Funeral in Berlin (British: spies and defectors; see Ipcress File)
The Ipcress File (British: British agent vs. Russians; first of series followed by Funeral in Berlin and Billion Dollar Brain)
The Jigsaw Man (British: hidden Soviet spies in Britain)
Letter to Brezhnev (British: comedy with two Liverpool girls who fall in love with Russian sailors)
The Nasty Girl (German: the difficulties of dealing with the Nazi past in modern Germany)
The Spy Who Came in From the Cold (British: Cold War intrigue in Berlin)
The Third Man (British, 1949: classic thriller set in occupied Vienna at the end of the war)

Asia since 1945

Bhowani Junction (American: the struggle between the British and Indian nationalists at the end of World War 2)
The Bridges at Toko-Ri (American: airforce in Korean War)
Gandhi (British: the life of the great Indian nationalist)
The Jewel in the Crown (British television series: the last days of the British in India)
The Killing Fields (American: the Communist takeover in Cambodia)
The Last Emperor (American-Italian: the life of the emperor of China who survived as a gardener in Communist Peking)
M.A.S.H. (American: the Korean war)
The Ugly American (American: US ambassador in Asia trying to deal with Communists)
The Year of Living Dangerously (American-Australian: attempted communist coup in Indonesia in 1965)

The Vietnam War

Apocalypse Now (American: madness and the War)
Born on the Fourth of July (American: Vietnam veteran turns anti-war activist)
Casualties of War (American: American brutalities)
The Deer Hunter (American: Americans in Vietnam)
Full Metal Jacket (American)
Go Tell the Spartans (American: a critical look at the early days of the Americans in Vietnam)
The Green Berets (American: one of the rare pro-war movies)
Who'll Stop the Rain (American: Americans in Vietnam and drugs in the United States)

Latin America

Missiles of October (American: docudrama about the Cuban Missile Crisis)
Missing (American: search for an American journalist who disappeared during coup in South American country)
State of Siege (French: left-wing guerrillas in Uruguay kidnapping American aid official)
Topaz (America: American attempts to gather information on Soviet involvement in Cuba)

The Middle East

The Battle of Algiers (Italian-Algerian: Algerian war of independence)
The Little Drummer Girl (American: Israeli attempts to trap Palestinian terrorist)